HANDBOOK

OF THE

POLISH ARMY

Compiled by the General Staff, The War Office

1st Edition

—

1927

The Naval & Military Press Ltd

In reprinting in facsimile from the original, any imperfections are inevitably reproduced and the quality may fall short of modern type and cartographic standards.

NOTES

Note 1.—In this handbook localities are always referred to by their Polish names, except Warsaw (Warszawa), Vistula (Wisla) and Silesia (Slask), where the English language has adopted its own special form of the name.

A list of Polish place names with their corresponding names under the partitioning powers is given in Appendix V.

Note 2.—The war establishments given in various chapters are in some cases an approximation (to the nearest 10). For this reason the totals do not always agree with the sums of the details.

J. R. E. CHARLES,
Major-General.

Director of Military Operations and Intelligence.

THE WAR OFFICE,
July, 1927.

TABLE OF CONTENTS.

Para.	CHAPTER I.—Historical Sketch.	Page
1.	Before 1914	1
2.	After 1914	5

CHAPTER II.—The Country.

1.	General description	9
2.	Mountains	9
3.	Rivers and canals	9
4.	Railways	10
5.	Roads	11
6.	Telegraphs and telephones	12
7.	Features of special military importance	12
8.	Population	13
9.	Ethnography	14
10.	National character	14
11.	Religion	15
12.	Education	15

CHAPTER III.—Constitution and System of Government.

1.	Executive	16
2.	Legislature	16
3.	Internal administration	17
4.	Justice	17
5.	Civil rights	17
6.	National minorities	18
7.	Revision of constitution	18

CHAPTER IV.—Material Resources.

1.	Finance	18
2.	Agriculture	18
3.	Industries	20
4.	Mineral wealth	21
5.	Commerce and shipping	22
6.	Horse supply	23
7.	Horse transport	23
8.	Mechanical transport	23

CHAPTER V.—Recruiting and Man-power.

1.	Law of military service	23
2.	Terms of service	24
3.	Recruiting organization	26
4.	Recruiting statistics and reserves available	27

CHAPTER VI.—Officers and Non-commissioned Officers.

1.	General	29
2.	Technical officers	30
3.	Provision of combatant officers	30
4.	Officers of the non-active list and reserve officers	30
5.	Promotion and retirement of officers	31
6.	Reports on officers	32
7.	Statistics	32
8.	Officers employed in foreign countries	33
9.	Non-commissioned officers	33
10.	Officials	33
11.	Interpreters	33

CONTENTS

CHAPTER VII.—Strength and Organization of the Army.

Para.		Page
1.	Peace strength and organization	34
2.	War strength and organization	35
3.	G.H.Q. and armies	36
4.	Composition and strength of a division	36
5.	Composition and strength of a brigade	37
6.	Mobilization	37

CHAPTER VIII.—Administrative Commands and Staffs.

1.	Administrative districts	38
2.	General notes on system of administration	39
3.	Military councils	39
4.	The Ministry of War	39
5.	The Higher Command	40
6.	The Inspectorate General	41
7.	Administration	43
8.	Special staff appointments	45
9.	Military attachés	45
10.	Foreign military missions	46
11.	Organization of general headquarters and army staffs	46
12.	Organization of corps staffs	47
13.	Organization of divisional and brigade staffs	47
14.	Chain of command	47
15.	Lines of communication	47
16.	Committees	48
17.	Intelligence corps	49

CHAPTER IX.—Infantry.

1.	Organization of the arm	49
2.	Organization of the regiment	49
3.	Rifle and mountain regiments	52
4.	Cyclists	52
5.	Reserve battalions	52
6.	Regimental specialists	53
7.	Designation and colours	53
8.	Personnel	54
9.	Transport	54
10.	Armament	56
11.	Equipment	56
12.	Ammunition	57
13.	Distribution of ammunition	57
14.	Grenades	57
15.	Tents and tentes-abris	57

CHAPTER X.—Machine Guns and Automatic Rifles.

CHAPTER XI.—Cavalry.

1.	General organization	58
2.	Regimental organization in time of peace	58
3.	Divisional cavalry	61
4.	Designation and colours	61
5.	Specialists	62
6.	Transport	62

CONTENTS

Para.		Page
	Chapter XI.—Cavalry—*continued*.	
7.	Personnel	63
8.	Equipment	64
9.	Armament	64
10.	Saddlery	65
11.	Technical equipment	66
12.	The horse	67

CHAPTER XII.—Artillery

A.—The Arm.

1.	General organization	68
2.	Artillery staffs	68
3.	Personnel	68
4.	Equipment	68
5.	Regimental specialists	69
6.	Rangefinders	69
7.	Directors	69

B.—Field Artillery (including Horse Artillery).

1.	Organization of the branch	69
2.	Organization of a regiment or group	70
3.	Organization of a battery	70
4.	Independent field artillery	70
5.	Ammunition column	70
6.	Anti-aircraft artillery	71
7.	Regimental transport	71
8.	Regimental specialists	72
9.	Personnel	72
10.	The field gun	72
11.	The field howitzer	72
12.	The horse artillery gun	73
13.	Ammunition	73

C.—Heavy Field Artillery (including Foot Artillery).

1.	Organization of the branch	73
2.	Organization of foot artillery	73
3.	Organization of a heavy (heaviest) artillery regiment	73
4.	Organization of foot artillery company	74
5.	Organization of heavy and heaviest batteries	74
6.	Ammunition columns	74
7.	Regimental transport	74
8.	Regimental specialists	74
9.	Personnel	74
10.	The heavy field howitzer	74
11.	The heavy gun	74
12.	Ammunition	75

D.—Mountain Artillery.

1.	Organization of the branch	75
2.	Organization of a battery	75
3.	Transport	76
4.	Regimental specialists	76
5.	Personnel	76
6.	The mountain gun (howitzer)	76

CONTENTS

E.—Trench Mortars.

F.—Close Range Batteries.

G.—Ammunition Supply.

Para.		Page
1.	Front line ammunition supply	76
2.	Ammunition transport columns	76
3.	Ammunition tractors	77
4.	Chain of ammunition supply	77
5.	Expenditure of ammunition	78
6.	Ammunition trains	78

Appendix to Chapter XII.—Armament of Polish Artillery.

CHAPTER XIII.—Technical Troops (Engineers).

1.	General	81
2.	Personnel	81
3.	Sapper regiments	81
4.	Electro-technical battalion	83
5.	Bridging battalion	84
6.	Units formed on mobilization	85

Chemical Warfare.

1.	General	86
2.	Chemical warfare units	86
3.	Manufacturing establishments and depots	86
4.	Gas shell in the artillery	87

CHAPTER XIV.—Tanks and Armoured Cars.

1.	Organization	87
2.	Tank depots	88
3.	Armoured car units	88
4.	Tank units	88
5.	Personnel	88
6.	Description of tank	89
7.	Description of armoured car	89

CHAPTER XV.—Signal Service.

1.	Organization	89
	(a) Peace.	
	(b) War.	
2.	Signal units	90
3.	Regimental communication detachments	91
4.	Telegraph units	91
5.	Telephone units	91
6.	Wireless telegraph units	91
7.	Wireless telephone units	92
8.	Listening set units	92
9.	Messenger dog units	92
10.	Carrier pigeon units	92
11.	Despatch riding	92
12.	Signal parks and depots	92
13.	Army wireless stations	92
14.	Army wireless telephone stations	93
15.	Personnel	93

CONTENTS

Para.	Chapter XV.—Signal Service—*continued.*	Page
16.	Technical equipment (telegraph and telephone)	93
17.	Listening sets	93
18.	Technical equipment (wireless sets)	93
19.	Wireless telephone sets	94
20.	Signal lamps	94
21.	Signal flags	94
22.	Very lights	94
23.	Message thrower's and projectiles	95
24.	Signal horns	95

CHAPTER XVI.—Mapping and Survey.

1.	Military geographical institute	95
2.	Organization of surveying in the field	95
3.	Organization and duties of surveying detachments	95
4.	Survey units with artillery	95
5.	Types and scales of maps in use	96
6.	Meteorological service	96

CHAPTER XVII.—Transportation.

A.—General.

1.	General notes on the transportation service	97

B.—Railways.

1.	General organization and administration of the service	97
2.	Railway personnel and units	98
3.	Organization of traffic	98
4.	Movement of troops	99

C.—Mechanical Transport.

1.	General organization and administration	100
2.	Organization in the field	100
3.	Motor transport columns	100
4.	Allotment of motor cars	101
5.	Mechanical transport troops	101
6.	Motor reserve	101
7.	Types of military motor vehicles	101
8.	Motor cars	101
9.	Caterpillars	101
10.	Steam lorries	101
11.	Petrol stores and supplies	102
12.	Motor lorries on rails	102
13.	Traffic regulations	102

D.—Horse Transport.

1.	General organization and administration	102
2.	Organization in the field	102
3.	Horsed transport columns	102
4.	Transport vehicles	103
5.	Colour of army vehicles	103

E.—Water Transport Service.

CONTENTS

CHAPTER XVIII.—Intendance and Supply.

Para.		Page
1.	General peace organization and strength	104
2.	Personnel	104
3.	Supply service	105
4.	Engineer services	107
5.	Organization of intendance and supply in the field	108
6.	Arrangements for feeding troops in battle	108
7.	Depot supply parks	109
8.	Field bakeries	110
9.	Field butcheries	110
10.	Scales of rations	110
11.	Forage rations	111
12.	Requisitions	111
13.	Billeting	112
14.	Travelling kitchens	112
15.	Design and care of barracks	112
16.	Water supply	113
17.	Army postal service	113

CHAPTER XIX.—Medical Service.

1.	Peace organization and strength of medical service	113
2.	Administration of medical services in peace	114
3.	Nursing service	116
4.	Medical organization in the zone of operations	116
5.	Medical organization on the line of communication	118
6.	Medical organization in home territory	118
7.	Transport of wounded and sick	118
8.	Hospitals	118
9.	Inoculation and vaccination	119
10.	Dentistry	119
11.	Travelling laboratories	119
12.	Red Cross brassard	119

CHAPTER XX.—Veterinary Service.

1.	Organization and strength	119
2.	Veterinary duties with troops	120
3.	Veterinary hospitals and other establishments	120
4.	Stables	121
5.	Remount services	121
6.	Horse breeding establishments	122
7.	Statistics	123

CHAPTER XXI.—Auxiliary Units and Semi-Military Forces.

1.	General	123
2.	The customs guard	123
3.	The frontier guard corps	124
4.	Rifle clubs and similar organizations	125
5.	The Związek Strzelecki (Rifle League)	129
6.	The Sokol Society	129
7.	The scout movement	130
8.	Women's organizations	131

CONTENTS vii

Para.   **CHAPTER XXII.—Police and Gendarmerie.**   *Page*
1. The civil police 131
    (a) Organization 131
    (b) Personnel 132
    (c) Duties 133
    (d) Relations with the army 133
    (e) Numbers 134
    (f) Uniform 134
2. The military gendarmerie 135
3. The provost service 135

CHAPTER XXIII.—Pay, Allowances, Gratuities and Pensions.
1. Pay of officers and professional N.C.O.s 136
2. Pay of other ranks 138
3. Pay of air service 139
4. System of issue of pay 139
5. Pay books 139
6. Gratuities 139
7. Pensions 140
8. Half-pay and similar payments to officers and professional N.C.O.s .. 143
9. Prisoners of war or those reported missing during military operations .. 143
10. Allowances 143

CHAPTER XXIV.—Discipline.
1. Military penal code 145
    (a) General 145
    (b) Support of civil power 145
2. Courts martial 146
3. Courts of honour 148
4. Interior routine of units 149
5. Military prisons 149
6. Leave and furlough 150
7. Moral 150

CHAPTER XXV.—Ordnance Department.
1. General 151
2. Personnel 153
3. Arsenals 153
4. Munition factories 154

CHAPTER XXVI.—Aviation.
1. General 155
2. Administration 156
3. Organization 156
4. Commands and staff 157
5. Recruiting, terms of service and training 158
6. Officers 158
7. Warrant officers and other ranks 159
8. Establishments 160
9. Strength and distribution of units 161
10. Types of aeroplanes in use 161
11. Building and supply of aeroplanes 161
12. Aerodromes 162
13. Balloon units 162
14. Aviation corps pay 163
15. Methods of communicating with aeroplanes 165

CHAPTER XXVII.—Military Education.

Para.		Page
1.	General	165
2.	Military orphanages	166
3.	Cadet schools	166
4.	Regimental officers' schools	166
5.	Technical schools and courses	168
6.	The Staff College at Warsaw	168
7.	Schools for N.C.O.s	168
8.	Military education in civil schools	169
9.	Study of foreign languages	171
10.	Welfare	171

CHAPTER XXVIII.—Uniform.

1.	General notes on uniform	172
2.	Details of uniform	172
3.	Badges of rank	176
4.	Staff distinctions	176
5.	Uniform worn by semi-military bodies	177
6.	Identity discs	177
7.	System of supply of uniforms	177
8.	Personal kit	177
9.	Medals and decorations	178

CHAPTER XXIX.—Navy.

1.	Historical sketch	178
2.	Administration	179
3.	Personnel	179
4.	Fleet organization	180
5.	Programme	180
6.	Ports	180
7.	Naval expenditure	181
	Appendix to Chapter XXIX—List of ships of the Polish Navy	181

APPENDICES.

Appendix	I.	Tactics and drill	182
,,	II.	Glossary of military terms	188
,,	III.	Abbreviations used in the Polish Army	196
,,	IV.	War establishments	198
,,	V.	List of Polish place names with their corresponding names under the partitioning powers	204
,,	VI.	Order of battle and peace stations of the army	205

PLATES.

Plate	I.	Distinguishing shields of headquarters	216
,,	II.	A.—Ordinary signals from aeroplanes	217
		B.—Infantry signals to aeroplanes with answers in morse	218
		C.—Signals made with cloths with answers in morse	219
,,	III.	Infantry private—marching order	220
,,	IV.	Cavalry trooper—marching order	221
,,	V.	Cavalry—machine gun detachment	222
,,	VI.	Infantry—machine gun section	222

In pocket at end of book—Order of battle map.

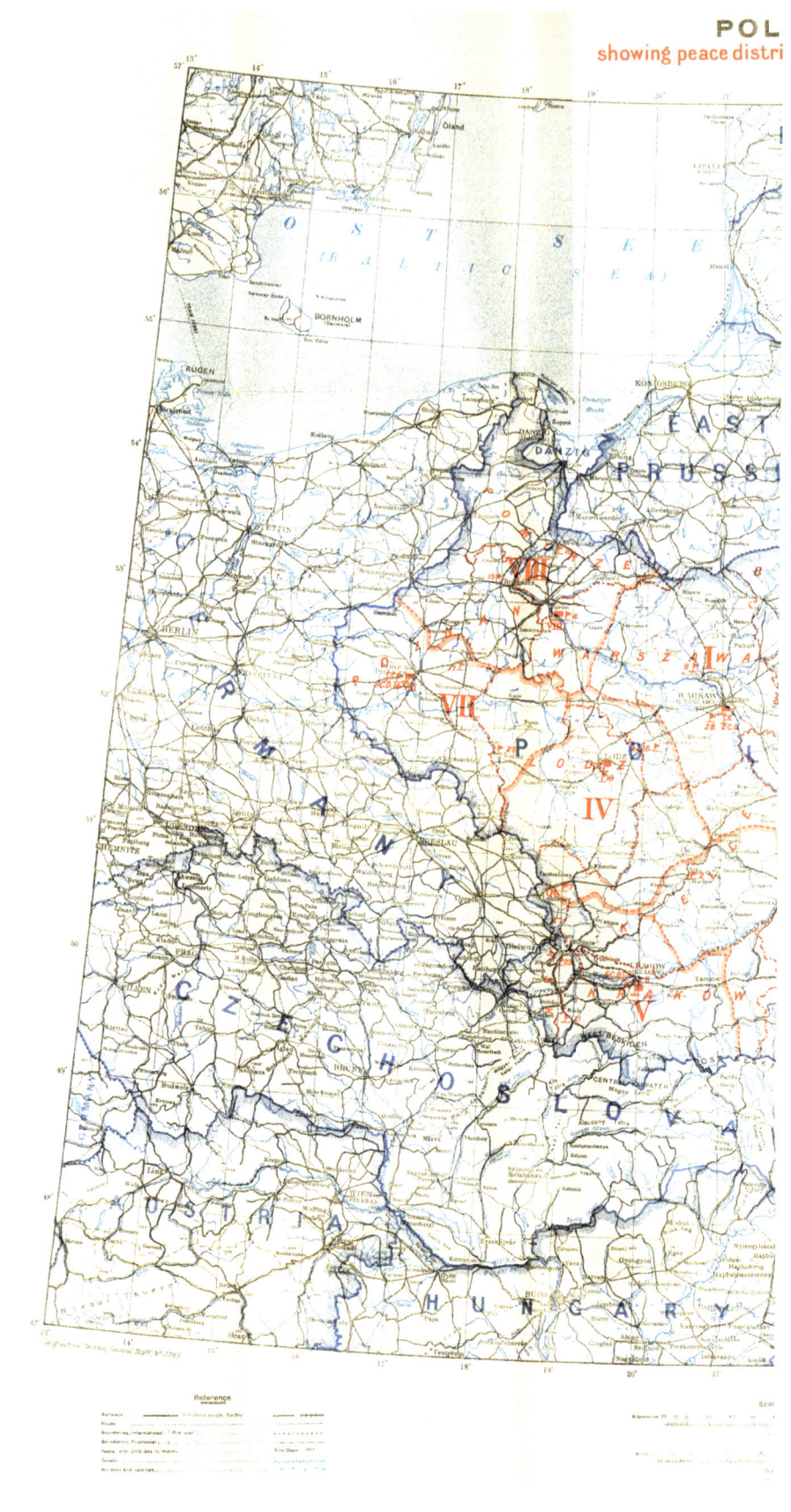

CHAPTER I.

HISTORICAL SKETCH.

Before 1914.

(1) Poland existed as an independent State in the Middle Ages, but its earlier history is lost in the mists of antiquity. The first reliable history begins in the 11th century, when we learn of the existence of a dynasty of semi-elective dukes, reigning at Krakow and claiming descent from a legendary ancestor, Piast. One of the Piast dukes was converted, together with his people, to Christianity by missionaries from Rome, and thus drew Poland towards Western civilization, while her Eastern neighbour, Russia, receiving her Christianity from Constantinople, was drawn away from the West. In this way the antagonism between the two great branches of Slavdom began. The dynasty gradually extended its dominion over tribes of kindred origin to the north and east, until their State reached the Baltic in East and West Prussia, included Poznan and Gniezno (the latter the seat of an Archbishop and senior prelate of the Polish State) and Upper Silesia. In 1320 the ruler took the title of King.

(2) The last Piast died in 1386 and was succeeded by his daughter, who was married to Jagiello, the pagan Grand Duke of Lithuania, a State that lay to the north and east of Poland, and included the Baltic sea-board and Riga, and the towns of Minsk (the capital), Wilno, Brzesc-Litewski, Kiev, and the Dniepr basin to the Black Sea. It is interesting to note that the majority of the inhabitants of this State were White Russians and Ukrainians, whose official language was White Russian, and that the tribe of true Lithuanians in the Kowno area were a very small part of the population. By this marriage the two States were united under the person of their ruler and were to have a common policy, though the union was very loose and had to be renewed more than once, notably by the Unions of Horodlo in 1413 and of Lublin in 1569. Even then the union was far from satisfactory. There were separate grand officers of State for the two portions, though the Diet was composed of the nobility of both parts, sitting together.

Under the Jagiellos the Polish State reached its greatest extent, including Riga, Smolensk, Kiev, Odessa in the east, the Baltic sea-board from Riga to beyond Danzig in the north, and part of Brandenburg in the west. The Teutonic Knights of East Prussia, after their defeat at Tannenburg in 1410, acknowledged the suzerainty of the Polish King, and their successors, the Hohenzollern Dukes of Prussia, continued to be vassals of the Polish King until 1656. During this period of expansion the Polish nobility carved out for themselves large estates in Lithuania and the Ukraine, where the peasant population never was, and is not now, Polish, and so laid the foundations of the Polish claim, which is never forgotten, to these outlying territories.

(3) Under the Jagiellos the privileges of the nobles, who alone were the governing class and formed the Diet, had been increased and the conditions of the peasants grew worse. They became mere serfs, the absolute property of the nobles, this system being extended to Lithuania also. Nothing was done to improve their state, until the time of the partitions, when the more Liberal among the nobles tried to carry through some

reforms. It was not, however, until 1864 that they were emancipated and then by the Russians. Another important fact to notice is that while Poland was Catholic, most of the Lithuanian peasantry was Orthodox ; and when Russia began to become powerful under the early Romanoffs she naturally coveted Lithuania. A further source of weakness of the Polish State was the selfishness of the individual nobles, and their jealous insistence on their individual liberties, of which the most pernicious was the " liberum veto," or the right of one man in the Diet to wreck a measure supported by every other member. It is noteworthy that even under the King the State was officially called a republic.

(4) The last Jagiello died in 1572 and was succeeded by Henry of Valois,* who fled the country in 1575, and then by his son-in-law, Stephan Batory of Hungary, by choice of the Diet, after which the crown became purely elective. Each election was an occasion for the nobles to extort more concessions from the candidate for kingship, and thus to lessen the central power, and in this strife the growing influence of the Russian Tsars became more and more powerful. The next kings were of the Swedish house of Vasa, and when they lost the Swedish throne Poland became involved in their struggle to regain it. A war with Moscow, both on religious questions and over the Pretender (Dmitri) to the Russian throne, and wars with rebellious cossacks of the Ukraine also took place about this time. Another danger to Poland was the growing power of the Turks, and wars with them were also frequent, terminating in the historic defeat given them by the Polish King Jan Sobieski at Vienna in 1683, which saved Europe from the Turks. In 1698, Sobieski was succeeded by the Elector of Saxony, the first of the two kings of that house who caused the ruin of Poland. It was in his reign that he, the Tsar, and the King of Denmark attacked Sweden, but the defeat of the Swedish King at Poltawa brought no gain to Poland, as a large party in Poland had been in favour of Sweden and had managed to drive the Elector out of Poland for some time. The second Saxon King, Augustus III, fell completely into the hands of Russia, and his reign was famous for the persecution of non-catholics and for the shameful neglect of the true interests both of the State and of the people, a condition of affairs which the few enlightened Liberals were powerless to alter.

(5) At his death in 1763, the Liberal party, headed by the Czartoryski family, considered that the only hope of introducing reforms, thereby strengthening the State, was to obtain the help of Russia. They therefore put forward as a candidate for the throne the favourite of Catherine of Russia, Stanislas Poniatowski, who was the last King of Poland. With Russian help he was elected king, and took the oath to an amended constitution. Catherine's ambition, however, was to increase the Russian Empire at the expense of Poland, and her support of reforms which would strengthen Poland did not last long. She found a willing ally in Frederick II of Prussia, and made a pretext for interfering with Polish internal affairs in demanding that Orthodox and Catholics in Poland should have equal rights. This demand led to the repeal of the recent reforms and the re-establishment of the old narrow constitution which Russia now guaranteed to preserve, and in 1772 a treaty was drawn up between Russia, Prussia and Austria, by which Russia obtained Vitebsk, Polock and Mogilev, Austria obtained Galicia (except Krakow), and Prussia obtained West Prussia (except Danzig) and the northern part of Poznan.

---

* Afterwards Henry III, of France.

This is known as the first partition of Poland. The Polish Diet was compelled to agree to it and had to admit the Russian ambassador to the Diet, accompanied by Russian troops to ensure that his wishes were being carried out.

(6) In 1787, however, a breach took place between Russia and Austria over the Turkish question. Poland was courted by both sides, and the Russian garrison was withdrawn to take part in the war against Turkey. The Poles seized the occasion to introduce a new Liberal constitution. However, Poland's favourable situation did not last long. Russia defeated the Turks and the Liberalism of the French Revolution induced the rulers of Russia, Austria and Prussia to settle their personal quarrels. To prevent the spread of new ideas in Poland, Catherine again invaded Poland and the Prussians followed later. Austria, too busy with her Napoleonic wars, took no part on either side. Poland was soon beaten, and, in 1793, the second partition took place, by which Prussia obtained Danzig and Thorn, Poznan and Lodz, while Russia obtained a huge stretch of country running from the Dwina in the north to the Dniester in the south. This led to the revolution under Kosciuszko in 1794, where the bravery of the Poles at Raclawice proved useless against the army of Russia and in 1795 the remaining territory of Poland was divided among the three Powers, Austria getting Lublin and Kielce; Prussia, Warsaw, and Suwalki; Russia, Courland, Kowno, Wilno, Grodno, and Volhynia. Poland had now completely disappeared from the map of Europe.

(7) After the defeat of the Austrians and Russians at Austerlitz and of the Prussians at Jena, the Poles saw in Napoleon a chance of regaining their liberty. The Treaty of Tilsit disappointed them, however, for Napoleon saw that to restore Poland would be a bar to an alliance with Russia, and all that was done for Poland was to create the Grand Duchy of Warsaw. In spite of their disappointments the Poles were completely loyal to Napoleon, even after 1812, when the rest of Europe was against him. Russia again occupied Warsaw, but it was not until the Congress of Vienna that Alexander revealed his plan of recreating a kingdom of Poland under his personal rule. In view of the opposition of Western Europe this plan was modified, and the Congress Kingdom as finally constituted did not contain either Poznan or Galicia, which remained in the hands of Prussia and Austria. The eastern boundary of the kingdom was drawn through Brzesc–Litewski.

(8) This State had a certain measure of autonomy within the Russian Empire, and had its own army, but the Russians maintained control through a Russian Imperial Commissioner and a Russian Commander-in-Chief. The arrangement was not popular on either side, and when the Tsar Nicholas came to the throne in 1825 he only awaited an excuse for cancelling it. This excuse came when the example of the French Revolution of 1830 encouraged the Polish Army to rise against the Russians. A temporary provisional government was formed in Warsaw, which sought to obtain a compromise with Russia, but the Russians demanded submission and sent an army to enforce it. The Powers of Europe protested on behalf of Poland, but Russia refused to listen, and in spite of the heroism of the Polish troops, their lack of discipline made them an easy prey and Poland was again conquered. The Tsar abolished the constitution and published a new Organic Statute, making Poland an integral part of the Russian Empire, but giving it a separate administrative and judicial system and other concessions. The statute, however, was never put into real operation; Poland was governed by the Viceroy

and by the Polish Department in Petrograd, and the most brutal measures were taken to punish the rebels. An amnesty that was granted was more remarkable for the names excepted from it than for the names it included, rebel soldiers were sent to distant parts of Russia, young sons of rebels were torn from their families and sent to Russia to be Russified, and Polish schools were closed. Paskievitch, the new Viceroy, was the instrument of these severities.

(9) A few years later the Organic Statute was abolished and the Russification of Poland by the Government of Russia became even stronger than before, though Liberal Russians felt a growing sympathy for her. The Pan Slav movement, which now began to develop, increased this sympathy, as did also the growing hostility of Russia to Austria, in which each side sought to conciliate their Polish subjects to use against the other. A party in Poland also, while not losing sight of the dreams of independence, were in favour of compromise with the partitioning Powers, a purely opportunist policy. Finally, Alexander II had himself crowned King of Poland in 1856 and relaxed his predecessors' severe system, political exiles being allowed to return. An agricultural society which was set up, though not neglecting agriculture, became an important political organization, and all over the country conspiracy flourished.

(10) The movement came to a head in 1861, riots occurred and a Polish Delegation was set up to govern Warsaw, followed by similar delegations in other towns. Alexander II tried conciliation, and made Wielopolski the instrument of his policy, hoping he could keep the Poles in order. But the extreme Poles took the bit in their teeth, claimed the restoration of Lithuania and White Russia to Poland, and forced Russia to take strong action. They also claimed the restoration of Poznan, West Prussia and Pomerania, and so brought the wrath of Prussia on their heads as well. Ever since 1815 Prussia had been trying to Prussianize her Polish subjects, at first by conciliatory measures; but, as each attempt failed, her methods became more brutal. An unsuccessful revolution in 1848 was suppressed with horrible cruelty. Accordingly, in 1863, the Prussians prevented any attempt of the Poznan Poles to join hands with their brothers in the Congress Kingdom by stationing troops all along the frontier. The Poles of Galicia made no attempt to join in the rebellion, as a previous rebellion in 1846 had been suppressed by the Austrians, who encouraged the Ruthenian peasants of Eastern Galicia to rise against the Polish upper classes and murder them wholesale. The Galician Poles then settled down to cultivate cordial relations with Vienna and to develop the idea of Polish nationality within that Empire. They obtained many great concessions, such as a special Minister at Vienna for Galicia, substitution of the Polish language in the administration, law courts, and schools, etc., in return for their support of the Hapsburg Monarchy against Russia and the idea of Pan Slavism. Consequently the Galician Poles limited themselves to furnishing arms and recruits to their rebellious brothers in the Congress Kingdom.

(11) When in 1863 Polish nationalism got beyond the control of Wielopolski, he was dismissed and the Tsar appointed General Berg in his place. A reign of terror followed. The Russian armies easily defeated the Polish insurgents, but the direction of the rebellion had passed into the hands of a secret organization, which punished all attempts at submission with assassination. When Alexander offered an amnesty no

Poles dared take advantage of it. The campaign devolved into a series of sporadic ambuscades and massacres, and was eventually stamped out with the greatest brutality. Naturally enough, after this, Alexander did his best to Russify Poland; the administration became purely Russian and the Polish language was prohibited everywhere. At the same time the peasants were made freeholders and village self-administration was set up. As the peasants had no experience, naturally all power came into the hands of the Russian officials and thus this reform, which was intended to create a new class of Russophil small-holders, only resulted in developing Polish national feeling at the expense of the Russian bureaucracy.

(12) After 1863, except for minor disorders in Russian Poland in 1906, there was no attempt at rebellion on the part of the Polish nation. In Prussian Poland the process of Prussification continued with conspicuous lack of success, German settlers became Polonised and the Kulturkampf directed against the Catholic religion ended in Bismarck's defeat. In 1885 Poles began to be expelled to other parts of Germany, the teaching of Polish was forbidden, and a Settlement Commission was formed to buy land from the Poles and sell it to German colonists. But all attempts failed ; Polish feeling grew instead of diminishing and the German population decreased in spite of the colonization. The only benefits which the Poles obtained from the Prussian domination were good economic development and efficient, if tyrannous, government.

(13) In Russian Poland, after 1863, the attempts of the aristocrats to be loyal to the Tsar and of the Polish Socialist Party to join hands with the Russian Socialist Party, only strengthened the middle party, the National Democrats, who stood for developing Polish culture in the people. Its success was rewarded by the fact that all the Polish deputies in the first Duma were of this party. The Pan Slav Congress at Prague in 1900, which was attended by several Russian Liberals, seemed to promise a reconciliation between Russian and Polish nationalism, but this was wrecked by the Polish support of Austria in the annexation of Bosnia, an act which was offensive to the Russians. This, and the abuses of the Russian officials, tended to discredit the National Democratic Party and increase the influence of the Socialists, who formed certain societies in which the idea of independence was fostered. Their spokesman was Pilsudski, who began to form in Galicia among the members a military organization, in which military training was given to young Poles to fit them for a fresh struggle for independence as soon as the occasion presented itself.

After 1914.

(14) In 1914 the occasion arrived, but found the Poles hopelessly divided. The National Democrats hoped for Poland's restoration with the help of the Allies, while Pilsudski adopted the cause of Austria. He considered that as Austria was the weakest of the partitioning Powers it would be easier to extort concessions from her, and consequently obtained her permission to take the field in August, 1914, with his military organizations, as an auxiliary of the Austrian army. These troops eventually developed into four brigades and obtained the name of the Polish Legion. There were two currents of opinion among the Legionaries. One party, headed by Pilsudski, aimed at complete independence of the Polish State, and was, with few exceptions, composed of Russian

subjects, while the other party aimed at independence within the limits of the Austrian Empire, and consisted mostly of Austrian subjects. These two tendencies persisted, until the peace of Brzesc–Litewski in 1918 caused the Austrophile Poles, under Josef Haller's command, to throw off their allegiance to Austria, as they could not agree to the partition of Poland as planned by the German Headquarters, to which Austria would have been forced to submit. They came to blows with the Austro-German forces and after a fight at Kaniew, on the Dniepr, they dissolved, many of the men making their way to join Dowbor-Musnicki's or Zeligowski's troops (*see* below), or to Arkhangel and Murmansk. The other section of the Legions fought until 1916, when the Germans proclaimed the independence of the Polish State, under a Council of Regency in Warsaw, and brought these units back from the front to form the nucleus of a new Polish army. The attempt to make this new army (or Polnische Wehrmacht) take the oath to Poland and the German Emperor met with opposition, and Pilsudski, as their chief, ordered them to refuse to take it. For this refusal the Legions were disbanded and Pilsudski imprisoned by the Germans in Magdeburg. Before the rupture he had organized among the Legions a secret military organization (Polska Organizacja Wojskowa, or P.O.W.) and through this he kept in touch with the ex-Legionaries until Poland's resurrection at the end of 1918.

(15) The Russians at the beginning of the war had issued a proclamation to the Poles, offering them in return for their support a certain degree of autonomy within the Russian Empire, but it was not until the overthrow of the Tsar's Government by Kerensky that any steps were taken to put these promises into effect. A Polish National Committee was set up in Petrograd, and the formation of Polish units out of the Polish soldiers in the Russian army was begun. These were under the command of Dowbor-Musnicki in the Minsk area. When Kerensky was in his turn overthrown by the Bolsheviks, Dowbor-Musnicki found that in addition to fighting Germans in front he had to oppose Bolshevized Russian soldiery all round. He was eventually compelled to obey orders issued from the Polish Regency in Warsaw (an organization nominated by, and completely under the control of the Germans) and capitulate. Other Polish units were formed in Arkhangel and Murmansk under British auspices, at Odessa by General Zeligowski, in Siberia under Kolchak's Government ; while Poles from Canada, America, etc., were recruited and formed into divisions in France, of which Haller took command after having made his escape from Kaniew to Arkhangel. Two of these six divisions fought under French control in the last six month's fighting in the Aisne area.

(16) When, therefore, the Germans capitulated on 11th November, 1918, there were a large number of trained Polish soldiers available in various parts of Europe to form a new Polish army. Pilsudski returned to Warsaw, was made Commander-in-Chief of the Army and Chief of State, and the formation of an army was started without delay. It must be remembered that at this time Poland was in the military occupation of the Germans, that the Bolsheviks on the eastern frontier were still aggressive in spite of the peace of Brzesc-Litewski, and that the Ukrainians, who had been specially favoured by the Austrians as a counterpoise to the Poles, and who had, under Austrian auspices, organized Ukrainian regiments, laid claim to a large tract of territory hitherto regarded as Polish, namely, Eastern Galicia and Volhynia. The armistice did not, therefore,

mean a cessation of hostilities so far as Poland was concerned, and an army was the first necessity for the new State to enable it to consolidate itself. Pilsudski's P.O.W. came back to the colours and three divisions of Legions were very quickly formed, followed by other divisions formed out of volunteers and by conscripts after the passing of a law introducing compulsory military service. The arms and equipment were obtained from the stocks left behind by the German and Austrian armies of occupation. Poznan (roughly the ex-German province of Posen) drove out the Germans on 31st December, 1918, and fresh divisions were formed there. Then in April the transport of Haller's army from France began, and about the same time Zeligowski marched the division he had formed from Odessa to Poland. The Polish division in Siberia, however, was unfortunate, as when forming the rearguard to Kolchak's troops in January, 1920, the greater part was taken prisoner and not released until after the signature of the Polish-Bolshevik peace treaty of October, 1920. Only a part of this division reached Vladivostock whence it was repatriated to Poland during the summer of 1920. Two more divisions were raised from the Wilno area when that district was taken from the Bolsheviks in 1919, and finally in 1920, at the time of the Bolshevik advance, a division of volunteers was formed and took the field. The strength of the army at the end of the Bolshevik war was 23 divisions and 9 cavalry brigades.

(17) Returning now to the operations of the newly-formed Polish army. After the restoration of the Polish State at the end of 1918, the situation was as follows : the German armies were holding a line from Riga through Dwinsk southwards facing the Russian Bolshevized armies, with whom relations were far from peaceful in spite of the Treaty of Brzesc-Litewski which had been concluded in February : the Ukraine was in the military occupation of Austria. When the revolutions broke out in Austria her army dissolved and the individual soldiers made their way home, except the Ukrainian regiments. The Germanophile Hetman of the Ukraine was succeeded by the revolutionary Petlura, whom the Ukrainian regiments recognized, and they proceeded to advance westwards to Lwow (Lemberg) meeting with resistance from the Polish inhabitants. In the north Pilsudski gave the occupying German armies facilities for returning to Germany, but this left the road open for the Bolsheviks to advance westwards. Therefore, at the very birth of the new State, it was invaded by two enemies. However, the invasion was checked at the beginning of 1919, Lwow was successfully held and the Bolsheviks and the Ukrainians were driven eastwards, leaving Wilno, Minsk, Bobruisk and Borisoff in Polish hands by the end of the summer. During the year the Supreme Council in Paris, as a temporary measure of safety against the Bolsheviks (who had by this time replaced Petlura in the Ukraine), authorized a military occupation of Eastern Galicia by the Poles up to the River Zbrucz, the old Austro-Russian frontier. There were also, at the beginning of 1919, minor operations against the Germans on the western frontier of Poznan, against the Czechs in Cieszyn (Teschen), and the Kowno Lithuanians over Wilno.

(18) The situation remained stable, however, through the winter of 1919–20, until the defeat of Denikin enabled the Bolsheviks to transfer reinforcements to their Polish front. Attacks began in February in the Mozyr area and in the Ukraine, but were repulsed. During all this period both sides professed to be anxious to conclude peace,

but the meeting of delegates was always postponed for a variety of causes, and the Poles, considering it dangerous to adopt a waiting attitude in face of the reinforcement of the Bolshevik army, resolved to strike a blow at the enemy before his concentrations were complete. To this end they made an agreement with their former enemy Petlura, and at the beginning of May, 1920, advanced on Kieff, which they entered on 7th May and held for about a month. The Bolsheviks then launched two attacks, one in the north, in the Lepel Drissa area, which, however, was repulsed. The other and principal attack was made with Buddenni's army of five cavalry divisions south-west of Kieff and was completely successful. The Polish front was broken and they began to retreat all along the line. The Bolshevik attack in the north was renewed, and during the summer months the Polish army was in constant retreat. Lwow alone held out successfully throughout the whole campaign. In the north, however, the Bolsheviks reached the lower reaches of the Vistula near Włocławek and arrived within six miles of Warsaw itself. In this critical situation General Weygand and Maj. Gen. Sir P. de B. Radcliffe were sent out to help the Poles to restore the situation, and with their advice, the Poles collected a reserve army south-west of Warsaw with which to make a counter-offensive while the retreating army stopped and held the line of the Vistula. This plan was completely successful. One counter-attack was made across the Vistula below Warsaw, by which a large part of the Bolshevik army in the triangle between the Vistula and the Prussian frontier was either captured or driven into East Prussia where it was interned, while the main attack above Warsaw, between that town and Dęblin, drove the Bolsheviks back in disorder. The Bolshevik troops never recovered and by the beginning of October were almost back on the line from which they had started, covering Minsk, Sluck and Szepetowka. An armistice and peace preliminaries were signed at Riga on 12th October, by which the frontier line between the two states was fixed.

(19) Wilno, however, remained a bone of contention, as the Bolsheviks, after capturing it from the Poles, ceded it to the Kowno Lithuanians, who transferred their government there. When the Polish army drove the Bolsheviks back from Lida, General Zeligowski with his division, mainly recruited from that area, severed his connection with the Polish army and marched on Wilno and captured it. From this arose the State of Central Lithuania, disowned officially by the Polish Government, though the private sympathies of every Pole, official or non-official, entirely approved of Zeligowski's action. After 18 months of quasi-independent existence, occupied the whole time by wrangles and conflicts with the Kowno Lithuanians, which the League of Nations vainly attempted to regulate, elections were held to a Central Lithuanian Diet, which voted for incorporation with Poland. The Polish Diet approved of this, and Central Lithuania was taken over in the summer of 1922 and General Zeligowski's troops were restored officially to the ranks of the Polish army, from which in reality they had never been separated.

(20) After the Peace of Riga had been signed, the Polish army, then having a ration strength of about a million and comprising 22 divisions, 2 independent brigades and 9 cavalry brigades, was gradually demobilized until in the spring of 1922 it reached its normal peace establishment of 275,000 men. At the same time a reorganization on a basis of three regiments to a division was put in hand. The present constitution of the army is 30 infantry divisions and 40 cavalry regiments, with auxiliary troops.

CHAPTER II.
THE COUNTRY OF POLAND.

1. General.

The Polish Republic has a superficial area of 386,273 square kilometres (150,888 square miles). The whole country is one vast rolling plain, with very few hills or rising ground exceeding 300 feet above its level. The central part, through Warsaw–Brzesc–Pinsk, is practically dead flat, but, in the other parts, the country is gently undulating without any noticeable features. In the south, where the Carpathians form the frontier, the foothills of these mountains form an agreeable change from the rather monotonous character of the rest of the country. Near Kielce is a short range of hills some 1,000 feet high, but this is the only noticeable feature in the broad expanse of rolling plain which extends throughout the country. The land is agricultural, but everywhere there are large tracts of forest, mostly pine or fir, though oak and beech are also common. Some of these, especially in the eastern provinces, are of vast extent, and in the marsh area of the Prypec the forest is continuous for hundreds of miles. From this fact it follows that, except in the south, all the frontiers of Poland are artificial and open, and are nowhere marked by any well-defined geographical feature forming a natural obstacle which can be easily defended.

2. Mountains.

The Carpathians alone form a defensible barrier between the Poles on the north, and the Slovak portion of the Czecho-Slovak State on the south. This range of mountains stretches uninterruptedly along the whole south frontier of Poland from south of Cieszyn to south of Kolomya, beyond which place its southerly trend takes it away from Poland into the State of Roumania. The highest portion of these mountains is in the Tatra district, south of Krakow, where the highest peak runs up to 2,663 metres above sea level (8,660 feet), but the average of the mountains is much lower, in fact, few peaks exceed 1,000 metres (3,250 feet) until the area east of Lwow is reached, where the average is higher again with several peaks rising to 1,700 metres (5,540 feet) and two even to 2,000 metres (6,500 feet).

The Carpathians, owing to their jumbled mass and the forests that cover them, rather than to their height, form a considerable obstacle to military operations; but there are numerous roads capable of taking all arms and light motors, and seven railway lines traverse the section which lies between Poland and Czecho-Slovakia.

3. Rivers and Canals.

The rivers of Poland nearly all drain into the Baltic; those draining into the Black Sea are only in the south-eastern corner.

The principal rivers draining into the Baltic are :—

Warta.—Rising south of Częstochowa and flowing through Poznan into Germany where it joins the Oder. It is navigable for vessels drawing 28 inches of water (70 cm.) as far as Poznan and for smaller vessels to Kolo. Its right bank tributary, the Notec, forms for a part of its course the frontier between Poland and Germany. This river is also navigable and with the Notec-Bydgosc canal gives a waterway to the Vistula valley for vessels drawing 28 inches of water.

Vistula (Wisla).—Rising in Cieszyn and flowing through the east of Poland to Danzig, with its right bank tributaries San, Bug and Narew. The Vistula is navigable for vessels up to 28 inches draught to Warsaw and for lighter barges up to Krakow. Its bed is full of sandbanks which often change their position. The Bug is navigable for craft up to 20 inches draught to Brzesc, from whence by the Muchawiec river and the Krolewski canal (70 cm. deep) vessels can get into the Prypec. The Narew is navigable as far as Lomza for vessels of not more than 18 inches draught. Its higher waters are joined to the Niemen by the Augustow canal, which, originally made for the lumber trade, is, however, in bad repair.

Niemen.—Rising in Russia, south of Minsk, and flowing through Polish Lithuania by Grodno into Kowno Lithuania near Memel. It is navigable as far as Grodno for vessels of 28 inches draught. Its left bank tributary, the Szczara, is connected with the Prypec by the Oginski canal which was also built for the lumber trade and is now in very bad repair as it formed part of a defensive line in the war.

Dwina.—For part of its course is the northern frontier of Poland, and forms an outlet into the Baltic. It is navigable as far as Polock for craft of 40 inches draught.

Draining into the Black Sea are :—

Prypec (Pripet).—Rising south of Brzesc and flowing through an extensive marsh to join the Dniepr in Russia. Right bank tributaries Stokhod, Styr and Horyn. Left bank tributary Jasiolda. It is navigable for vessels of 28 inches draught.

Dniestr.—Rising in the Carpathians south of Lwow, and running east to become the frontier of Russia and Roumania. Its left bank tributary, the Zbrucz, is the frontier between Poland and Russia. It is not navigable in Poland owing to its swift course and rocky bed.

As a general rule Polish rivers flow in a broad valley, in which they have carved a devious channel, often breaking up into several branches. The valley is marshy and liable to be flooded. The actual banks of the river itself are low, and not more than a few feet above the water. All rivers become icebound during the winter. Bridges have very often to be built of great length, so as to bridge over part of the valley where the ground is marshy, and bridge piers have always to be provided with outworks to protect them from damage by the ice.

4. Railways.

Railways in Poland were constructed when Poland was divided between the three partitioning Powers, and so were designed to suit the needs of the three separate Powers, who were in opposition to one another, and not to suit the needs of Poland as a whole.

We see, therefore, in the former Russian area seven strategic railways from the interior of Russia converging in Poland, namely :—

Petrograd–Wilno–Warsaw.
Polock–Lida–Siedlce.
Moscow–Smolensk–Brzesc.
Briansk–Homel–Brzesc.
Kieff–Kowel–Dęblin.
Ekaterinoslav–Berditcheff–Rowno.
Odessa–Proskurow–Tarnopol–Lwow.

In Poznan, which, like the whole of the former German Empire, was well provided with railways, we see that most lines on meeting the old frontier stopped ; and through communication over the frontier was possible only at very few places. The same is noticeable on the old Russo-Austrian frontier. A further difference is that in 1914 all lines east of Warsaw were Russian gauge, and all lines west of that place and in Galicia were normal gauge.

During the occupation of Poland by the Central Powers certain of these defects were removed as it was in their interests to have good communications. The main Russian lines were converted to normal gauge ; Lwow was connected with Lublin, and Suwalki with Margrabowa. The process of filling up such gaps has since been continued, but even now the general plan of the railways leaves much to be desired. A main railway may cross and re-cross the same frontier ; for instance the main line from Katowice to Poznan runs for a short distance in German territory.

The main lines of communication, beyond those already mentioned leading into Russia, are :—
    Warsaw–Danzig.
    Warsaw–Bydgosc–Poznan–Berlin–Paris.
    Warsaw–Lodz–Kalisz–Breslau.
    Warsaw–Częstochowa–Dziedzice–thence to Czecho-Slovakia–Vienna.
    Warsaw–Lwow–thence to Roumania and Hungary.
    Krakow–Lwow.
    Baranowicze–Luniniec–Sarny–Rowno.

A new railway has been opened by which the Poles can reach the port of Gdynia without having to pass through the territory of the Free State of Danzig.

The following statistics refer to the year 1924 :—

	Kilometres.
Length of lines in exploitation	16,780
Rolling stock in possession—	
Locomotives	5,054
Passenger coaches, luggage vans and post vans	11,546
Goods wagons (covered)	48,605
Coal trucks	52,679
Flat trucks	13,379
Tank wagons	5,441
Special	2,144

The programme for new railway construction includes the following main lines :—
    Upper Silesia to Danzig without passing through Germany.
    Upper Silesia to Warsaw.
    Upper Silesia eastwards to Kowel.

5. Roads.

The same difference, as with railways, is noticeable in connection with the road system in the three different parts of Poland. In Poznan and in Silesia there are numerous metalled roads ; in Galicia there are also plenty, even up to the eastern frontier ; but in Russian Poland there are very few metalled roads ; even some of the most important towns such as Wilno are not joined up by them, and the further east one proceeds the more their absence becomes noticeable.

In Poznan the roads have good foundations, and with their strong permanent bridges are capable of taking heavy continuous traffic, but the Galician roads and those in the ex-Russian part are made of local stone and have bad foundations. Consequently they vary according to whether the local stone is hard or soft, and they would soon break up under heavy continuous traffic. Moreover, in this area the state of war that existed from 1914 to 1920 meant the destruction of numberless bridges, and few of these have as yet been repaired by permanent structures. On any of these roads one is liable to meet a temporary bridge in weak condition, which would not take heavy traffic. They are, however, being steadily replaced by permanent bridges of wooden pile work, which are capable of taking heavy traffic.

In the Russian portion a few of the main roads are supplemented by a network of "traktats" which, though suitable for the local country cart, are unmetalled and mere sandy or muddy tracks according to the weather.

It is important to notice that there are only two metalled roads crossing the eastern frontier from Poland to Russia, namely, Brzesc–Sluck–Bobruisk and Rowno–Jitomir–Kieff. Other roads run towards the frontier—mainly in the southern part—but do not connect with the Russian road system beyond.

6. Telegraphs and Telephones.

The telegraph system unites even the small villages in the west, but does not extend as yet into the villages in the east. The larger towns are connected by telephone and within them there is a good local system.

Wireless stations exist at Warsaw, Poznan, Krakow, Torun, Danzig and Grudziądz, and there is at Warsaw an installation capable of communicating with America. There are temporary stations at Lwow and Wilno which are to be replaced by more powerful permanent installations, and at various other towns there are stations set up and worked by the Army, partly for instructional purposes.

The Indo-European Telegraph Company owns three lines (eventually they will possess four) through Poland, as part of the direct British-owned cable way from England to India. The section through Poland passes by Schneidemühl–Kutno–Warsaw–Brzesc–Rowno; the company's own wires are put up on its own poles along its own route, and are quite separate from the Polish telegraph system.

7. Features of Special Military Importance.

Poland is so flat that there are few features of special military importance. The Carpathian mountains forming the southern frontier have already been described. The marshes of the Prypec, however, deserve special mention.

This river, rising south of Brzesc, flows through an area of marsh and forest, afterwards through Pinsk and eventually joins the Dniepr north of Kieff. Its tributary on the left bank, the Jasiolda, is the extremity of an extensive marsh bordering it and the Prypec, and stretching in a zone of some 50 miles broad right into Russia. On the right bank of the Prypec the Styr, Stokhod, Horyn, and the Ubort traverse a similar zone of rather greater width to the south. Throughout this belt of marsh, some 120–150 miles broad, there is no road communication at all, neither north and south between the Bobruisk–Sluck–Brzesc road and the Kowel–Rowno–Kieff road, nor east and west between the road junction of Brzesc–Litewski and the river Dniepr. The east and west railway Brzesc–Pinsk–Mozyr is built through this marsh, but accompanied only by the roughest of tracks, while the north and south railway Baranowicze–Luniniec–Sarny is accompanied by no track at all. The country is very sparsely inhabited. Only in winter, when all water and mud is frozen hard, is the country at all passable. This extensive marsh therefore breaks up an attack from the east into two independent movements, while the possession of Brzesc, at the head of the marsh, is important for the defence as being the first point where communications north and south of it converge.

Worthy of notice also are the two " corridors," the narrow strips of Polish territory giving access to the Baltic, west of Danzig, and to the river Dwina, east of Dwinsk, respectively. The Danzig corridor is well provided with roads and railways, and cuts off East Prussia from the rest of Germany.

The other corridor, leading to Dwinsk, is devoid of good roads, but is valuable to Poland as giving access to the river Dwina (a navigable waterway to the sea) by the important railway Wilno–Dwinsk; it also contains the less important railway Molodeczno–Polock.

The western frontier of Germany is marked for some 35 miles north of Poznan by the course of the river Notec, and for some 20 miles west of Poznan by a series of lakes, but otherwise it is completely open from the Baltic to the junction of the States of Germany, Czecho-Slovakia and Poland. At this south-western corner of Poland lies Upper Silesia, with its rich deposits of coal and iron and its well developed industries. This area was claimed by the Poles after 1918, and finally a decision was given by the League of Nations that the industrial area should be divided between Poland and Germany. A frontier to carry out this decision has been established. As, however, the industrial area was developed as a whole, the frontier cuts right across the system, with the result that, for instance, a town is in Germany and its waterworks in Poland, or a mine is in Poland and the workers who come every day to work it live in Germany. Hence many regulations to admit free crossing of the frontier have had to be made. But the district is of importance to Poland, as it contains the coal and iron and other mineral wealth which are necessary to Poland, and would have to be defended in case of war.

8. Population.

The population of Poland (1921 figures) is as follows :—

Poles.	Other Races.	Total.	Remarks.
	Polish Republic in September, 1921.		
17,359,883	8,012,564	25,372,447	Census of 30.9.1921.
	Polish Upper Silesia.		
677,896	302,400	980,296	German census of 8.10.1919.
	Former Central Lithuania.		
336,344	152,624	488,968	Local census of 1919.
	In Military Establishments.		
285,870	—	285,870	
	Total.		
18,659,993	8,467,588	27,127,581	

9. Ethnography.

In the figures in para. 8, the number of Poles includes all those who so described themselves at the time of the census, and may therefore include people of Jewish, Ruthenian, White Russian or other nationalities who acknowledged themselves as Polish. The figure for "Other Races" represents the Jews, Germans, Ruthenians, White Russians, etc., who did not elect to claim Polish "nationality" (as opposed to Polish "citizenship").

The Polish inhabitants are mostly concentrated in Poznan, Western Galicia and in the Congress Kingdom. They are mixed with Germans in Poznan and Upper Silesia, with Jews in the whole of the rest of Poland, with White Russians in the north-eastern provinces (in Novogrodek the Poles are only 50 per cent.), and with Ruthenians in the south-eastern provinces (in Stanislawow, Polesia and Volhynia the Poles vary from 14 to 22 per cent. only).

Both the White Russians and the Ukrainians, though quite distinct from one another, are a mixture, as it were, of the true Poles and the true Russians; each of their languages has something in common with both Polish and Russian, and it is hard to lay down a definite boundary line between either of them and the Poles on one hand, or the Russians on the other.

With exception of the Jews, there is very little ethnographical difference between the different nationalities inhabiting Poland. The racial type is the brachycephalic Alpine or Celto Slav, sturdy and of medium stature. (The small stunted Jew, however, lowers the average considerably, and taking the whole of the population together, the average stature is low.) The pigmentation varies between a blonde type with light brown hair and blue or blue-grey eyes, and a brunette type with dark hair and light brown or brown eyes. The majority, especially in the centre and north, are of the former type, the latter type being in a majority only in the south and south-west. Occasional dolichocephalic individuals are met, with blue eyes and fair hair, both among the aristocracy and among the peasants.

The Jews, who have always kept free from intermixture, are a long-headed, black (occasionally ruddy) haired race with brown eyes, stunted growth and poor physique, yet showing extraordinary power of resistance to disease and insanitary conditions.

10. National Character.

At the present time the character of the Pole is undoubtedly suffering from the influence of 150 years' subjection to alien rulers, which has developed in him a spirit of low cunning and deceitfulness and a love of secret methods in preference to open dealing.

The Pole is individually brave, and hard-working; in Russia, before 1914, he was always considered more sober and more honest as a workman or servant than the Russian. He is clever in theory and has good ideas, but is bad at putting them into practice and at organization. Yet in Russia, before 1914, Polish engineers were directing many Russian concerns, in preference to Russian engineers.

The principal characteristic of the Pole, however, is his insistence on his individual rights, and his consequent inability to modify his opinions and to work in co-operation with others for the public good. This weakness brought about the partitions in the 18th century, and is most marked in the political life of the State since its regeneration.

The Pole shows at his best as an agricultural worker, in a lesser degree as an industrial worker, and at his worst as a clerk or business man, where his lack of organizing ability, lack of method, and openness to bribery are most conspicuous. Consequently the administrative and Government officials are inefficient and dilatory, and this reflects itself in the whole State administration. By contrast with the other public departments, the Army is more efficient, and office work is carried on with greater speed, exactitude, and relevancy.

11. Religion.

The true Pole is, in public, a very devout Roman Catholic, and the priesthood have a very great influence, even among the socialists. During the time of the dismemberment of Poland the Roman Catholic priesthood showed very great patriotism, and in spite of persecution did much to maintain the sentiment of nationality, and to carry on Polish hedge-schools in defiance of the Russian and German Governments. Consequently their influence is not ill-merited.

Other religions have, however, full rights, there being Lutheranism among Poles of German extraction, the Jewish religion among the Jews, the Orthodox Church among the White Russians and Ukrainians, while the Uniate Church (*i.e.*, the Greek Orthodox Church, recognizing the Pope as Head, however) flourishes in the south-eastern districts of Poland. Over the latter a great struggle raged in the last quarter of the 19th century; the Russians tried to force or bribe them into Orthodoxy, while the Roman Catholic clergy tried to oppose this. The attempt was a failure, for when Nicholas II established the principle of religious liberty, many Orthodox Ukrainians returned to the Uniate Church, and many Uniates returned to Roman Catholicism.

12. Education.

Education is very backward. At present 70 per cent. of the recruits are illiterate. Previous to 1914 the Polish language was forbidden in all Russian schools, and a large majority of the Polish population never went to school. In Poznan, it is true, education was good, but again the Polish language was forbidden. In Galicia the educational system was bad though Polish schools were regularly established. Consequently, throughout the State education was at a low ebb. Universities, however, existed in all these parts, and Poles who consented to learn in a foreign tongue could and did receive a good education.

Now elementary State schools have been opened all over the country, the Universities and technical schools are well attended, and, in the army, illiterate recruits, and those from the eastern districts who know no Polish, are being taught the Polish language and the three " R's." In a few years time a great improvement will be noticeable.

All schools are supervised by the State Educational Department. Education is standardized everywhere—so that to have finished a certain class in an elementary or secondary school (gymnasium) means throughout the country the attainment of a certain definite level of education.

CHAPTER III.

THE CONSTITUTION AND SYSTEM OF GOVERNMENT.

Poland is a republic. The head of the State is the President and the legislative chambers are the Senate and Diet (Sejm). The official name of the State is the Rzeczpospolita Polska.

1. Executive.

The President of the State is elected for a period of 7 years, by the Senate and Diet sitting together as a National Assembly, and is chosen by an absolute majority of votes. Only Polish citizens are eligible, which does not exclude Polish citizens of non-Polish nationality, *e.g.*, Jews. The President is also Supreme Chief of the Armed Forces of the State, but is forbidden to exercise supreme command in time of war; on the advice of the Council of Ministers, given through the Minister of War, however, he appoints the Commander-in-Chief, who is then responsible to the Diet for all matters concerning the waging of war.

The President is not responsible for his acts to the Diet, and is not a member of either Senate or Diet, but can be impeached for high treason, infringement of the constitution or penal acts, by a motion passed in the Diet by a three-fifths majority, at least half the members of the Diet being present.

The Diet alone authorizes the President to declare war or conclude peace.

In the event of the absence or incapacity of the President to act, his functions are executed by the Marshal, or Speaker, of the Diet.

2. Legislature.

The Diet consists of 444 members; 372 of these are elected for a period of 5 years by universal, direct, secret, and equal suffrage on proportional representation principles. Votes are given for lists of candidates presented by the various political parties, not for the candidates themselves. All citizens are eligible to vote who are over 21 years of age, but soldiers serving with the colours may not vote; all citizens are eligible to be elected who are qualified voters and over 25 years of age, including soldiers. The remaining 72 members are nominated by the Electoral Committee from the various party lists, in proportion to the number of successful candidates of each party among the 372 elected members.

The Senate consists of 111 members, 93 being elected and 18 nominated. Senators are elected by each province (Wojewodstwo) forming an electoral district. All citizens, including soldiers, over 40 years of age who are qualified voters may be elected, and all citizens over 30 years of age are qualified voters, except serving soldiers.

The Senate and Diet are coterminous; and no one can be a member of both Senate and Diet.

The first Diet and Senate were elected on the 5th and 12th November, 1922.

The Diet must meet on the third Thursday after its election and every year not later than October in order to vote the Budget. The President convokes, opens, and adjourns the Senate and Diet and can dissolve the Diet before its term if two-thirds of the members present vote for dissolution, or if the Senate so votes, by three-fifths of its members; in both cases at least half of the legal number of members being present. The Senate is then dissolved also. New elections to both Houses must take place within 90 days.

All sittings are public, except on the motion of the Marshal of the Diet, a member of the Government, or on a motion brought forward by 30 deputies.

Every bill put forward by the Diet must be submitted to the Senate, which must express any objection within 30 days. In the event of modification by the Senate, the bill must be returned to the Diet within 30 days. The second decision of the Diet is final.

Ministers are appointed and dismissed by the President according to the expressed wish of the majority of the Diet. Ministers need not be members of the Diet, but have a right to speak and participate in its sittings; but may only vote if members.

The Marshal of the Diet is appointed by the Diet and carries out duties similar to those of the Speaker in the British House of Commons. He replaces the President when necessary, and is the official channel for communications between the President and the Diet.

3. Internal Administration.

The whole country is divided into 16 wojewodstwos (provinces) dependent on the Ministry of the Interior. The head of the province, the wojewoda, is appointed by the Central Government and is assisted by a local council, partly elected locally and partly composed of the leading local officials. The Ministry of the Interior controls by means of inspectors. The council deals with local finance, police, schools, etc. The municipality of Warsaw is counted as equivalent to a wojewodstwo.

The wojewodstwo is sub-divided into districts (starostwos or powiats) presided over by a starosta, assisted by a local council, and the starostwo is sub-divided again into communities, headed by a soltys. All soltys are members of the starostwo council.

4. Justice.

The method of carrying out justice is fixed by law and controlled by the Minister of Justice. Judges are appointed by the President for life, and are above the law in the exercise of their functions; and their decisions cannot be altered. Trial by jury is obligatory for all serious or political charges.

5. Civil Rights.

All persons born of Polish parents or who become naturalized are citizens of the Polish Republic and are equal before the law and have equal opportunities for all public positions. Citizens without distinction of origin, race, language, or religion enjoy full liberty, rights of property, and inviolability of domicile.

Privileges of birth, titles and armorial bearings are not recognized, except scientific distinctions and professional and official titles.

Complete freedom of religion exists, but the Roman Catholic Church is recognized as predominant.

Liberty of the press, secrecy of correspondence, etc., are guaranteed, as are the retention of national languages and customs.

6. **National Minorities.**

Special provision for the protection of national minorities exists according to the various Treaties of Peace of 1919 and 1920.

7. **Revision of Constitution.**

The Constitution can only be altered by a two-thirds majority of the Diet, half of the members at least being present. Every 25 years the Diet and Senate in joint assembly can revise the Constitution by an absolute majority vote.

CHAPTER IV.

MATERIAL RESOURCES.

1. **Finances.**

Poland is a country whose wealth lies mainly in her agriculture.

Her financial situation is not yet stable, but a policy of rigid economy combined with high taxation is now being followed, with the result that the latest (1925) budget has been balanced. A new currency was introduced in April, 1924, consisting of the zloty, which is equivalent to a gold franc, divided into 100 grosze.

Poland's debts are (1925) :—

	£
Internal debts	4,171,000
External debts	75,965,000
Total	£80,136,000

or about £2 15s. 6d. per head of the population.

The revenue of the State in 1924 amounted to 1,702,800,000 zlotych (£68,112,000) and the expenditure to 1,660,900,000 zlotych (£66,436,000), leaving a surplus revenue of 41,900,000 zlotych (£1,676,000). This is the first year in which there has been a surplus. The incidence of taxation amounts to about £2 7s. 0d. per head.

2. **Agriculture.**

Poland is mainly an agricultural and timber-producing country, its mineral wealth being concentrated in certain well-defined areas (see para. 4 below).

Of the total surface of Poland 48·5 per cent. is arable land, 17·2 per cent. pasture land, 24·4 per cent. forests, and 9·9 per cent. under buildings, roads, etc., or waste land.

Most of the land is in private ownership, very little belonging to the State.

The principal crops are rye, barley, oats and potatoes.

The yield of the different crops in 1924 was as follows :—

	Metric tons.	Metric tons in 1923.
Rye	3,823,000	5,962,000
Wheat	894,000	1,354,000
Barley	1,254,000	1,655,000
Oats	2,571,000	3,522,000
Potatoes	26,574,000	26,494,000
Beet	344,844	268,347
Hay	Satisfactory	—
Clover	Satisfactory	—

The 1924 crop of cereals was much below the average on account of the severe winter and unfavourable summer.

Forests cover an area of 9,960,000 hectares, of which one-third is State-owned. The principal large forests are the Niemen forests, 134,425 hectares, between Slonim and Mosty; the Bialowiez forest north of Brzesc-nad-Bugiem of 125,858 hectares; the Wolhynian Klewan area of 61,700 hectares; the Wolhynian Karpilowicze area of 35,400 hectares; the Augustow forests of 111,200 hectares; and the State forests of the Wojewodstwo of Stanislawow of 243,000 hectares. Besides this the Pinsk marshes are covered with trees, but owing to the marshy soil these are mainly small and not worth exploiting.

The trees in Bialowiez are about 50 per cent. pines, 20 per cent. firs, 10 per cent. oaks, 20 per cent. others, of which birch trees are predominant. In uncontrolled forests the trees are nearly all pines, firs, and birches.

Several saw mills have been erected in forests for the conversion of timber into planks. In other forests the timber is felled, and floated down rivers to ports. In this way timber is floated down the Bug and Vistula to Danzig, and, when the political friction with Lithuania is settled, it will be floated down the Nyeman to Memel. Bydgosc is a big timber port on the Vistula, with numerous saw mills, and is a centre of export.

The character of the timber exports is as follows:—red pine (fir) in the round, white pine, ash (in the round or sawn), oak staves, sleepers, oak (in the round and hewn) paper wood, pit props, telegraph poles, deals, and battens. The total export in 1922 was nearly one million tons.

Live Stock.—Much live stock perished during the Great War, and during the Bolshevik invasion. Statistics give the following figures for 1921:—

Horned cattle	7,900,000
Sheep and goats	2,200,000
Pigs	5,200,000
Geese	9,000,000
Poultry	40,000,000

Fisheries.—Poland is poor in fish on account of her small sea coast, and the river fish are not very good. There are about 900–1,000 men engaged in sea fishery with 76 steam boats and 200 sailing boats. The average monthly catch is about 40,000 kilogrammes of fish, mainly sprats and herrings.

Industries connected with Agriculture.—*Milling.*—There are 19,000 mills (mechanical, wind, or water) grinding in all 4,350,000 tons of corn. The yearly requirements per head of the population are 160 kilogrammes of rye and 60 kilogrammes of wheat, which can be produced in German Poland and the Kingdom alone.

Sugar.—Sugar factories are established all over Poland. In 1924 they produced 534,000 tons of beet sugar.

Distilleries.—In 1922 there were 1,179 spirit distilleries, producing 1,110,000 million hectolitres; and this represents even less than half the pre-war production. A large proportion is exported to Germany.

Breweries.—The production was 3,912,000 hectolitres in 1912, but has fallen to half that quantity since the war.

Tobacco.—This is now a monopoly of the Polish Government. Sixty per cent. of the tobacco used in making cigarettes is imported from Italy.

Agricultural Imports and Exports.—Poland is practically self-supporting and the agricultural imports are limited to non-necessaries, fruits, fish, and so forth, with the exception that rye flour, used in making rye bread, is imported in large quantities.

The agricultural exports are mainly geese (5,000,000 yearly, having fallen from 9,000,000 in pre-war times), eggs (7,000 wagons yearly), meat (63,000 wagons), potatoes, cheese and butter.

Lack of transport facilities and the necessary factories prevent the full development of trade in agricultural products of a perishable nature.

3. Industries.

As mentioned above, industries in Poland are only beginning to develop. The principal are :—

(a) Textiles at Lodz.
(b) Petroleum in Galicia.
(c) Metallurgy and mining in Silesia.
(d) Metallurgy in the Kielce area.
(e) Timber.

All industries are at present (1925) undergoing a crisis on account of high wages and high cost of production. The number of unemployed registered at the end of 1924 was 150,000, though the unemployment problem is not so serious in a country whose population is chiefly engaged in agriculture.

The textile industry gets its raw cotton mainly from America, but about 25 per cent. from India, and its raw wool mainly from Australia, purchased in Bradford. There were 928 factories in 1924, employing 124,191 workmen, of which over 50 per cent. are for wool, about 40 per cent. for cotton, and the remainder for silk, flax and jute.

The Chemical Industry.—There were, in 1924, 324 factories employing 26,155 workmen. The main products are superphosphates, acids, carbides, wood and rectified spirits, turpentine, disinfectants, soap and glycerine.

Metallurgical Industry.—There were, in 1924, 773 works and factories (including mines) employing 72,721 workmen. The principal branches of the metallurgical industry in 1922 were :—

	No. of Establishments.	Production in tons.
Iron works	29	480,000
Steel works and blast foundries	62	1,002,000
Zinc works	24	85,000

4. Mineral Wealth.

The country possesses a rich mineral area in that part of Upper Silesia allotted to Poland in 1921, and in the neighbouring area of the Dąbrowo basin and Cieszyn. In this area coal, iron, copper, zinc, lead and cadmium are mined.

Brown coal is worked in the above areas, and also in smaller quantities along the river Notec in Poznan, in the Kolomja district of Eastern Galicia, and in Podolia between Lwow and Krzemieniec.

Salt is worked in the well-known salt mines of Wieliczka, near Krakow, and in other mines in the same area.

Sulphur is obtained from Posadza in small quantities. Iron pyrites are found in Upper Silesia. The pyrites deposits in Olkusz and Wloclawek are not worked.

Phosphates are found in Podolia but are not worked.

The yearly production of these substances is as follows (in metric tons) :—

	1924.	1923.
Coal	29,384,401*	36,097,997
Brown coal	80,871*	171,035
Coke	873,110*	1,376,194
Salt	244,096*	363,307
Sulphur	300 tons yearly.	
Iron ore	198,381*	459,740
Copper	600 tons.	
Zinc ore	388,406*	1,007,574
Lead ore	—	15,047
Cadmium	42 tons in 1921, or 8 per cent. of world production.	
Ozokeryte	400 tons in 1922.	

* First eleven months of 1924.

Oil Industry.—The condition of the oil industry in 1924 was very critical, owing to withdrawal of much foreign capital, increased cost of production, financial shortage owing to stabilization of the currency and decreased output of the wells. Many new wells failed to realize expectations.

The main oilfield is situated in the Drohobycz, Boryslaw, Trustanowice, Mraznica area, south-west of Lwow, with smaller fields at Jaslo, south-east of Tarnow, and around Stanislawow ; all these places being in the foothills of the Carpathians in Galicia.

The following statistics show the work in the three main oil fields during 1924 :—

Oilfield.	Net production in metric tons.	Number of wells at work.
Drohobycz	564,641	1,299
Jaslo	53,479	1,110
Stanislawow	39,841	198
Total	657,961	2,607

5. Commerce and Shipping.

1924 was an unfavourable year for trade. The following figures show the trade for that year:—

	Weight in metric tons.	Value. £
Exports	15,739,762	50,537,680
Imports	2,408,995	57,207,920

The imports and exports during the year 1923 were as follows:—

Description.	Imports.	Exports.	Principal Articles.
Live stock (head)	9,800	213,063	—
Foodstuffs (tons)	246,209	425,476	Corn, 17 per cent.; meat, 8 per cent.
Raw material (tons)	2,386,771	14,947,716	Combustibles, 80 per cent.; vegetables, 15 per cent.
Semi-manufactured goods (tons)	175,620	1,502,242	—
Finished articles	385,557	772,253	—

The greatest imports are: from Germany 37 per cent., U.S.A. 15 per cent., Austria 10 per cent., Great Britain 7 per cent., Czecho-Slovakia 7 per cent.; the greatest exports are: to Germany 50 per cent., Austria 11 per cent., Roumania 11 per cent., Czecho-Slovakia 5 per cent., England 3 per cent., Russia 3 per cent.

The principal articles of import are:—

	Zlotych.
Finished articles in metal, machinery, etc.	234,000,000
Raw cotton	141,000,000
Raw wool	80,000,000
Rye flour	15,000,000
Fats	15,000,000
Fish	28,000,000

There is also a local import of raw materials from the mines in German Upper Silesia to the metallurgical works in Polish Upper Silesia.

The principal articles of export are:—

	Zlotych.
Coal	313,000,000
Prepared timber	67,000,000
Rough timber	46,000,000
Cotton goods	108,000,000
Woollen goods	49,000,000
Oil products	51,000,000
Eggs	10,000,000
Potatoes	7,000,000

The only port is Gdynia, through which 123,000 tons passed in 1924. The majority of the commerce passes through Danzig.

THE POLISH ARMY

6. Horse Supply.

The census of horses in 1921 showed a total number of 3,200,000. It is stated that there are now about four million. Some of these are small, undersized horses, used on the farms, but there is a large number of good, strong, if rather light horses, suitable for transport and for riding.

The heavy draught horses are mainly used in the towns and are mostly imported, as are the best riding horses.

The army is practically entirely dependent on the local horses; only officers' chargers are regularly bought abroad, though lately purchases have been made in Ireland and Hungary for cavalry and horse artillery.

7. Horsed Transport.

The horse is used exclusively in the country for transport work, and very generally in the towns.

For heavy loads in towns flat platform wagons are used, but for all other loads and all over the country districts one type of cart, evolved after long experience, is in use. It is a long, low, four-wheeled vehicle, made of wood, with pole draught, generally drawn by two horses. The wheel-base is from two to three yards, and width of track about 3 feet 6 inches or 4 feet. The sides slope inwards towards the bottom to keep within the wheels. It is very strong, light, and handy, and stands a lot of rough wear. Its carrying capacity is about 400 kilogrammes.

8. Mechanical Transport.

Owing to lack of good roads the use of motor vehicles is not very great. The proportion is one motor vehicle (including motor cycles) to 2,350 inhabitants. There are altogether, according to statistics of the beginning of 1925, in Poland :—

7,369 passenger motor cars,
2,352 motor lorries,
1,607 motor cycles,

of which the greater number of cars are in Warsaw town (1,963), Poznan province (1,403), and Silesia (1,094). Lorries are most numerous in Warsaw (568) and Silesia (508).

CHAPTER V.

RECRUITING AND MAN-POWER.

1. Law of Military Service.

The Law of Military Service was signed by the President on 23rd May, 1924, and took effect from the date of publication, namely 18th July, 1924.

Military service is obligatory on all male citizens of the Polish State, between the ages of 21 and 50 years. In the event of general mobilization, men of 19 and 20 years of age can also be called up for service.

The peace strength of the Regular Army will be fixed by the Legislature.

2. Terms of Service and Periods of Training.

(*a*) *General.*—All male citizens are liable as stated for a period of 29 years, divided as follows :—

    (i) Active Army : 2 years, from 21–23 years of age (in cavalry and horse artillery $2\frac{1}{12}$ years).

    (ii) Reserve Army : Up to the end of the year in which the man completes 40 years of age, divided into two periods :—

        (i) From 23–30 years of age.
        (ii) From 30–40 years of age.

    (iii) Levee en masse (Pospolite Ruszenie) : For 10 years, up to the end of the year in which the man completes the age of 50 years.

The "wiek poborowy" or age of enrolment, begins on 1st January of the year in which the man completes 21 years of age, and ends on the last day of the year in which he completes 23 years of age, lasting thus 3 years.

(*b*) *Reductions and Postponement of Service.*—(i) Recruits who have attained the necessary educational standard (six classes at a State middle school or recognized private school) may claim a reduction of service to 18 months in two periods, the first of 15 months, during which he has to do a 6 months' course of training and becomes a podchorązy (ensign) of reserve, the second of 3 months after which he becomes a 2nd lieutenant of reserve. Should he, however, not pass the prescribed examinations to obtain this rank, he goes back to the ranks as an ordinary conscript and has to complete 2 years' service. These men are called up to carry out their first period of colour service between 20th and 25th June of the year in which they finish their school.

(ii) Postponement of service for one year at a time may be granted to :—

    (*a*) The sole support of a family dependent on his earnings.
    (*b*) Owners of hereditary property of small size, worked by the owner himself and alone.

For these two categories, if the postponement is continued till the man reaches the age of 23 years, he is then called up in the following October for a short period of 5 months.

    (*c*) Students, of universities and equivalent training establishments up to 26 years of age, and of middle schools up to 23 years of age.

(iii) Ministers of religions recognized by the State (Christian, Jewish, Mahometan) and monks are passed into the Levee en masse without medical examination. If called up for service they do duty as clergymen, or can serve in the medical corps.

These reductions and postponements are granted by the recruiting commissions to applicants, who make their applications, supported by the necessary documents, before the examination and classification by the recruiting commissions.

During mobilization and war all postponements of service are automatically cancelled.

(*c*) *Reserve Training.*—(i) *Officers.*—Officers of the reserve (including regular officers transferred to the reserve) are liable to training as follows :—

    (*a*) In the first 4 years : two periods of 6 weeks each.
    (*b*) In the second 4 years : two periods of 8 weeks each.
    (*c*) Subsequently : two periods of not more than 4 weeks each.

THE POLISH ARMY

After completing 40 years of age reserve officers can only be called up for training by order of the Cabinet, for special reasons such as the introduction of new weapons or of new field service regulations.

(ii) *Soldiers.*—All men passed to the reserve must carry out training as follows :—
   (a) Two periods of 4 weeks in the first 4 years in the reserve.
   (b) Two periods of 3 weeks in the second 4 years in the reserve.

After this period they are not liable to further training except in special cases as may be decreed by the Cabinet.

Each man on being transferred to the reserve is given by the P.K.U. (*see* below) a document on which is noted the unit to which he is to be posted in the event of mobilization or reserve training.

(iii) *Levee en masse.*—There are no training periods for officers or men passed to the Levee en masse.

(d) *Voluntary Enlistment.*—Voluntary enlistment is allowed to Polish citizens of good character over 17 years of age and under 28. They may choose their arm of the service, and serve for 2 years in the ranks. Men who have reached the age for compulsory service and have been enrolled are not permitted to join as volunteers.

Foreigners may only be enlisted as volunteers with the consent of the President of the Republic and this service does not give them the rights of citizenship.

(e) *Yearly Contingent.*—The yearly contingent will be fixed by law, but in order that all citizens may receive military training, leave will be granted by the Minister of War to a certain portion of the yearly contingent, and in their place will be called up men who have been granted postponement (*see* above) and men who were not called up at the proper time owing to being surplus to the yearly contingent.

(f) *General Regulations.*—Men liable to military service will not be given visas for travel abroad without the consent of the military authorities.

Polish citizens living abroad who attain the age of conscription must report to the nearest Polish consulate, who will give the necessary instructions regarding the carrying out of military service.

Reservists are obliged to report all changes of address to their proper P.K.U. (Reinforcement Districts—*vide* para. 3 (b) below).

Reservists are called up, after mobilization has been proclaimed, by order of the Minister of War.

During emergencies affecting the safety of the State the Cabinet can order the mobilization of reservists, or of certain classes of reservists, even in time of peace.

(g) *Release from Liability to Military Service.*—A man will be released from liability to military service—
   (i) On 31st December of the year in which he attains 50 years of age. (For an officer, 60 years of age.)
   (ii) If completely unfit for military service. In this case he is released by the P.K.U.
   (iii) If found to be of foreign citizenship.
   (iv) After certain judicial sentences. In these cases by order of the Ministers of War and Interior.

(h) *Auxiliary Service.*—The law regarding military service also provides that in case of war, besides military service, the duty of auxiliary service is incumbent on all citizens (without distinction of sex) between the ages of 17 and 55. The method of carrying out this auxiliary service will be fixed by special decree.

3. Recruiting Organizations.

(a) The preliminary arrangements for conscription are performed by the civil and military authorities in concert. Orders regarding preliminary registration, and the summons to appear before the recruiting commissions, called the " pobor " (*see* below), for examination and enrolment are issued over the signature of the civil authorities.

(b) The military authority is the headquarters of the area of reinforcement (Komenda Okręgu Uzupełnien or K.O.U.) under the commander of the corps district. Each area of reinforcement is divided into reinforcement districts (Powiatowa Komenda Uzupełnien or P.K.U.) of which there are 103 for the whole country. The staff of a P.K.U. consists of a colonel or a lieutenant-colonel in command, an officer for instructional duties and one registration officer for each of the sub-divisions (2 to 4) of the district.

(c) In each reinforcement district a recruiting commission is set up, whose duties are to make arrangements in co-operation with the civil authorities for the medical examination of men attaining the conscription age, to allot them to different categories, and to post those classed fit for service to units. Later they carry out the transfer of soldiers to the reserve, keep registers of reservists and call them up for military training and for mobilization. The commissions are composed of :—as president, a civil official appointed by the Wojewode (or in municipalities by the mayor), the commander of the P.K.U. or a field officer appointed by the military district, a member of the civil administration, and a civil or military medical officer. Their decisions are final, except as provided in the next paragraph.

(d) In military districts a revision commission (Komisja Rozpoznawcza) is set up, similar in composition to the recruiting commissions, but with senior officials and officers, namely, the wojewoda or deputy appointed by him, a general or colonel appointed by the military district commander, senior civil and military medical officers, and a field officer. The duties of this revision commission are to decide questions regarding the physical fitness of recruits in case of disagreement in the recruiting commission; to re-examine men classified as unfit if there is reason to question the legality of the classification of the recruiting commission; and to examine male members of the recruit's family if the recruit claims release on account of being the sole support of his family.

(e) The sequence of events in calling recruits to the colours is as follows :—
  (i) Each year the civil authorities of the commune register all men residing in the commune who complete 18 years of age in that year.
  (ii) Men approaching the age of conscription are obliged to call personally, during the months of December and November preceding the year in which they complete 21 years of age, at the communal office with their documents. The communal authorities before 1st February of the next year make up from this a nominal roll which, after being publicly exhibited for two weeks, is sent to higher civil authorities who draw up an enrolment list for each P.K.U.

THE POLISH ARMY

(iii) The civil authorities then order the men on the enrolment lists to report for examination before the recruiting commissions at the P.K.U. headquarters. This is called the "pobor." This should normally take place during the months of May and June of the year in which the man completes 21 years of age. From this examination he is classified according to his fitness, and those selected for military service (category A) are enrolled, posted to units, and dismissed to their homes to await the individual summons to join their unit for actual military service, being reckoned as soldiers on leave at the disposition of the Minister of War.

(iv) The Minister of War then, by summons to each individual, orders these men to join their units between 1st and 7th October in the same year.

(*f*) Recruits, after the medical examination mentioned in (*e*) (iii) above, are divided into five categories :—

A.—Fit for service in the active army.
B.—Temporarily unfit for service in the active army. These men have to appear before the recruiting commission in the next and subsequent years, until found either fit or reduced to a lower category.
C.—Fit for service with arms in the Levee en masse.
D.—Fit for service without arms in the Levee en masse.
E.—Totally unfit for service.

There is no appeal allowed on the part of the recruit against these decisions, but they may be revised by the revision commission as stated in (*d*) above.

4. Recruiting Statistics and Reserves available.

The population of Poland in 1921 was 27,200,000 inhabitants, but since then it has been steadily increasing, and at the end of 1925 was estimated to have passed 30,000,000, and may now be approaching 32,000,000.

It has been calculated, both by American relief workers as well as Polish authorities that the population of what is now Poland was in 1910 practically 30,000,000, and that with the average increase it would have been in 1924 34,000,000. The war period, 1914–1920, thus produced in 1921 a direct loss of 3 million inhabitants and an indirect loss of some 4 or 5 million by 1925. Further, the physical standard of all persons born after 1900, who were children during the war, has been considerably lowered, and the birth rate during the period 1915–1921 was much reduced, so that these classes are not expected to give more than about 160,000 men all told.

The proportion of male inhabitants who in any one year reach the age of 21 was, according to pre-war statistics in Germany and Austria, about 1·73 per cent. of the total male population. But this does not seem to hold for Poland, as official figures give the number of young men who attain this age in any year as from 300,000 to 320,000, *i.e.*, about 2 per cent. of the total male population. This may be due to the fact that the average life is shorter in Poland than in Germany or Austria. Of this number it is stated that—

    50–60 per cent., *i.e.*, 150,000–192,000, are fit for active service (average, say, 170,000).

    15–20 per cent., *i.e.*, 45,000–64,000, are fit for service in the Levy en Masse with arms.

    About 10 per cent., *i.e.*, 30,000–32,000, are fit for service in the Levy en Masse without arms.

    About 10 per cent., *i.e.*, 30,000–32,000, are totally unfit for any form of service.

Therefore, at the present date, 1927, the fighting man-power of the State can be reckoned as follows :—

2 classes, 19 and 20 years of age, liable for service but not yet called up, at 170,000	340,000
2 classes serving, or on indefinite leave, at 170,000	340,000
8 classes of reserve, category 1, aged 23–30. Of these :—	
Classes 1901–1903, who were too young to fight in the war, at 150,000	450,000
Classes 1896–1900 fought and suffered casualties in the war, at 100,000	500,000
10 classes of reserve, category 2, at 70,000..	700,000
Total man-power available	2,330,000

But the whole of those classes born before 1905 are not trained for service. The reason is that many Poles were not called up by the Russians for military service. Further, during the Great War the Russians evacuated large numbers of inhabitants, most of whom were not able to return to Poland till after 1921, and so did not serve during the war.

The number of men serving in the Polish Army at the end of the war in 1920 was approximately 1 million; this number has now been reduced by death and by the attainment of the limit of age for military service, and it may be taken that 800,000 remain.

Since then the following classes have been called up for service :—

1899 and 1900, who avoided service before for reasons mentioned above..	50,000
1901–1905, at 165,000	825,000
	875,000
Less casualties, say	800,000

In other words, there are at present 1,600,000 trained men available.

These would be distributed as follows on mobilization :—

30 divisions, at 13,000	390,000
Cavalry formations	65,000
Army troops, artillery, engineers, aviation, signals	45,000
Field army	500,000
Line of communication units, say	100,000
Establishments and services in home area	50,000
	650,000

leaving 950,000 and the untrained men for forming new units and to enter reserve units to replace casualties.

Men engaged in important work who would not be called up for service, are not allowed for in the above calculations.

CHAPTER VI.

OFFICERS AND NON-COMMISSIONED OFFICERS.

1. General.

The position, rights, and conditions of service of officers are laid down by a law called for short the " Pragmatyka " of officers.

All citizens of the Polish State without distinction of nationality or religion can become officers, provided that they have the necessary educational and physical qualifications. Thus Jews, or men of Russian or German nationality, but citizens of Poland, are equally eligible, with the native Pole, to become officers. As a general rule only men of good social position are taken into the cavalry and horse artillery.

The Corps of Officers is divided into several branches, infantry, artillery, intendance, etc., but all branches have equal rights, and officers of all branches are on an equal footing. There is no special corps of general staff officers, but officers are seconded from their units for temporary service on the staff.

An officer can only be transferred from one branch to another at his own request. He can only be transferred to the reserve at his own request, or after two unsatisfactory reports. He can only lose his commission as a result of loss of citizenship, or after conviction by the civil power, or by a court of honour or court-martial.

All officers who were previously officers in the old Russian, Austrian or German armies were accepted into the Polish Army in the same rank as they held in their previous army. The work of establishing their rank and seniority was of some difficulty, and commissions were set up to deal with the question for each of the former armies. These commissions have finished their work and the order of seniority is now definitely established.

The ranks of officers (with their Polish names) are as follow :—

Marshal	Marszałek.
General	Generał broni.
Lieutenant-General	Generał dywizji (of a division).
Major-General	Generał brygady (of a brigade).
Colonel	Pułkownik.
Lieutenant-Colonel	Podpułkownik.
Major	Major.
Captain	Kapitan, or in cavalry Rotmistrz.
Lieutenant	Porucznik.
2nd Lieutenant	Podporucznik.

The rank of Aspirant Officer, or young man who is passing through a military school with a view to becoming an officer, exists under the Polish name of Podchorąży.

2. Technical Officers.

Technical experts employed in connection with arms, ammunition, engineer material, signal stores, aviation equipment, and so on, are officers belonging to the arm in question. They acquire the necessary technical knowledge by passing through special courses, for instance, at the Armourers' School, at the Signal School, at the Air Mechanics' School, or at a university or equivalent educational establishment, such as a polytechnic. They are liable to be returned to regimental duty before receiving promotion to higher rank.

3. Provision of Combatant Officers.

A young man may become a regular officer of the Polish Army either by direct entry as such or by passing through the ranks.

Young men wishing to obtain a direct commission in the regular army must pass through the prescribed courses at a Podchorąży or Officers' School. The candidate must have finished the course at a middle school with the final matriculation examination or have passed an equivalent examination, and must pass a medical examination. He then joins the Podchorązy School at Ostrow for a general military educational course lasting 10 months (1st September to 30th June). At the end of this he is allotted to an arm of the service and receives the rank of serjeant and the title Podchorązy. He is then attached to an infantry regiment for 3 months, at the end of which he joins the special school of his arm for a 2 or 3 years' course. If he passes this course satisfactorily he is made 2nd lieutenant at the end of the second year.

The various officers' schools are described in Chapter XXVIII.

Non-commissioned officers who desire to obtain a commission must fulfil the following conditions :—

    (*a*) Have completed 3 years' service as a N.C.O.
    (*b*) Have reached the rank of Plutonowy.
    (*c*) Be specially recommended.
    (*d*) Have passed through three classes of a middle school, or have had war service.

Those whose candidature is accepted are sent for a 2 years' course at the officers' school for N.C.O.s at Bydgosc.

The 2 year course at this school is intended to raise the education of the pupil to a level approximating to that attained at the end of the middle school course (matriculation). After completing this course the candidate is commissioned as 2nd lieutenant, but, for all arms except the infantry, he has to undergo a further short course at the special officers' school of his own arm. The school will eventually contain 600 pupils in each yearly course, but at present there is only one course of 300 pupils.

4. Officers of the Non-Active List and Reserve Officers.

(*a*) *Officers of the Non-Active List.* (*Stan Nieczynny.*)—Officers may be put on the non-active list—

    (i) At their own request for long-term leave (6 months to 3 years).
    (ii) For temporary unfitness.
    (iii) On reduction of establishments.
    (iv) When prisoners of war.
    (v) If elected member of the Senate or Diet.

Officers on the non-active list can be called up in peace time for two training periods of 4 weeks each.

(b) *Officers Transferred to the Reserve.*—Officers can be transferred to the reserve at their own request, or after two consecutive unfavourable yearly reports, or for physical unfitness.

Officers on the non-active list and in the reserve have right of precedence, among other candidates of equal qualifications, in obtaining employment in Government service, or in subsidized undertakings.

(c) *Reserve Officers.*—Reserve officers are those citizens, subject to the law of universal service, who have obtained reduction of service to 18 months with the colours on account of educational qualifications, on the condition of becoming officers of the reserve. This period of 18 months is subdivided into two sub-periods, the first of 15 months, the second of 3 months during the following summer training season.

A young man, liable to military service, who desires to become a reserve officer has to have an education not lower than the standard of six classes of a middle school. After doing 3 months' service with his unit he is admitted to a school for Podchorążys of reserve where he spends 6 months, and then returns to his unit for the remaining 6 months of his first period of service. If he passed a satisfactory examination at the school he is nominated Podchorąży of Reserve, and as such appears with his unit during the next summer training season for the second period of 3 months' service, at the end of which he is granted the rank of 2nd Lieutenant of Reserve.

One school for reserve officer candidates is established for the infantry in each military district, and three, for cavalry and artillery, in selected military districts; these schools taking the form of instructional companies, squadrons, or batteries. The school for reserve officers of Engineers is at the Engineer Training Camp at Modlin, those for reserve officers of other arms at the Training Centres of Signals, Railways and Motor Transport. A few of the best pupils at these schools are specially allowed to enter a regular Officers' School with a view to becoming professional officers.

Professional men (doctors and veterinary surgeons) are not called up for service till they have passed their university examinations. They then do the first 9 months' service as above, after which they are employed at their profession in a military establishment or unit corresponding to their profession, and are finally appointed officers of the medical or veterinary reserve.

Reserve officers must do the following training periods :—
- (i) Two periods of 6 weeks in the first 4 years of reserve service.
- (ii) Two periods of 8 weeks in the second 4 years of reserve service.
- (iii) Two periods, of not more than 4 weeks each, in the remaining years; training periods to be at an interval of at least 2 years.

After attaining 40 years of age and being under 50 years, a reserve officer may only be called up for one period of not more than 4 weeks' training on the introduction of new weapons or new regulations.

5. Promotion and Retirement of Officers.

An officer can only leave the Officer Corps by ceasing to be a Polish subject, or after judgment by the civil power or a court of honour.

Promotion is by seniority or by selection. 2nd lieutenants are promoted to lieutenant after 2 years' service. Further promotions are as follows:—

    Lieutenant to captain after at least 4 years' service as lieutenant: 20 per cent. by selection in peace, 50 per cent. by selection in war.

    Captain to major after at least 4 years' service as captain: 60 per cent. by selection in peace, 80 per cent. by selection in war.

    Major to lieutenant-colonel after at least 3 years' service as major: 80 per cent. by selection in peace, all by selection in war.

    Lieutenant-colonel to colonel after at least 4 years' service as lieutenant-colonel: all by selection in peace and war.

Above the rank of colonel, promotion is by selection after at least 3 years' service in the officer's existing rank. Marshals are only made for exceptional services to the State.

In war time service in the field of operations counts as double for the purposes of promotion.

To qualify for promotion to major, captains must have passed successfully a course for field officers. Officers of the general staff, after promotion, must do 1 year's regimental duty. Officers of the fighting arms before promotion must have commanded for at least 2 years the unit corresponding to the rank they hold.

The ages of retirement are: for generals and major-generals 61 years completed; brigadiers 59; colonels 57; lieutenant-colonels 55; and for majors and juniors 53 years completed.

6. Reports on Officers.

Commissions are appointed yearly by the Minister of War at the Ministry of War, and in each of the military districts to report on the qualifications of officers for promotion. If these commissions report unfavourably on an officer in two successive years, he is transferred to the reserve.

7. Statistics.

The peace strength of the officers of the Polish Army is fixed at 17,905 officers (budget for 1927–28). The latest Army List, that for 1924, shows—

    143 general officers,
    6,500 infantry officers,
    1,558 cavalry officers,
    2,156 artillery officers,
    692 engineer officers,
    490 aviation officers,
    353 signal corps officers,
    1,264 medical officers,
    1,436 intendance officers,

the remainder including railway, ordnance, transport, gendarmerie, veterinary, justice, accountant, and topography officers, chaplains and the navy.

According to the same Army List the officers of the reserve number about 27,300.

8. Officers employed in Foreign Countries.

No Polish officers are employed outside Poland, except military attachés in certain capitals, and a few officers attending courses of instruction in the military schools of foreign Powers. These latter are all in France, where there are Polish officer-students at the *Ecole Supérieure de Guerre*, and others at certain military and aviation schools. Occasionally a Polish officer is sent to a course in England or Italy.

9. Non-commissioned Officers.

The following are the gradings that exist in the Polish Army, with their corresponding English equivalents :—

Szeregowiec	Private.
Starzy szeregowiec	} Lance-corporal.
Bombardier (artillery)	
Kapral	Corporal.
Plutonowy	Serjeant.
Sierzant	Staff serjeant.
Sierzant Sztabowy	Warrant officer.

The last two must be long-service volunteers.

Four months after a yearly class has been embodied in a unit, the best recruits are picked out and formed into a special school within the regiment for training to become N.C.O.'s. This training lasts 4–5 months, after which the soldier becomes a corporal.

At the end of their first year's service, those that volunteer for long service and are over 18 years of age are sent to training schools for N.C.O.s where they undergo training for about 6 months. They are then sent back to their regiments as professional N.C.O.s. For these schools *see* Chapter XXVIII, para. 7.

10. Officials.

The grading of "Military Official" given formerly to certain people holding the position of officer, and performing administrative duties in certain arms and services has been abolished. They have been transferred to the Corps of Officers of Administration.

11. Interpreters.

There are no interpreters, appointed as such, in the Polish Army. Every Polish officer, however, knows fluently either Russian or German, according as his education was carried out in the old Russian, Austrian or German parts of Poland. A certain number of officers of better education or social position, especially in the cavalry, know French—some of them perfectly—but it is by no means uncommon to find a general or high staff officer ignorant of that language. A few officers know English, but other languages are practically unknown, unless the officer's previous career in one of the old armies brought him into contact with another race.

With a view to encouraging the study of foreign languages yearly examinations in languages are to be held, beginning with 1925, for officers not above the rank of major, which if passed successfully, will give the officer a diploma as military interpreter. The officer who passes highest in Roumanian, Italian, Czech, Lettish, Esthonian, Finnish and Turkish will be given 3 months' leave with special allowances and free passage to those countries.

Officers having this diploma are to be given preference in selection for appointments on the staff where their language qualification would be likely to be useful.

CHAPTER VII.

STRENGTH AND ORGANIZATION OF THE ARMY.

1. Peace Strength and Organization.

The peace strength of the Polish Army has not yet been fixed by law, but will be approximately 270,000 all ranks, including 17,000 officers, two yearly classes with the colours, and the permanent staff of about 35,000 professional N.C.Os. and specialists.

This army is organized in peace into the following units :—

> 90 infantry regiments,
> 40 cavalry regiments,
> 30 regiments field artillery,
> 10 regiments heavy field artillery,
> 10 " divisions " horse artillery,
> 1 regiment mountain artillery,
> 1 regiment heaviest artillery,
> 1 regiment and 6 groups anti-aircraft artillery,
> 4 companies foot artillery,
> 1 tank regiment,
> 10 engineer regiments,
> 1 bridging battalion,
> 1 electro-technical battalion,
> 2 regiments and 3 independent signal battalions, signal service,
> 2 regiments railway troops,
> 10 divisions motor transport,
> 10 squadrons horse transport,
> 6 aviation regiments,
> 1 balloon battalion,
> 10 divisions gendarmerie,
> 10 medical battalions,

with permanent hospitals, magazines, stores, and miscellaneous institutes (*e.g.*, chemical battalion, geographical institute, etc.).

To each of the 10 military districts (*see* Chapter VIII) is assigned a tenth part of the above units, where the number is divisible by 10, except the cavalry (*see* Chapter XI). Other units are allotted to districts as convenient. The infantry and field artillery in each district are organized into 3 infantry divisions (3 infantry regiments and 1 field artillery regiment).

THE POLISH ARMY

2. War Strength and Organization.

The war strength of the Polish Army is in practice limited to the war material available for arming and equipping the reserves called to the colours.

The man-power of the nation will admit of the regular formations being doubled on the outbreak of war, and the provision of a suitable proportion of army troops, line of communication and home area establishments, and this probably represents the ideal to which the preparations are directed, though at the present date it cannot be carried out.

It may be taken that 40 divisions represent the total that could be mobilised to-day, but that this figure will be gradually increased. Even these 40 divisions would be lacking in certain important articles, its artillery would be equipped with old pattern guns, and there would be a great deficiency of light machine guns. These disadvantages, however, would not prevent the mobilization.

On this basis the mobilized army would consist of the following:—

Combatant troops:—

40 divisions at 13,000..		520,000
4 cavalry divisions } 5 cavalry brigades }		65,000

Army troops:—

13 regiments artillery (11 heavy and 2 mountain) and A.A. batteries	24,000	
Aviation	15,000	
Engineers	15,000	
Signals	3,000	
Various headquarters	3,000	
Total army troops ..		60,000
Total combatant troops		645,000

Line of communication troops:—

Medical	25,000	
Supply	10,000	
Railway	2,000	
Veterinary	5,000	
Transport	30,000	
Ordnance	5,000	
Labour units and miscellaneous	50,000	
Frontier and guard units	25,000	
Total L. of C. troops, say ..		152,000
Total Field Army ..		800,000
Establishments in home area		75,000
Reserve training units, about two-thirds of the field army		525,000
Total army ..		1,400,000

This number can otherwise be divided as follows :—

Total army, ration strength	1,400,000
Field army	800,000
Combatant troops	645,000
Infantry and cavalry	397,000
Bayonets and sabres (2,000 bayonets per regiment, 750 sabres per cavalry regiment)	288,000

3. G.H.Q. and Armies.

General headquarters consists of the general staff (all branches being represented), the commanders (and their staffs) of the "general reserves," or, more properly speaking, of headquarter troops (*i.e.*, artillery, signals, engineers, tanks, aviation, and armoured trains), and heads of services and departments. The strength of general headquarters is not known.

The armed forces are grouped into armies. The army is the biggest unit of operation and administration, and as such must be a completely self-contained formation. The boundaries of the army zones are fixed by general headquarters. The army is normally composed of :—

(*a*) 3–5 divisions of infantry, brigades or divisions of cavalry.
(*b*) Artillery reserves.
(*c*) Engineer reserves.
(*d*) Tanks.
(*e*) Aviation.
(*f*) Administrative services.

It may be found necessary to put two or more armies under a single command, in which case a G.O.C. Front is appointed. As his duties are almost exclusively strategical and tactical his staff only contains the operations and intelligence branches, and at his headquarters there are not the usual heads of administrative services, such as are appointed to army headquarters.

4. Composition and Strength of a Division.

The division is the smallest formation of all arms ; it must be provided with all means of fighting and administration, light enough to be mobile and easily handled.

A division at war establishment consists of :—

Divisional headquarters.
3 regiments infantry.
1 regiment field artillery.
2 squadrons cavalry.
1 engineer battalion.
1 telegraph company.
1 W/T platoon.
Administrative services.

The total ration strength of the division may be taken at about 13,000, the combatant strength at about 11,000, or 6,000 bayonets, 300 sabres, 36 field guns and howitzers,

134 heavy machine guns, and 332 light machine guns or automatic rifles, though the full complement of guns and machine guns could not be issued at present (April, 1925).

A cavalry division at war establishment consists of :—

    3 cavalry brigades (6 regiments).
    2 divisions horse artillery (6 batteries).
    Telegraph company.
    Wireless platoon.
    Pioneer squadron.
    Squadron light armoured cars.
    Administrative services.

The total strength may be taken at about 9,000 all ranks and 9,600 horses, with 24 guns, 84 heavy and 96 light machine guns.

5. Composition and Strength of a Brigade.

Brigades of infantry do not normally exist, but if a fourth regiment be added to a division on mobilization they would be organized into two brigades.

Independent cavalry brigades consist of :—

    3 regiments cavalry,
    1 division horse artillery,
    Telegraph company,
    Wireless platoon,
    Pioneer squadron,
    Administrative services,

or some 4,500 all ranks and 4,900 horses with 12 guns, 42 heavy and 48 light machine guns.

Eventually independent cavalry brigades will also have a squadron of light armoured cars.

6. Mobilization.

On declaration of war such reserves as are required are called to the colours.

Each unit of the army is completed up to war establishment and throws off a depot unit, which remains at the peace station after the unit has moved off to the front. This depot unit is then responsible for training reservists and recruits and for filling up casualties in the front line unit.

Units of the transport, medical, veterinary, and similar services are very extensively augmented on mobilization. For instance, the transport divisions of a D.O.K. have to find the transport columns of the three divisions belonging to the district, and also a proportion of the transport columns required by cavalry formations and for armies.

The medical battalion (the only medical unit in the D.O.K. during peace) forms medical companies and field hospitals for the divisions and cavalry formations in the district, besides a number of medical units (trains, hospitals, disinfecting units) at the disposal of the army, and others remaining in the district for the reception and treatment of cases from the front.

CHAPTER VIII.

ADMINISTRATIVE COMMANDS AND STAFFS.

1. **Administrative Districts.**

The territory of Poland is divided into 10 so-called "corps" districts (Okręg Korpusowy), in each of which are stationed in peace time three infantry divisions, together with certain cavalry and army troops.

At the head of each military district is a general officer, who is in peace time entirely responsible for the administration of his district and the troops and establishments stationed in it, also for all the mobilization arrangements and preparations both of those units that exist in peace, and of those that will be created for war, and in war for preparing reinforcements for the troops despatched from his district to the front, and for the administration of all units and establishments that remain behind. He has hitherto exercised a general supervision over the training of the troops, in spite of the fact that the various Army Inspectors have been responsible for this; but now the status of the Inspectors has been altered and they have all been merged in a Central Inspectorate General (*see* paragraph 6 below) at Warsaw, and the responsibilities of the District commander in this respect, and in general his relations with the Inspectorate General, have not yet been established.

The general-in-command is assisted by a deputy, and has a staff of 21 officers divided into two branches, namely, general and training, and a sub-section for intelligence. The general branch deals with the organization, recruitment, mobilization, discipline and security, while the training branch looks after not only the training and education of the troops, but, keeping in touch with the civil authorities, and authorized societies, supervises the arrangements for the military education of the nation. In addition to the staff there is the office personnel and the staff detachment. The total district headquarters in peace amounts to 32 officers, 87 other ranks, and 33 horses.

The heads and personnel of administrative services of a military district do not form part of the district headquarters, but are subordinate through the staff to the district commander, in the same way as the divisions belonging to the district. Some of the heads of administrative services are at the same time commanders of corresponding troops not included in the subordinate formations. These administrative services are: artillery (armament), engineers, signals, intendance, medical, veterinary, and chaplains. The officers commanding the units of mechanical transport, horse transport, railway troops and aviation, if any, act as the heads of the corresponding administrative services of the district.

The districts are as follows :—

	Headquarters.		*Headquarters.*
No. 1	Warsaw.	No. 6	Lwów.
No. 2	Lublin.	No. 7	Poznań.
No. 3	Grodno.	No. 8 (Pomeranian)	Toruń.
No. 4	Łódź.	No. 9	Brześć.
No. 5	Kraków.	No. 10	Przemysl.

Although these districts are called corps districts, the troops stationed in them do not form army corps either in peace or war, nor does the commanding general take command over them in war, but remains at his district headquarters to carry on the administration of the district.

2. General Notes on System of Administration and Policy.

The President is the head of the Executive, and is therefore the supreme Chief of the Army, and as such grants commissions to officers, makes appointments to commands from divisional commander upwards, awards promotion and confirms retirements. For other matters he delegates his authority to the Minister of War, who is the Commander-in-Chief of the Army in peace.

The Ministry of War is the governing authority in all matters connected with the Army, including its training, armament supply, provision of man-power, etc., but for purposes of decentralization gives large powers, especially in administration, to the military districts, who are intended to be self-supporting, and who only refer to the Ministry of War in case they are unable to supply their needs from their own resources. The Ministry of War lays down the policy to be adopted, leaving the execution to the districts, but keeping powers of supervision and control.

In matters connected with recruiting, *e.g.*, registering the male population, calling them up for medical examination and classification into categories, the Ministry of War works in close touch with the Ministry of the Interior, and it is the latter who actually issues the orders for these measures.

3. Military Councils.

The Council of State Defence, which was constituted in October, 1926, is the supreme authority in all questions affecting the defence of the State, the principles of mobilisation, and the organization of the State's resources. It consists of the President of the Republic as chairman, the Prime Minister as vice-chairman, and the Ministers of Foreign Affairs, War, Interior, and Finance, and the Inspector General of the Armed Forces as members, though other Ministers and experts can be called upon to attend meetings if their presence is required.

The Inspector General is the reporter of all questions submitted to the Council and no decision can be taken without his opinion having been heard.

To prepare the material for discussion, and to generally execute the necessary office work, a Bureau of the Council of State Defence has been set up, which is entirely composed of military officers, and which works under the direct orders of the Inspector General.

The Council elaborates the general programme of work in the domain of preparations for the defence of the State; works out projects of laws in such matters; gives its opinion in matters of importance to State defence which affect the sphere of action of several Ministers, and co-ordinates their work.

4. The Ministry of War.

The Ministry of War is divided into three branches :—
  (*a*) The Inspectorate General.
  (*b*) Administration Branch.
  (*c*) Army Control Branch (Finance and Accountancy).

According to the decree of 6th August, 1926, the Minister of War commands the armed forces and directs all their affairs. He bears constitutional and parliamentary responsibility for his actions in office.

The Inspector General is the permanent deputy of the Minister of War in all questions concerning the preparation of the armed forces for defence and he works out all mobilisation and concentration plans.

The relations between the Minister of War and the Inspector General are left very vague, and at the present moment it is not known whether the Inspector General carries out his work quite independently, without submitting it for approval to the Minister of War, or whether the Minister of War is constitutionally responsible for the preparation of the armed forces for war, on the plans drawn up by the Inspector General, which plans may never have been submitted to him.

The system has not yet been tested, because since the issue of the decree referred to above, the posts of Minister of War and Inspector General have been held by the same man, Marshal Piłsudski.

The origin of this system is to be found in a question of personalities. All previous attempts at defining the duties of the Higher Military Authorities endeavoured to submit the Inspector General (who was, *ipso facto*, the officer designated as future Commander-in-Chief in war, and for which post no other person was ever considered except Marshal Piłsudski, the creator of the Polish Army and the leader of it once already to victory) to the Minister of War; who was to be constitutionally responsible for all Army matters, including the preparation for war. The Marshal has always objected to this submission and has maintained that the drawing up of the war plans should be left entirely to the Inspector General and that the War Minister should have no authority over them at all. When Piłsudski returned to power as a result of the *coup-d'état* of May, 1926, he proceeded to put his ideas into execution, but obviously found that to claim openly the independence of the Inspector General from the Minister of War was impossible, so the definitions of their respective duties and responsibilities were left in vague terms in the decree.

The Minister of War has at his immediate disposition a small Military Cabinet, whose functions are representation and liaison with the civil legislative and executive powers.

The Navy Department is also subordinate directly to the Ministry of War, *vide* Chapter XXIX.

5. The Higher Command.

The supreme authority over the armed forces is vested by constitution in the President of the Republic, but in time of war he is not allowed to exercise the functions of command. On the proposal of the Cabinet, the President nominates the Commander-in-Chief of All the Armed Forces of the State, whose headquarters are designated "Naczelne Dowodstwo," or Supreme Command. It is established by decree, on the authority of the constitution, that the general appointed in peace as Inspector General is designated as the future Commander-in-Chief in War.

The Inspector General, who, as stated in the previous paragraph, is responsible in peace for making all preparations for war, decides upon the general plan of operations; draws up the arrangements for the mobilization and concentration of the armed forces;

fixes the composition of the different armies working under his orders, and prepares magazines and depots in suitable places in accordance with the plan of operations. The territory in which the armies are operating is proclaimed as the Zone of the Armies, " obszar wojenny," by order of the Minister of War, and the Commander-in-Chief is given absolute command over this territory. The remaining territory of the State, " obszar krajowy," home area, remains under the normal government of the country, and all military units and establishments therein are directly under the Minister of War.

6. The Inspectorate General.

The Inspector General is the supreme authority for making all preparations for the use of the armed forces in war, and the Inspectorate General is the organ through which he works.

The Inspector General's duties in detail are :—

(1) Carrying out studies of military operations.
(2) Preparation of war plans.
(3) Training of higher commanders.
(4) Laying down principles of training.
(5) Recommendations in matters of peace organization, location, armament, matériel; and, as regards military industry, fortifications and the budget.
(6) Supervision and inspection.
(7) Confidential reports on officers from regimental commander upwards, and recommendations for nominations to these posts.
(8) Co-operation with civil authorities and social institutions in preparing for State defence.
(9) Participation in work of Committee of State Defence and supervision of its office.

The Inspectorate General consists of :—
(a) The Inspectors and their staff.
(b) Four offices, namely :—
   (i) The Cabinet of the Inspector General.
   (ii) The Bureau of Inspection.
   (iii) The Independent Sub-section for Personnel.
   (iv) The Bureau for the Work of the Committee of State Defence.
(c) The General Staff.

The work of all these organs is directly controlled by the Inspector General.

(a) The full establishment of Inspectors is 14. Only Generals of Division have the right to the title of Inspector; Generals of Brigade appointed to this duty are designated " Generals for Duty with the Inspectorate General." Each of these fourteen generals has a staff of 3 officers (one a general) and an orderly officer, with a small office personnel. At present 12 only have been appointed, of which 8 are at Warsaw, 2 at Wilno, 1 at Lwów, and 1 at Toruń. The eight at Warsaw have no territorial dependence, but are sent by the Inspector General to carry out inspections as he wishes. It is expected that as the Inspectorate settles down in the saddle a programme will be drawn up for the year's inspection work for each of the Inspectors and Generals for Duty.

The inspectors carry out their duties with the authority of the Minister of War, on the orders of the Inspector General as the Minister's permanent deputy. They have no right to issue orders to the General Commanding the district in which they are inspecting, either before, or in consequence of their inspection, but the General Commanding the district is bound to give such orders to the troops and establishments as will enable the inspection to be carried out according to orders. After the inspection the Inspector renders a report to the Inspector General, who then gives such orders as he may think necessary, based on the recommendations of the Inspector.

There are no Inspectors of Arms, such as Inspector of Cavalry, Inspector of Artillery, and so forth.

(b) The four offices have the following duties :—

- (i) The Cabinet of the Inspector General contains his personal staff, officers to whom he gives special tasks or missions as required. It is not yet quite clear what these tasks and missions are, but it is supposed they act more or less as the Marshal's confidential agents.
- (ii) The Bureau of Inspection draws up the programme of inspection, collates the results, works out recommendations, and supervises the execution of such as are put into force.
- (iii) The Independent Sub-section for Personnel keeps a register of all senior officers, from those commanding regiments upwards, draws up their confidential reports and carries out appointments. It also prepares the appointments to be made on mobilization.
- (iv) The Bureau for Work of the Committee of State Defence prepares the material for the sittings of this committee.

(c) The General Staff is divided into four bureaux, namely, organization, information, operations, and supply and transportation.

These bureaux (oddział) are sub-divided as follows :—

I Bureau : Organization.

Section 1—General organization.
    ,,   2—Mobilization of personnel and horses.
    ,,   3—Mobilization of stores and material, and industrial mobilization.

II Bureau : Information.

Section 1—Organization.
    ,,   2—Collation of intelligence.
    ,,   3—Collection of intelligence.
    ,,   4—General.

THE POLISH ARMY

III Bureau : Operations.

Section 1—General operations and use of special arms.
,, 2—East.
,, 3—West.
,, 4—Arrangements for covering mobilization and frontier defence.
,, 5—Fortifications.
,, 6—Training and experiments.
,, 7—League of Nations.
,, 8—Physical training and military instruction of the nation.

IV Bureau : Supply and Transportation.

Section 1—Supply.
,, 2—Lines of communication.
,, 3—Communications and transportation.

This fourth bureau is in the same position with regard to the administrative services as the third Bureau is with regard to the fighting troops. In peace it executes the plans of the Inspector General as far as they affect the administrative services; it establishes depots and magazines at suitable places in accordance with the plan of operation; arranges movements and generally organizes the rearward services and establishments of the Army. Under this bureau are military commissars appointed to work in conjunction with the public services, namely, railways, waterways, post and telegraphs, roads, and aviation.

Under the Chief of Staff are also the Supreme War School (Staff College), Supreme Intendance School, Military Scientific and Publishing Institute, and Military Geographical Institute.

The total peace establishment of the Inspectorate General is 39 generals, 249 officers, 410 other ranks, 103 civilian employees, and 267 horses.

7. Administration and Control.

(a) *Administration Branch*—The administration branch of army headquarters is directly under the Minister of War, who is assisted by two Vice-Ministers, and who all work through the ten administrative departments of the Ministry of War. The first Vice-Minister is also entitled Chief of Administration, and is responsible for the provision of all personnel and material needs of the army, while the second Vice-Minister is in charge of its training and peace organization. The first Vice-Minister is assisted by a Deputy Chief of Administration.

Though each of the Vice-Ministers has the power to deal directly with each of the ten departments as regards matters within his competence, yet it is laid down that the first four departments, which are those, more or less, of the combatant arms, are directly under the second Vice-Minister, while the six other departments are directly under the first Vice-Minister.

The ten departments of the Ministry of War are—

I Department : Infantry.

(1) Infantry, and tanks.
(2) Gendarmerie.
(3) Recruiting for all arms, and reservists.

II Department: Cavalry.
(1) Cavalry.
(2) Horse transport.
(3) Veterinary.
(4) Remounts.

III Department: Artillery.
(1) Artillery.
(2) Organization.
(3) Weapons.
(4) Ammunition: (*a*) rifle, (*b*) gun.
(5) Chemical and gas.

The last three sub-sections of this department are responsible for supplying all armed forces with all the weapons and ammunition they require.

IV Department: Aviation.
(1) Organization.
(2) Equipment.
(3) Aeronautical (balloon) service.

There is also a sub-section dealing with anti-aircraft defence.

V Department: Technical Troops.
(1) General (organization, mobilization and personnel).
(2) Engineer and railway troops.
(3) Fortifications.
(4) Signal troops.
(5) Mechanical transport (excluding armoured cars).

This department is also responsible for the supply of all technical material for these services and each section contains a sub-section for financial control of that section.

VI Department: Buildings.
(1) General.
(2) Building and maintenance.
(3) Architecture and designs.
(4) Financial control,
and a sub-section for keeping a register of all military buildings.

VII Department: Intendance.
(1) Organization.
(2) Food supplies.
(3) Clothing.
(4) Pay, provision of money, pensions.
(5) Financial control branch.
(6) Transportation in conjunction with Ministry of Railways.

This department includes the Interior Economy, Equipment, and Clothing Commissions.

VIII Department: Health.
(1) Organization of medical services and provision of equipment.
(2) Hygiene and medical.

IX Department: Justice.
(1) General.
(2) Regulations.
(3) Courts-martial, punishments, prosecutions.
(4) Legal—opinions on draft laws, etc.

X Department: Military Industries.
(1) Organization.
(2) Commercial.
(3) Technical.
(4) Mechanical.

In the competence of each department come all questions regarding the training, organization and mobilization of the arms concerned, together with promotion and personal questions up to the rank of battalion commander (inclusive).

(b) *Financial Control Branch.*—This branch is under a military officer of the rank of brigadier-general, who is called the Chief of the Corps of Controllers.

It prepares the military budget, controls military expenditure, and is divided into four sections :—
(1) Preparation of estimates and budget.
(2) Control of expenditure.
(3) Financial control of central organs and corps districts.
(4) Accountancy and book-keeping.

8. Special Staff Appointments.

Besides the above bureaux and departments necessary for the preparation for war and maintenance of the army, there exist also the following organizations :—

(a) Under the Inspector General :
Centre of Higher Military Studies.
Historical Bureau.
(b) Under the Chief of Administration :
Chaplain General's office.
Chaplain's office for religions other than Roman Catholic.
War Museum.

9. Military Attachés.

Poland keeps military attachés at :—

London.	Moscow (2).	Prague.	Helsingfors.
Berlin.	Angora.	Bucharest.	Riga.
Paris (2).	Tokio.	Belgrade.	Reval.
Rome.			

There are three officers in each course at the French Ecole de Guerre, and other officers (including naval officers) are sent from time to time to study in various schools or military factories in France.

10. Foreign Military Missions.

A French Military Mission is at present (1926) in Poland, giving advice on the organization and equipment of the Polish Army, and giving instruction in certain of the higher military schools, such as the Supreme War School, Artillery School at Torun. It includes a naval branch of some four naval officers. The total strength is about 30 officers.

11. Organization of General Headquarters and Army Staffs.

(a) At the head of each staff is a chief of staff, who is responsible for the co-ordination of all staff work. He signs certain orders " by order " of the commander of the formation, but orders containing fundamental decisions, and papers involving money charges on the public, or awarding praise or reprimand, must be signed by the commander himself.

In every formation each arm or service has its own chief, who is the technical adviser to the commander of the formation, as well as commander of the troops of that arm or service.

A distinction is drawn between commanders of arms, cavalry and infantry, who have no administrative functions, and commanders of arms and/or services (artillery, signals, transport, etc.) who have administrative duties as well. Commanders of arms and services have access to the commander of a formation only through the chief of staff or his deputy.

(b) The headquarters of every formation consists of the staff and the directors of the arms and services of the formation, and is divided into two echelons :—

   (1) G.O.C., chief of staff, chief signal officer, and the major portion of the staff, with a minimum of the personnel of the arms and services.
   (2) The minor portion of the staff and the majority of the personnel of the arms and services.

Every headquarters has an officer called " O.C. Headquarters," who corresponds to a camp commandant.

(c) The services satisfy all the requirements of the troops. The chiefs of services are kept informed of the intentions of the commander of the formation, and foresee his requirements and take steps to satisfy them. They take their general orders from the commander, and technical orders from the chief of the service in the next highest formation. They have at their disposal specially trained troops of their own service.

The following are the services :—

(1) *Armament* (provides also gas and anti-gas matériel).
(2) *Engineers.*
(3) *Intendance.*
(4) *Signals.*
(5) *Motor transport.*
(6) *Aviation.*
(7) *Horse transport.*
(8) *Medical.*
(9) *Railway.*
(10) *Remounts.*
(11) *Veterinary.*
(12) *Justice.*
(13) *Chaplains.*
(14) *Field mapping.*
(15) *Gendarmerie.*
(16) *Field post office.*

No information is available regarding the strength of General Headquarters. The war establishment of an army headquarters is given in Appendix IV.

12. Organization of Corps Staffs.

Corps do not form part of the normal organization of the Polish army. If a corps is formed in war, the corps headquarters would consist of officers of the general staff only, the administration continuing to be carried out by the army. Such corps would only be formed for tactical reasons if the number of divisions in an army were too large.

The war establishment of a corps headquarters is given in Appendix IV.

13. Organization of Divisional and Brigade Staffs.

In peace time the staff of a division (cavalry or infantry) or independent cavalry brigade consists of two officers, who divide the work between them. War establishments are given in Appendix IV.

The headquarters of a cavalry brigade forming part of a cavalry division consists only of the commander and two other officers, with 13 other ranks and 17 horses.

14. Chain of Command.

The tactical unit on which is based the composition of a field army is the division. From 3 to 5 divisions, with cavalry, form an army, and the "armies" are directly under Supreme Headquarters.

Divisions and armies are self-contained organizations, and are fully provided with all the administrative staffs and services required to make them entirely self-supporting.

If the field army is called upon to fight on more than one front, "front headquarters" would be formed, according to requirements.

If, again, the number of divisions in an army exceeds 5, intermediate "corps headquarters" would be established, but front and corps headquarters are for tactical purposes only, and have no administrative staffs or services.

"Group headquarters" were sometimes formed during the Bolshevik war, when a small force of all arms was required for a special operation for which the normal organization was unsuitable. The groups varied from the equivalent of a couple of divisions down to a small mixed brigade.

15. Lines of Communication.

As stated in para. 5, the country in war is divided into the home area, which remains under the Ministry of War, and the army zone under the Supreme Headquarters; while the latter is sub-divided into operation and lines of communication sub-zones. The army commander fixes this dividing line in his own army zone, and an officer is appointed as O.C. lines of communication for each army.

In accordance with the plans of operations drawn up in peace time, a certain number of depots are established in suitable localities. On the outbreak of war some of these, situated in the army zone, are put at the disposal of armies and the remainder, the most important, at the disposal of the Commander-in-Chief. These latter are kept full by the Ministry of War, and the Commander-in-Chief is relieved of the task of maintaining them himself.

The arrangements for supplying the troops with their requirements in food, munitions, and stores are made by the IV Bureau of the General Staff of the various formations, working through the administrative services as their executive organs. This branch of the staff at the Ministry of War is responsible for obtaining the requirements from the producer, and for storing them and for maintaining the Commander-in-Chief's depots, in accordance with the plan drawn up in peace, amended, if necessary, to suit the requirements of the Commander-in-Chief. The IV Bureau at General Headquarters is responsible for foreseeing the requirements of the armed forces, for keeping the Ministry of War informed as to what is required, and for meeting the demands of the various armies. The IV Bureau at Army Headquarters is responsible for making known to the General Headquarters its requirements, and for distribution of the stores received to the troops.

Behind each army is a regulating station (Stacja Regulająca) under an officer known as the regulating commissar. He is directly under the Commander-in-Chief through his IV Bureau, but remains in close contact at all times with the army commander. His duty is to supply the army in question with all requirements for its maintenance and operations. He is the director of all military transport (rail, road, waterways) in the army area, for personnel and material.

He has at his disposal :—

- (a) Certain magazines, magazines of the regulating commissar, situated in his army area.
- (b) Credits in main reserve magazines of the Commander-in-Chief, situated in the home area.
- (c) Certain trains of fixed composition, calculated to carry one day's supplies or one day's ammunition, or other stores for large formations depending on him, circulating in front of the regulating station.
- (d) Certain march routes in the railway time table from the home area to his area.

In addition to forward supply he is responsible for organizing evacuations to the rear.

The procedure is that the army commander, through the IV Bureau of the General Staff, informs the regulating commissar of his requirements, by formations, and fixes in conjunction with him the railheads and the times at which the various formations will draw their requirements.

The regulating commissar then arranges for the requirements to be met from the magazines at his disposal, or from his credits at the main reserve magazines, taking care to refill his own magazines without delay.

The regulating commissar is assisted by a considerable staff of officers, which includes representatives of various services. The total establishment of a regulating station amounts to 33 officers, 119 other ranks, 32 horses, 10 wagons and 2 motor cars.

16. Committees.

The following special committees exist for supplying technical advice, and for working out technical problems, on behalf of the Ministry of War.

(*a*) *Under the General Staff:*—
Armament Committee (permanent institution).
Experimental Institute for Gas Warfare (permanent institution).
Military Technical (Wojenno-Naukowa) Committee. Meets when required to give technical opinion on purely military matters (*e.g.*, failure to execute orders in the presence of the enemy), when called upon by a military court of justice.

(*b*) *Under the Administrative Staff:*—
Food Committee. A permanent committee for supervision of food supplies, fuel supplies, execution of contracts, and the feeding of the army in war.
Clothing Committee. With functions similar to the Food Committee.
Council of Military Industry. Representatives of various Ministries and industries.
Military Medical Council.
Military Scientific Publishing Institute. Publishes regulations, handbooks, etc.
Bureau of Technical Investigations. Works in connection with the Intendance.

(*c*) *General :*—
Society of Military Knowledge (T.W.W.). A society with headquarters at Warsaw and branches in the districts, whose object is to promote the study of military matters. It arranges lectures, demonstrations, and so on.

17. Intelligence Corps.

No such corps exists in the Polish army. The gendarmerie perform the duties of intelligence police, while the work of intelligence officers of all sorts is performed by special officers seconded from their units.

CHAPTER IX.
INFANTRY.

1. Organization of the Arm.

The infantry of the Polish army consists of 90 regiments, numbered 1 to 86 (omitting Nos. 46 and 47) and 1 to 6 mountain rifle regiments (pułk strzelców podhalańskich). The regiments which used to be numbered 46 and 47 are now the 5th and 6th mountain rifle regiments. For brevity the initials " p.p." (= pułk piechoty—regiment of infantry) and " p.s.p." are commonly employed after the number of the regiment.

2. Organization of the Regiment.

A regiment in peace consists of :—
    Headquarters.
    Signal platoon.
    Pioneer platoon.
    Three rifle battalions.

Regimental headquarters comprises the C.O.'s staff and the administrative staff, which, however, is equally under the C.O.

The C.O.'s staff consists of :—
> Commanding officer, colonel.
> Second in command, lieutenant-colonel.
> Adjutant, captain.
> Medical officer and 6 medical personnel.
> 3 clerks.
> 5 mounted orderlies.
> 9 batmen.
> Bandmaster and 36 bandsmen.

The medical officer is on the establishment of the medical service, not on that of the regiment.

The administrative staff consists of :—
> Quartermaster (major) in charge and 3 clerks.
> Officer for personnel (captain) and 6 clerks.
> 2 officers for equipment (captain and subaltern) with 2 N.C.Os. and 6 storemen and clerks.
> Paymaster and 3 clerks.
> Supply officer and 3 clerks.
> 1 librarian.
> 2 canteen men.
> 6 armourers.
> 2 tailors.
> 2 shoemakers.
> 3 farriers.
> 1 wheeler.
> 1 saddler.
> 3 N.C.Os. (for pay, armament, and supplies).
> 2 cooks.
> 4 officers' mess men.
> 6 batmen.

The second in command is specially charged with training. The quartermaster is in charge of all administrative, supply, and mobilization arrangements. The total headquarters in peace amounts to 10 officers, 34 N.C.Os. and 75 privates, with 11 riding horses and 1 vehicle.

The signal platoon consists of :—
> Lieutenant in command.
> N.C.O. in charge of stores.
> Wireless section :—
>> (a) 1 wireless patrol of 4 men.
>> (b) 2 earth telephone patrols (4 men each).
>> (c) 1 two-horsed cart.

Telephone section :—
- (a) 4 telephone patrols (4 men each).
- (b) 2 two-horsed carts.

Special section :—
- (a) 3 signal patrols (2 men each).
- (b) 2 men for pigeons and messenger dogs.

The total platoon amounts to 1 officer, 41 other ranks, 4 draught horses and 3 carts.

The pioneer platoon consists of an officer (captain), with two sections each of 13 men, totalling 1 officer and 27 other ranks.

Each rifle battalion consists of headquarters (a major in command, adjutant, serjeant-major, and 2 batmen, with 1 horse), 3 rifle companies, and 1 machine gun company. If a battalion is detached the headquarters is increased by a quartermaster and 5 other ranks.

A rifle company, commanded by a captain, consists of headquarters (2 observers, 2 buglers, 2 drummers, 2 cooks, tailor, shoemaker, 2 N.C.Os. for pay, arms, and supplies, and 2 company officers, who are not definitely allotted to platoons) and 3 platoons. Each platoon has an assistant platoon commander (staff serjeant) and two groups, each group composed of a commander (serjeant) with a light machine gun section of 6 men and a grenadier section of 6 men. The total company amounts to 3 officers, 25 N.C.Os., 73 privates. In war a platoon has four groups, and the total combatant strength of a company is 4 officers, 200 other ranks, 11 horses and 4 vehicles, with 12 light machine guns or automatic rifles. The vehicles are 1 S.A.A. wagon, 1 baggage wagon, 1 field kitchen and 1 cook's wagon.

A machine gun company, commanded by a captain, consists of headquarters (range-taker, 2 observers, 2 buglers, 2 cooks, tailor, shoemaker, armourer, serjeant-major and 3 N.C.Os. for pay, arms, and supplies, together with 2 company officers not definitely allotted to platoons) with two platoons (each of 4 machine guns) and one platoon of special weapons. The machine gun platoon, under an assistant platoon commander, consists of two sections (each composed of a commander and 2 gun detachments of 6 men) and 4 drivers. The platoon of special weapons contains a detachment for a 37 mm. gun and a detachment for a mine-thrower or Stokes mortar. The total strength of the company is 3 officers, 24 N.C.Os., 83 privates, with 12 draught horses and 12 vehicles. In war the machine gun company consists of 3 machine gun platoons and a fourth platoon of special weapons. Its combatant strength amounts to 5 officers, 160 other ranks, 37 horses, 18 vehicles, with 12 machine guns, 1 gun, and a mortar. Besides the 12 one-horsed carts for the machine guns, there are 2 vehicles for the infantry gun and mortar, a S.A.A. wagon, baggage wagon, field kitchen, and cook's wagon.

When a regiment is stationed near the frontier it is not considered desirable that its mobilization store should be at its peace station, and it is placed in some other town further inland—in this case a mobilization store staff of 2 officers and 17 other ranks is allowed.

Certain regiments stationed near the Eastern frontiers are given an increased establishment by 367 N.C.Os. and men, 47 horses and 27 vehicles. The difference is made up by adding one more group to each platoon of the rifle companies and by doubling the number of vehicles in the machine gun companies and certain minor increases.

3. Rifle and Mountain Regiments.

There is no difference between the organization of ordinary infantry regiments and mountain rifle regiments except that the latter have a modified transport establishment. They are stationed in or near the Carpathians, and are specially trained in mountain warfare, and in the use of skis ; and as a distinction they wear a special badge, composed of a silver swastika in a wreath. This badge is worn on the collar patch and also at the left side of the cap, where in addition it has three feathers pointing to the rear.

4. Cyclists.

Field service regulations state that a company of cyclists forms part of an independent cavalry brigade. No steps have, however, yet been taken to provide any cyclist units, though a project existed at one time for the organization of an instructional cyclist cadre in each military district, to be attached to one of the regiments, which should be the nucleus of cyclist units on mobilization.

5. Reserve Battalions, etc.

On mobilization each infantry regiment leaves behind at its peace station a depot, which expands into a reserve battalion. These reserve battalions furnish a certain number of second line battalions, of which the following are the war establishments :—

(a) *Line of Communication (Etape) Battalion.*

	Officers.	Other Ranks.	Horses.	Vehicles.	Light Machine Gun.	Heavy Machine Gun.
Headquarters	4	40	36	14	—	—
4 companies, each	4	194	12	7	3	—
Platoon of heavy machine guns	1	33	8	4	—	4
Total battalion	21	849	92	46	12	4

(b) *Guard Battalion.*

	Officers.	Other Ranks.	Horses.	Vehicles.	Light Machine Gun.	Heavy Machine Gun.
Headquarters	4	30	11	5	—	—
4 companies, each	4	180	5	2	—	—
Total battalion	20	750	31	13	—	—

(c) *Fortress Battalion.*

	Officers.	Other Ranks.	Horses.	Vehicles.	Automatic Rifles.	Light Machine Gun.	Heavy Machine Gun.	37 mm. Gun and Mortar.
Headquarters	4	40	45	18	—	—	—	—
Signal platoon	—	30	—	—	—	—	—	—
3 companies, each—								
(a) With automatic rifles.	4	200	11	4	12	—	—	—
(b) With light machine guns.	4	205	17	10	—	6	—	—
Machine gun company	4	120	30	14	—	—	8	2
Total battalion (a)	20	790	108	44	36	—	8	2
Total battalion (b)	20	805	126	62	—	18	8	2

6. Regimental Specialists.

All infantry soldiers are supposed to be trained in the rifle, the light machine gun or automatic rifle, the V.B. grenade rifle attachment, and in bomb throwing.

Specialists' training is only given to the men employed with the infantry gun, the heavy machine gun, the bomb-thrower, and to the pioneers and the regimental signallers. The pioneers are supposed to be capable of carrying out demolitions, wiring, and the construction of small concrete emplacements.

For the signallers, courses are held for officers at the signal school at Zegrze, and for N.C.O.s and selected men at the instructional signal company at military district headquarters. Others are trained regimentally.

The training of the other specialists is carried out in the regiment. Courses are held as well in the N.C.Os'. courses at the central musketry school at Torun and at courses arranged in military districts for duty N.C.Os., and, with engineer formations, for pioneer N.C.Os.

7. Designation and Colours.

Many of the infantry regiments have a secondary name (and sometimes a secondary number) recalling their history; for instance, the first nine regiments are called the " Legion " regiments as they were formed from the remnants of the Polish Legions; the 28th to the 31st Regiments are called in addition the " Kaniewski Rifles " as they were formed from the remains of the troops that fought at Kaniew; many regiments from Poznan bear in addition to their number a secondary number and the name " Wielkopolski " (Great Poland) as they were originally formed in Great Poland, *i.e.*, Poznan.

Each regiment has a standard, one metre square, with a red Maltese cross on a white ground. On the obverse in the centre is a Polish eagle surrounded by a wreath of laurel leaves and in each of the four corners is the number of the regiment, similarly surrounded by a wreath. On the reverse in the centre are the words " Honor i Ojczyzna " (Honour and Fatherland) surrounded by a wreath, and in the four corners are blank shields. On the top of the staff to which the colour is attached is a plate of white metal bearing the number of the regiment, surmounted by a Polish eagle. The standard is fringed with gold.

8. Personnel.

The peace strength of an infantry regiment is 54 officers and 1,394 other ranks (of a reinforced regiment 54 officers and 1,759 other ranks) and its war strength is 74 officers, 2,700 other ranks, 425 horses, 172 vehicles, with 36 heavy and 108 light machine guns.

Peace Establishment.

	Officers.	N.C.Os.	Other Ranks.	Total.	Horses. R.	Horses. L.D.	Horses. Total.	Vehicles.
Regimental headquarters	10	39	75	124	11	—	11	1
Signal platoon	1	10	31	42	—	4	4	3
Pioneer platoon	1	6	21	28	—	—	—	—
1st battalion—								
Headquarters	2	1	2	5	1	—	1	—
3 companies	9	75	219	303	—	—	—	—
Machine gun company	3	24	83	110	—	12	12	12
2nd battalion	14	100	304	418	1	12	13	12
3rd battalion	14	100	304	418	1	12	13	12
Total	54	355	1,039	1,448	14	40	54	40
Mobilization store	2	7	10	17	—	—	—	—
Reinforced regiment	54	436	1,323	1,813	19	82	101	67

War Establishment.

	Officers.	Other Ranks.	Horses.	Vehicles.	Automatic Rifles or light M.G.	Heavy Machine Gun.	37 mm. Gun.	Mortar.
Regimental headquarters	12	160	125	50	—	—	—	—
Signal platoon	1	105	6	4	—	—	—	—
Pioneer platoon	1	60	3	1	—	—	—	—
Battalion headquarters	3	30	27	9	—	—	—	—
Line company	4	200	11	4	12	—	—	—
Machine gun company	5	160	37	18	—	12	1	1
Total battalion	20	800	97	39	36	12	1	1
Total regiment	74	2,700	425	172	108	36	3	3

Note.—The above figures are sometimes an approximation to the nearest 10, consequently the totals are not quite exact.

9. Transport.

The greater part of the transport consists of long, low four-wheeled carts, of the pattern used by the country peasants, and therefore the most suitable for the country. They are capable of carrying 400 kilogrammes (1,100 lb.). These carts are used for

THE POLISH ARMY

carriage of supplies, baggage, entrenching tools, ammunition and other stores. Special two-wheeled carts are used for the carriage of signalling equipment, while the machine guns are carried on carts the pattern of which varies with the equipment.

The total number of vehicles accompanying a regiment in war is 172. This is divided into fighting transport, which again is divided into two echelons, and regimental supply column. The supply column is divided into two sections, each of 18 wagons, including a number of wagons specially detailed for carrying meat. This column carries the third and fourth days' rations for the regiment, while the first day's (unexpended portion) and second days' rations are carried in the fighting transport.

The distribution of the wagons among battalions, companies, etc., is as follows:—

	Fighting Transport 1st echelon.	*Fighting Transport 2nd echelon.*	*Supply Column.*
Per line company—			
For S.A.A.	1	—	—
Field kitchen	—	1	—
Cook's wagon	—	1	—
Baggage wagon	—	1	—
Per machine gun company—			
For machine guns	12	—	—
For 37 mm. gun	1	—	—
For mortar	1	—	—
For S.A.A.	1	—	—
Field kitchen	—	1	—
Cook's wagon	—	1	—
Baggage wagon	—	1	—
Per battalion headquarters—			
For S.A.A.	4	—	—
Tool wagon	1	—	—
Ambulances	2	—	—
Baggage wagon	—	1	—
Officers' mess	—	1	—
Per signal platoon	4	—	—
Per pioneer platoon	1	—	—
Per regimental headquarters—			
For engineer stores	3	—	—
Ambulance	1	—	—
Field kitchen	—	1	—
Cook's wagon	—	1	—
Baggage and office	—	3	—
C.O.'s wagons	—	2	—
Treasury	—	1	—
Canteen	—	1	—
Officers' mess	—	1	—
Supply column and meat wagons	—	—	36
Total	**84**	**52**	**36**

The total road space of the 1st echelon of fighting transport is 1,200 metres, and of the 2nd echelon 900 metres.

The horses vary considerably and are generally of the same type and quality as the local peasants use. That is to say, in Western Poland they are bigger, stronger, and better looked after than in Eastern Poland.

10. Armament.

The armament of the infantry consists of—

Rifle and bayonet,
Automatic rifle or light machine gun,
Heavy machine gun,
Mortar,
Infantry gun,

but the type of all five weapons varies in different units.

As regards rifles the French Lebel, the Austrian Mannlicher, and the German Mauser are in use, but are to be replaced gradually until the German Mauser is general throughout the army. It is a repeating rifle, the recoil ejecting the fired cartridge and bringing a fresh one into the chamber. It is being manufactured in small quantities in Poland. The calibre is 7·9 mm.

The bayonet also varies, the type corresponding to the rifle at present in use.

The light machine gun or automatic rifle is either the French Chauchart, the German light Maxim, or the Lewis gun. Attempts have been made to convert the Lewis gun to take Mauser ammunition, but without success. All types are eventually to be replaced by a regulation type firing Mauser ammunition. The Browning had been selected, but until the question of constructing a factory in Poland for its manufacture has been settled with the makers, no orders have been placed.

The heavy machine gun in present use is of three types : Maxim, Hotchkiss and Schwarzlose. The type selected for general introduction is the Hotchkiss, firing Mauser ammunition. It is intended to build a factory for the manufacture of these in Poland.

The weapons of accompaniment are at present a 37 mm. gun and a Stokes mortar (French pattern). The 37 mm. gun, however, is eventually to be replaced by a fresh type which has not yet been decided upon. The choice lies between three types of 47 mm. gun, made respectively by Pocisk factory in Poland, Beardmore in England, and Driggs in America.

N.C.Os. down to the rank of serjeant are armed with a dagger and pistol, other ranks with rifle, sword bayonet, and dagger. Officers have sword and pistol.

11. Equipment.

(a) The *personal equipment* of the infantry soldier comprises belt with braces supporting a knapsack and carrying 6 ammunition pouches for 120 rounds S.A.A., gas helmet, haversack, water-bottle, entrenching tool, section of cloth and short pole for forming a *tente-abri*, steel helmet, a spare pair of boots, and greatcoat (when not in use rolled round the knapsack). The knapsack contains his spare personal kit and part of his ammunition.

THE POLISH ARMY

(b) *Gas helmets* at present in use are of various types, the French type predominating, but the Polish Chemical Institute has invented a new pattern which will eventually be introduced throughout the army.

(c) The *steel helmet* is of the same pattern as in the French Army.

(d) The *telephone equipment* varies in different regiments. A Polish pattern, made in Warsaw, is gradually to replace all other types.

(e) *Tools.*—Each battalion has a tool wagon carrying 80 shovels, 20 picks, 50 hatchets, and 10 saws. Regimental headquarters has a similar wagon, also a wagon for barbed wire, and a wagon for light bridging equipment. The pioneer platoon wagon carries explosives and carpenters' tools.

(f) *Binoculars.*—Binoculars are carried by officers and by certain N.C.Os. in the machine gun companies.

(g) *Rangefinders.*—Rangefinders are only in use in the machine gun companies.

12. Ammunition.

Six days' supply is carried within the division, of which 4 days' are in the regimental and 2 days' in the divisional transport columns. A day's supply is 40 rounds per rifle, 1,000 per light machine gun and 2,000 per heavy machine gun.

13. Distribution of Ammunition.

The soldier carries 120 rounds on the person, which represents 3 days' expenditure, and another 40 rounds per rifle are carried in the company and battalion S.A.A. wagons.

The light machine gun is accompanied by approximately 1,000 rounds with the personnel of the light machine gun section, and 3,000 rounds in the S.A.A. wagons.

The heavy machine gun is accompanied by about 2,500 rounds on the machine gun carts, with further supplies in the company S.A.A. wagons, amounting to about 8,000 rounds all told.

The actual amount of ammunition carried per machine gun (light and heavy) varies with the type, but the above figures represent an average. For instance, the S.A.A. for the Hotchkiss machine gun is carried in boxes which hold 288 or 250 rounds, according to whether they are contained in rigid or pliable loading strips.

A regiment carries also 6,000 grenades, 4,600 shell for the infantry gun and mortar, and 200 Verey lights.

14. Grenades.

Various patterns of hand grenades are in use, which have been obtained from stocks left behind by the German or Austrian armies, or captured from the Russians.

The Vivien-Bassier grenade attachment to the rifle is in general use throughout the infantry, having been supplied from France.

Hand grenades and rifle grenades are normally carried in the transport of the company, with a reserve in the battalion and regimental wagons. When action is imminent they are given out to the men of the grenadier sections.

15. Tents and Tentes-abris.

Each soldier carries a short pole and a strip of waterproof canvas, and by combining a number of these a small shelter can be constructed.

CHAPTER X.
MACHINE GUNS AND AUTOMATIC RIFLES.

The organization of the Polish Army does not as yet include machine gun units, but their formation is being contemplated. An experimental battalion has been organized in the Poznan military district, with which tests are being carried out in order to arrive at a definite organization which will be suitable for the operations that the army is likely to engage in; no decision has yet been made. Otherwise, machine gun and automatic rifles form part of the armament of infantry and cavalry, and are dealt with in the chapters devoted to those arms.

CHAPTER XI.
CAVALRY.

1. General Organization.

The Polish cavalry consists of 40 regiments, namely, Nos. 1 to 27 Uhlans (Lancers), 1 to 3 Szwoleżerzy (Chevauxlegers), and 1 to 10 Konni Strzelci (Mounted Rifles). The organization and establishment of each type of regiment is exactly the same.

These regiments are organized into :—
   4 cavalry divisions, each of 3 brigades of 2 regiments.
   5 independent cavalry brigades, each of 3 regiments.

The Cavalry Divisional Headquarters are located at Bialystok, Warsaw, Poznan, and Lwow, *i.e.*, in Nos. 3, 1, 7, and 6 military districts respectively, but some of the units in the divisions are stationed outside the limits of these military districts. The Independent Cavalry Brigade Headquarters are located at Rowno, Wilno, Krakow, Stanislawow, and Baranowicze, *i.e.*, in Nos. 2, 3, 5, 6 and 9 military districts respectively, and all their units are stationed in their respective districts. It will be observed that four of these 5 brigades are close to the eastern frontier.

There is also an independent light brigade (numbered 8), which has been recently formed in the Pomeranian military district, which is partly composed of cavalry and partly of provisionally organized light infantry battalions, but the definite composition and organization of this brigade has not yet been settled.

2. Regimental Organization in Time of Peace.

A regiment consists of —
   Regimental headquarters.
   Signal troop.
   4 line squadrons.
   1 machine gun squadron.
   1 reserve squadron.

The regimental headquarters comprise the C.O.'s staff and the administrative staff, which, however, is equally under the C.O.

THE POLISH ARMY

The C.O.'s staff consists of—
  Commanding officer (colonel).
  Second in command (lieutenant-colonel).
  Adjutant (captain).
  Medical officer and 3 medical personnel.
  Veterinary officer and 3 veterinary personnel.
  Trumpeter.
  2 clerks.
  7 pioneers.
  6 batmen.

The medical and veterinary officers are included in the establishment of the medical and veterinary services, and not on the establishment of the regiment.

The administrative staff consists of—
  Quartermaster (major) in charge and 3 clerks.
  Officer for personnel (captain) and 3 clerks.
  Officer for equipment (captain) and 6 clerks and storemen.
  Paymaster and 3 clerks.
  Supply officer (lieutenant) and 4 supply personnel.
  3 armourers.
  2 tailors.
  2 bootmakers.
  2 saddlers.
  3 farriers.
  1 wheeler.
  3 N.C.Os. (pay, rations and forage).
  2 cooks.
  3 officers' mess men.
  3 canteen men
  1 librarian and postman.
  6 batmen.

The duties of these officers are as follows. The second in command is specially charged with training. The quartermaster is in charge of all administration, supply, and preparations for mobilization. Under him the officer for personnel is in charge of administration and of mobilization arrangements as regards personnel (including officers and men of the reserve) and horses. The officer for equipment is in charge of all stores and workshops, and of mobilization arrangements as regards materiel. The duties of the other officers are obvious. The total headquarters amounts to 8 officers, 27 N.C.Os. and 47 men, with 25 riding horses and 3 vehicles, for which no draught horses are allowed.

The signal troop consists of an officer (captain), an N.C.O. for stores, and two sections, the first of which contains a W/T patrol (5 men), 3 signal patrols (6 men), a pigeon patrol (2 men), and a cart, and the second 4 telephone patrols, 20 men and 2 carts. The troop amounts to 1 officer, 8 N.C.Os. and 30 other ranks, with 39 horses and 3 carts.

A line squadron consists of the commander, his staff and four troops.

THE POLISH ARMY

The C.O.'s staff contains—

    Commanding officer (captain).
    3 squadron officers.
    Serjeant-major.
    2 trumpeters.
    4 N.C.Os. (pay, arms, rations, forage).
    Farrier.
    Tailor.
    Bootmaker.
    Saddler.
    2 cooks.
    4 batmen.

with 13 riding horses and 2 unhorsed wagons.

Each troop consists of—

    Staff-serjeant.
    3 sections (24 men).
    Light machine gun section (5 men).

with 30 riding and one pack horses.

The total squadron amounts to 4 officers, 27 N.C.Os., 110 other ranks, 137 horses and 2 carts.

A machine gun squadron consists of the commander, his staff and three troops.

The C.O.'s staff comprises—

    Commanding officer (captain).
    3 squadron officers.
    Serjeant-major.
    2 trumpeters.
    Rangetaker.
    2 observers.
    3 N.C.Os. (pay, rations, forage).
    Armourer.
    Farrier.
    Tailor.
    Bootmaker.
    Saddler.
    2 cooks.
    4 batmen.

with 17 riding horses and 2 unhorsed wagons.

In the first and second troops the 4 machine guns are carried in pack, and each troop consists of—

    Staff-serjeant.
    Saddler.
    4 gun squads ; each of 11 men, with 11 riding and 4 pack horses.

THE POLISH ARMY

The third troop has the 4 guns carried on light vehicles, and consists of—
Staff-serjeant.
Saddler.
4 gun crews of 3 men.
4 drivers for 4 three-horsed vehicles carrying gun.
4 drivers for 4 two-horsed vehicles carrying S.A.A.

The total machine gun squadron amounts to 4 officers, 20 N.C.Os., 110 other ranks, 167 horses and 10 vehicles.

The reserve squadron consists of 3 officers, 15 N.C.Os., 58 other ranks, with 96 horses and 2 carts, and contains a cadre for a depôt and personnel for looking after and training remounts. The C.O. is also in charge of mobilization arrangements and stores of units not existing in peace, but formed at regimental headquarters in war.

3. Divisional Cavalry.

There is at present no divisional cavalry. It is intended, however, that in war divisional cavalry squadrons shall be formed out of cavalry reservists, of whom there is a large surplus. To this end each military district is to form a mobilization store in which all the material required by these squadrons is to be held. A scheme is also to be adopted by which suitable cavalry horses are hired out to selected peasants, cavalry reservists, who will obtain the use of these animals in peace time, and bring them with them on mobilization.

Officers are also provided from the reserve of cavalry officers.

Divisional cavalry will consist of a division, or wing, of two squadrons and a machine gun platoon, with a war establishment as follows :—

	Officers.	Other Ranks.	Horses.	Vehicles.	Automatic Rifles.	Machine Guns.
Wing headquarters	2	50	58	18	—	—
2 squadrons	10	308	328	12	8	—
Machine gun platoon	1	21	23	3	—	2
Total wing	13	379	409	33	8	2

4. Designation and Colours.

Cavalry regiments are numbered from 1 upwards on three separate lists : Uhlans, Chevauxlegers, and Mounted Rifles.

There is no difference, except in name, between any of these. When the Polish Army began to be formed at the end of 1918, three cavalry regiments, numbered 1 to 3, were formed out of the P.O.W., and two regiments, numbered 1 and 2, from the disbanded soldiers of Dowbor-Musnicki's troops. As neither were willing to give up the honour of being the 1st Regiment, the establishment of the two types, Uhlans and Chevauxlegers was ordained, the ex-P.O.W. regiments becoming the Chevauxlegers. As in the past all Polish cavalry were "Uhlans" and their uniform had become the type of all lancer regiments in other parts of Europe, subsequently formed regiments of cavalry of the line were put on the Uhlans list. The Mounted Rifles were originally raised to provide divisional cavalry, but are now on the same footing as other regiments and take their place in the higher cavalry formations.

Many regiments of line cavalry possess territorial names, either from their recruiting areas or from battles at which they distinguished themselves in the past. Poznanian regiments, in addition to their consecutive number, are also called the 1st, 2nd "Wielkopolski" regiments, etc., dating from the time when the ex-German provinces of Poland formed their own army independent of Warsaw.

Each regiment has a standard, exactly similar to that of the infantry, but of smaller dimensions, 65 cm. square.

Each regiment has a pennon on the lance of its own distinguishing colours. On the collar of the jacket a patch of the same shape and colours as the pennon is sewn within the zig-zag braid worn by all ranks of the army. The cap band is also of the predominant colour of the pennon.

5. Specialists.

All cavalry soldiers are trained in the use of the sword, lance, carbine, and bayonet, and of the automatic rifle or light machine gun. Specialist training is given to :—

(a) Heavy machine gunners in the regiment, while certain N.C.Os. are sent to go through a course, which includes musketry, at the Central Musketry School, Torun.

(b) Signallers. Courses are held for officers at the Signal School at Zegrze, and for N.C.Os. and selected men (non-professional) at the instructional signal company at military district headquarters. Others are trained regimentally.

(c) Veterinary N.C.Os. Trained at courses held at military district veterinary establishments.

(d) Farriers and shoeing smiths. Courses are held in military district veterinary establishments and at the Central Shoeing School at Warsaw for selected farriers, but the remainder are trained regimentally from among the soldiers whose civil occupation is that of shoeing smith. One man in each troop is trained as a shoeing smith.

(e) Armourers. Armourers are personnel of the Armament Corps attached to the unit, and are assisted by learners provided by the regiment.

Other tradesmen as far as possible are selected from those engaged in the trade concerned in civil life.

6. Transport.

During peace only the technical carts of regimental headquarters are horsed, no horses being provided for transport wagons either of headquarters or of squadrons.

THE POLISH ARMY

In war the total number of vehicles accompanying a regiment of cavalry is 88. Most of them are two-horsed transport wagons, but some are only light one-horsed carts.

The allotment of vehicles is as follows:—

	Fighting Transport 1st echelon.	Fighting Transport 2nd echelon.	Supply Column.
Per squadron—			
For S.A.A.	1	—	—
Field kitchen	—	1	—
Cook's wagon	—	1	—
Baggage wagon	—	1	—
Forge wagon	—	1	—
For forage	—	—	2
Per machine gun squadron—			
For S.A.A.	4	—	—
Field kitchen	—	1	—
Cook's wagon	—	1	—
Baggage wagon	—	1	—
Forge wagon	—	1	—
For forage	—	—	2
Per regimental headquarters and signal troop—			
For medical equipment	1	—	—
For veterinary equipment	1	—	—
For technical equipment	1	—	—
For signal equipment	5	—	—
Field kitchen	—	1	—
Cook's wagon	—	1	—
Baggage wagon	—	1	—
Forge wagon	—	1	—
Treasury wagon	—	1	—
C.O.'s carriage	—	1	—
For forage	—	—	2
Regimental supply column	—	—	34
Total (per Cav. Regt.)	16	26	46

The above applies to regiments that have machine guns of the machine gun squadron on pack saddlery, but to regiments which have the machine guns of the machine gun squadron on vehicles, 8 vehicles drawn by 4 horses each are allotted in addition, replacing 32 pack horses (*see* War Establishment).

7. Personnel.

In peace the establishment of a cavalry regiment is 32 officers, 866 other ranks, with 875 horses.

Peace Establishment.

	Officers.	N.C.Os.	Other Ranks.	Total.	Horses.		Total.	Vehicles.
					Riding.	P. & D.		
Headquarters	8	27	46	81	23	2	25	4
Signal troop	1	8	30	39	36	3	39	3
4 squadrons	16	108	440	564	582	16	548	8
Machine gun squadron	4	24	110	138	115	52	167	10
Reserve squadron	3	15	58	76	96	—	96	2
Total peace establishment	32	182	684	898	802	73	875	27

War Establishment.

	Officers.	Other Ranks.	Horses.	Vehicles.	Automatic Rifles or light M.G.	Heavy Machine Guns.
Regimental headquarters	11	100	125	45	—	—
Signal troop	1	30	30	5	—	—
Line squadron (each)	5	160	165	7	4	—
Machine gun squadron	5	140	180	10	—	8
Total regiment	37	910	995	88	16	8

8. Equipment.

The equipment of a soldier includes a belt with four ammunition pouches carrying 60 rounds S.A.A., bayonet, entrenching tool, gas mask, haversack, water-bottle, and steel helmet. It is proposed also to give him a bandolier to carry the additional 60 rounds of S.A.A.

Field glasses are issued to certain N.C.Os. and men.

In each section of a troop one man has a V.B. attachment to his carbine.

9. Armament.

Officers and N.C.Os. down to and including serjeants and certain specialists are armed with sword and pistol.

Other ranks are armed with a sword (except certain administrative personnel), carbine, and bayonet, and the front rank personnel of the line troops below the rank of serjeant have in addition lances.

The carbine is usually the Austrian Steyer carbine, but other types are also in use. Eventually all variant types will be replaced by a weapon firing Mauser ammunition.

The lance is of hollow steel, German pattern, with a four-edged point of forged steel in one piece with the shaft. Its length is 10 feet 6 inches, weight 4 lb., point of balance about 5 feet from the point. It has a leather loop attached near the centre. A pennon of the regimental colours is carried in peace. Some regiments have a French wooden lance.

The sword is for cutting and not for pointing. The blade is 80 cm. long, curved, with a greatest divergence from the straight of 3·1 cm. The hilt is of brass, 11 cm. in length, without handguard.

The light automatic weapon in use is either the Browning automatic rifle or the Chauchart gun, which is to be replaced eventually by a new type, not yet decided upon, taking 7·9 mm. ammunition. The detachment for a light machine gun in war consists of 6 men (including 2 horseholders), 6 riding and 1 pack horses.

The heavy machine gun is either the Maxim or Hotchkiss. The type for eventual adoption throughout the army will be the Hotchkiss.

In the machine gun squadron each troop (with pack transport) consists of two sections, each of 2 machine guns. The machine gun detachment in war consists in all of 11 men and 15 horses, namely, gun commander, layer, belt numbers, 3 ammunition numbers, artificer, and 5 horseholders, with 12 riding and 3 pack horses. The first pack horse carries the machine gun, tripod, and 2 boxes of S.A.A., and the remainder carry 8 boxes of S.A.A. and spare parts each. The box carries either 300, 288, or 250 rounds S.A.A., according to the pattern of the machine gun.

Experiments are being made to find a form of vehicle for the machine gun that shall at the same time be its firing platform and carry two men of the detachment. Such a vehicle is expected to be very useful in Eastern Poland, where it could move over country that would be impossible for armoured cars.

The ammunition carried in the field is as follows :—

> Six days' expenditure (a day's expenditure being 40 rounds per rifle, 1,000 per light machine gun, and 2,000 per heavy machine gun) is carried in cavalry formations, of which 4 days' are carried with the regiment, and 2 days' with the division (or brigade) transport columns.
>
> Each soldier carries 120 rounds, the remaining 40 being carried in the squadron S.A.A. wagons.
>
> The light machine gun is accompanied by about 2,000 rounds distributed among the men and horses of the section, a further 2,000 being in the squadron S.A.A. wagon.
>
> With the heavy machine gun, approximately 4,500–5,000 rounds are carried on the pack animals, and a further 3,000 in the squadron S.A.A. wagons.

10. Saddlery.

The pattern of the cavalry saddle varies in the different regiments. Some have the Austrian pattern, high above the horse's back, high cantle, and badly shaped seat which tends to push the body forward. Others use the Russian saddle which is nearer to the

English pattern and is more comfortable. In both the panels are lined with numnah and a saddle blanket is worn folded underneath. In front are carried two large holsters, while behind, over the arch of the saddle, are the rolled greatcoat and personal blanket, with mess tin on top in the centre. The girths are of plaited web, and over all is a leather surcingle. A breastplate is worn with both types of saddlery.

It is laid down that the sword is to be carried under the saddle-flap on the near side, hilt to the front and projecting past the holsters, the point reaching to about the bottom rear corner of the folded blanket, but not all regiments have yet adopted this system.

The bridle is of ordinary pattern with T bit and big bit. It has brass mountings for officers.

The following personal equipment is carried on the saddle :—
- (a) *In front.*—Two holsters with personal kit, containing section of picketing rope, brush (each three men carry between them 1 clothes brush, 1 blacking brush, and 1 polishing brush), hair brush, tooth brush, soap, towel, cloth for repair of uniform, rifle cleaning material, iron ration, shirt, pair of drawers, pair of foot-cloths or socks, knife, fork, and spoon, bread and condiments, and 60 rounds of S.A.A. Every fourth man carries a canvas bucket on the outside of the holsters.
- (b) *In rear.*—Rolled greatcoat, blanket, and mess tin.
- (c) *At the side.*—Filled nose-bag and shoe-case on the near side, entrenching tool on the off side.

The total weight of these is 22 kilogrammes, or nearly 50 lb.

Together with the weight of the saddlery, armament, and the soldier himself, the weight carried by the horse is some 120–130 kilogrammes, or 265–285 lbs. (19 or 20 stone).

11. Technical Equipment.

The technical equipment of a cavalry regiment consists only of signal stores. No explosives or tools are given to regiments, but are concentrated in the pioneer squadrons.

Pioneer squadrons are an integral part of cavalry divisions or of independent cavalry brigades. They are normally attached to one of the regiments of the division (or brigade).

The squadron consists of a commander (captain) and his staff, and four platoons in the case of a divisional squadron or three platoons in the case of a brigade squadron.

The commander's staff consists of 2 trumpeters, a serjeant-major, tailor, bootmaker, saddler, 2 cooks, shoeing smith, 4 N.C.Os. (pay, armament, rations, forage), with 2 carts. Three officers (two in a brigade squadron) are also attached to this staff. A troop consists of a serjeant, three sections each of 8 men, with a one-horsed cart for explosives and a cart for tools. The total strength of a divisional squadron amounts to 4 officers, 23 N.C.Os., 102 other ranks, with 121 horses and 10 vehicles, and of a brigade squadron of 3 officers, 19 N.C.Os., 78 other ranks, 92 horses and 8 vehicles.

The pioneer squadrons are composed of cavalry recruits who, after doing recruit training in regiments for 3 months, are seconded to the pioneer squadrons for the rest of their military service. It is intended that after receiving these recruits pioneer squadrons shall be sent to an engineer camp for technical training, which will comprise field works, wiring, demolitions, and bridge building.

The personnel wear collar pennons of crimson and black, with black cap bands.

The equipment of the squadrons includes entrenching tools, other tools, *e.g.*, saws, wire cutters, and so forth, and explosives, but no bridging material.

The war establishment of pioneer squadrons is :—

	Officers.	Other Ranks.	Horses.	Vehicles.
Cavalry brigade pioneer squadron (3 troops)	4	118	122	16
Cavalry division pioneer squadron (4 troops)	5	150	150	18

In the first case the 16 vehicles include 7 with tools and 3 with explosives, and in the second the 18 vehicles include 8 with tools and 4 with explosives, the remaining wagons being one for S.A.A., field kitchen and cook's cart, and baggage and supply wagons, in both cases.

12. The Horse.

The horse of the Polish cavalry is considerably lighter than the British cavalry horse. He is a native of the country, and has great strength and endurance, which have been transmitted from the time when the Tartars of the Golden Horde occupied the greater part of Poland in the 14th century, when they brought large numbers of their horses from Central Asia. These Tartar horses are renowned for their endurance and have given this quality to their descendants, which are the present locally bred horses of the country. Bad breeding and feeding among the horses of the poorer peasants have greatly reduced their size, and those used by the poorer classes are very small, though retaining much strength and endurance. The horses, however, of the better class peasants have not deteriorated so much and have been kept up to standard by breeding from good stallions which the various landowners and Government institutions in the past have kept. This is the horse which mounts the cavalry and supplies the draught horses for the artillery, and though they look too small and loose for the weight they have to carry, or pull, they have proved to be the best suited for military purposes in this part of Europe. It is said that the Germans in 1917 and 1918, finding their own military horses could not stand either the climate or the country, replaced them all by local horses, of which they requisitioned 200,000. But there is considerable difference in quality in regiments; those formed in Poznan, which were able to take the horses of the retreating Germans, or get horses from studs which did not suffer in the war, are much better mounted than regiments formed in ex-Russian Poland, from whence all good horses had already been taken by the various armies that operated there during the war.

CHAPTER XII.
ARTILLERY.
A.—The Arm.

1. **General Organization.**

 The artillery of the Polish Army consists of—
 - 30 regiments of field artillery (1 per division, field guns and field howitzers).
 - 10 regiments of heavy (field) artillery (1 per army corps).
 - 13 groups* of horse artillery.
 - 1 regiment of mountain artillery.
 - 4 companies of foot artillery.
 - 1 regiment of heaviest artillery.
 - 1 regiment of anti-aircraft artillery.
 - 6 groups of anti-aircraft artillery.

 It is possible that eventually the divisional artillery will consist of a regiment of field guns (9 batteries) and a group of field howitzers (3 batteries)—but owing to financial conditions this reorganization is not likely to take place for some years to come.

2. **Artillery Staffs.**

 Under the Minister of War is an inspector of artillery with two sub-inspectors and a staff.

 In each military district is an inspector of artillery of the district, a brigadier-general or colonel.

 The divisional artillery is, through the regimental commander, immediately under the divisional commander. The two groups of horse artillery in a cavalry division are under an officer commanding horse artillery of a cavalry division.

 In war time, when general headquarters takes the field, and when front headquarters and army headquarters are formed, a senior artillery officer is attached to these headquarters as artillery adviser and as commander of such artillery as is directly under the orders of these headquarters.

3. **Personnel.**

 The personnel of the artillery is drawn from the same classes of population as the infantry. Efforts are made to obtain men whose civil occupation is that of shoeing smith, carpenter, or saddler, to carry out similar duties in the artillery, and to allot a proportion of men with some education to be trained as telephonists and signallers.

4. **Equipment.**

 Officers are armed with sword and pistol.

 Mounted N.C.Os. and trumpeters are armed with sword and pistol, other N.C.Os. and the rank and file with a carbine and bayonet. In the horse artillery all ranks are armed with a sword, carbine, and bayonet, except the senior N.C.Os., who have sword and pistol only.

 The carbine is carried slung over the left shoulder.

 All other ranks wear a leather belt with pouches, haversack, waterbottle, gas mask, and steel helmet.

---

* The word "group" is used as a translation of the Polish word "dywizjon," which must be carefully distinguished from the word "dywizja," which is translated "division."

THE POLISH ARMY

The greatcoat, blanket and mess-tin of mounted men, including drivers, are attached to the rear arch of the riding saddle. Outriders have a pair of wallets for small kit on the front of the saddle. Drivers carry their wallets on the off horse on the pad. The greatcoat, blanket, mess-tin, and small kit of gunners, who ride on the vehicles, are strapped to the vehicles.

The harness is not uniform in pattern. Some batteries have French type with breast harness, with a small pad on the off horse. Others have Russian or Austrian with large neck collar and complicated harness, and a regular saddle on the off horse. A blanket for the horse is folded underneath all saddles and pads. The traces are of rope, with steel chains and hooks. The traces of the centre horses are attached to a swingletree, which is hooked to the point of the pole. There is no such thing as a quick release, and to unhook the centre horses from the pole needs much manipulation to free the swingletree hook with its spring clip from the ring at the end of the pole. The Russian harness gives much longer distance between each pair of horses, especially between the centre and wheel horses.

5. Regimental Specialists.

The greater part of the specialists are professional N.C.Os. with a long service engagement, but some of them are taken from the annual class of recruits who have the necessary qualifications.

Armament artificers and armourers are selected from recruits who are mechanics, and after a preliminary training in the regiment are sent to the Central School of Armourers (Centralna Szkola Zbrojmistrzow) at Warsaw for a 6 months' course, after which they are appointed to units. They must be on a long service engagement.

Shoeing smiths are trained in the regiment, but if they wish to become farriers on a long service engagement they go through a course arranged by the military district.

Wheelers and saddlers are taken from among those of the yearly class whose civil occupation is the same.

Veterinary personnel are trained at a course arranged in each military district.

As regards signallers, courses for officers are held at the Central Signal School at Zegrze, and for N.C.Os. and selected men at the instructional signal companies in military districts. Others are trained in the unit.

6. Rangefinders.

It is proposed to introduce the Barr and Stroud rangefinder into the artillery, at first one per group, but eventually one per battery. In the meantime ranges are measured either by means of the map or by calculation.

7. Directors.

The director used by the Polish artillery is the French pattern director with compass, graduated in millièmes (6,400 millièmes make up a circle). Batteries are supplied with two of these directors.

Batteries are also supplied with a periscopic director (with a magnifying power of 12) but this instrument is not considered accurate and is generally only used for observation.

B.—Field Artillery (including Horse Artillery).

1. Organization of the Branch.

The field artillery is allotted to divisions. It consists of 30 regiments, of 3 groups of 3 four-gun batteries. Two of these groups should be armed with 75 mm. 1897 pattern

French field guns and one with 100 mm. Skoda howitzer. Owing to shortage of equipment, however, many regiments have only 2 guns per battery and only 1 howitzer per battery.

The horse artillery is allotted to cavalry divisions (2 groups) and to independent cavalry brigades (1 group). A group consists of 3 four-gun batteries armed with Russian 3-inch horse artillery guns, 1902 pattern, of which there are sufficient to arm all 13 groups. It is proposed to reline these guns to take 75 mm. French ammunition.

2. Organization of a Regiment or Group.

A regiment consists of regimental headquarters, signal platoon, and 3 groups. A group of field artillery consists of group headquarters, 3 batteries, and on mobilization a group ammunition column. If a group is detached from regimental headquarters the group headquarters is increased. A horse artillery group consists of headquarters, signal detachment, 3 batteries, and on mobilization an ammunition column.

The peace establishments are as follows :—

> Regimental headquarters consists of 10 officers and 102 other ranks, group headquarters of 2 officers and 10 other ranks, and horse artillery group headquarters of 9 officers and 84 other ranks.

Medical and veterinary officers are furnished to field artillery regimental headquarters and horse artillery group headquarters from the establishment of the medical and veterinary services.

3. Organization of a Battery.

A battery is commanded by a captain and consists of 2 platoons, each of 2 guns and 2 ammunition wagons. It also has 2 machine guns for anti-aircraft protection. In peace, except in frontier stations, only 1 platoon is horsed.

The peace establishment of batteries is :—

	Officers.	Other Ranks.	Total.	Riding Horses.	Draught Horses.	Total.	Vehicles.
Field battery (horsed).. ..	3	87	90	20	53	73	13
Field battery (1 section only horsed).	3	84	87	20	29	49	13
Horse battery	3	109	112	70	55	125	14

The detachment for each gun or howitzer consists of gun commander and N.C.O. for ammunition (both mounted) and 6 gunners for work at the gun and the ammunition wagon. The battery staff includes an N.C.O. for fire duties, 3 scouts, 4 telephonists, and 2 trumpeters as combatant staff, and an administrative staff of serjeant-major, pay, supply, and forage N.C.Os., armourer, 2 cooks, tailor, shoemaker, saddler, and 2 farriers.

4. Independent Field Artillery.

All field artillery is included in the divisional organization, and no independent regiments, groups, or batteries exist.

5. Ammunition Column.

A field artillery group ammunition column carries approximately 2 days' supply per gun in the group. A group ammunition column of a 75 mm. group consists of 45 transport wagons for the carriage of ammunition, and that of a 100 mm. group of 60 wagons, besides

5 vehicles for the use of the column. The wagons are of the ordinary pattern used by the peasants. Ammunition columns do not exist in peace. In war they will be commanded by captains.

A horse artillery group ammunition column carries 1½ days' supply for the group, or a total of 1,152 shell. These shell are contained in 12 ammunition wagons.

6. Anti-Aircraft Artillery.

The anti-aircraft artillery consists of 1 regiment at Warsaw and 6 independent groups stationed in military districts which have aviation regiments.

The regiment consists of headquarters, signal section, company of machine guns, searchlight section, listening section, and 2 groups of 3 batteries each. One group consists of modern anti-aircraft guns, mechanically transported; the other group consists of ordinary field guns, which have been mounted on improvised mountings. These batteries are capable of being rapidly dismounted and transported on travelling carriages drawn by horses.

The regiment has a peace establishment of 38 officers and 658 other ranks, with 51 horses, 12 horse-drawn vehicles, 12 motor vehicles, and 4 tractors.

The armament of the regiment consists of (each battery has 4 guns):—

(a) 1 battery 75 mm. French guns, on 4-wheeled De Dion Bouton 60 h.p. lorries. For direct fire only.

(b) 1 battery 75 mm. French guns, on a 2-wheeled tractor drawn by Latile-Suresnes 60 h.p. tractor lorry. For direct and indirect fire.

(c) 1 battery 88 mm. German Krupp guns, on 4-wheeled trailer drawn by F.W.D. 60 h.p. lorry.

(d) 3 batteries with 75 mm. and Russian 3-inch field guns, with reinforced buffers and springs, on semi-permanent revolving platforms.

The batteries (a) and (b) above have up-to-date French instruments; battery (c) has German ones. The batteries under (d) with 75 mm. guns have French instruments, but the battery with Russian 3-inch guns has only home-made instruments made to the design of an officer of the regiment.

The listening section has new apparatus recently received from France.

The 6 groups of anti-aircraft artillery each consist of 2 batteries of Russian 3-inch guns on semi-permanent mountings, with a technical section.

7. Regimental Transport.

Each horse or field battery, besides its 4 guns and 4 ammunition wagons, has at war strength 2 carts for machine guns, 2 telephone carts, a cart for battery stores, a field kitchen, and 4 transport wagons, carrying respectively a forge, baggage, supplies, and forage. Ammunition columns also have 5 wagons for the use of the column, *vide* para. 5 above.

Group headquarters have 2 telephone carts, 1 wagon with medical and veterinary equipment, and 2 transport wagons for baggage and forage.

Regimental headquarters have a telephone cart, a wagon for medical and veterinary equipment, 8 transport wagons for the carriage of baggage, forage, and stores, and in addition a supply column divided into two sections, each of 28 vehicles, and carrying 1 day's supplies.

72   THE POLISH ARMY

The whole of the transport is divided into fighting transport, 1st and 2nd echelons, and the supply column.

8. Regimental Specialists.
The specialists in a field artillery regiment and a horse artillery group are :—

	Horse Artillery Group.	Field Artillery Regiment.
Armourers (small arms)	2	3
Armament artificers (guns)	2	3
		(also 1 per battery)
Farriers	3	3
		(and 3 shoeing smiths per battery)
Wheelers	2	2
Saddlers	2	3
		(1 per battery in addition)
Medical personnel	3	6
Veterinary personnel	1	3
Wireless operators		in signal platoon
Telegraphists		distributed throughout regiment.

9. Personnel.
Regiments are commanded by colonels, with lieutenant-colonels as seconds-in-command. The quartermaster, head of the administrative branch of regimental headquarters, and group commanders in the regiment are majors, but one of them may be a lieutenant-colonel. Commanders of independent groups of horse artillery are generally lieutenant-colonels. Batteries are commanded by captains.

For the armament and equipment of personnel *see* Section A, para. 4.

10. The Field Gun.
The field gun is the French 75 mm. gun, 1897 pattern. The principal details are given in the Appendix at the end of this chapter.

The limber contains 24 shell, with small stores. Three men are carried on it, facing the front.

The wagon body carries 72 shell in two compartments, and has a corn box, spare parts box, fuze box, and fuze setter. In action it is unlimbered, the top then opens and discloses the shell in a horizontal position. It is supported by two props, which in the travelling position are on the rear of the wagon body.

11. The Field Howitzer.
The field howitzer is a 100 mm. howitzer, type 14, manufactured at the Skoda works. The principal details are given in the Appendix.

The limber is divided into 8 compartments for ammunition, telephone gear, and spare parts. Three men are carried on it.

The ammunition wagon contains 12 compartments for ammunition, each holding a box containing 3 rounds.

THE POLISH ARMY

12. The Horse Artillery Gun.
The gun is a 3-inch Russian field gun, 1902 model, of the lightened type, formerly used in the Russian Horse Artillery. For details *see* the Appendix at the end of this chapter.

The limber carries 24 shell, and the ammunition wagon, with limber, 96 shell.

It is said that this gun is being relined and altered to take the same ammunition as the French 75 mm. gun.

13. Ammunition.
The ammunition includes both shrapnel and high explosive shell. In addition gas shell are held in store for horse and field artillery.

The ammunition carried for the 75 mm. gun is as follows :—
>120 rounds per gun in the battery, representing 2 days' expenditure, and about
>120 rounds per gun in the group ammunition column ;

for the 100 mm. howitzer—
>80 rounds per gun in the battery, and
>100 rounds per gun in the group ammunition column ;

and for the 3-inch horse artillery gun—
>120 rounds per gun in the battery, and
>96 rounds per gun in the ammunition column.

For further reserves of shell within the division *see* Section G below.

C.—Heavy Field Artillery (including Foot Artillery).

1. Organization of the Branch.
The heavy field artillery is organized in 10 regiments of heavy artillery, each of 3 groups of 3 four-gun batteries, and 1 regiment of heaviest artillery of similar composition.

These heavy regiments are in peace time stationed one in each military district. In war they are allotted to armies as required. The heaviest regiment is stationed at Warsaw.

Shortage of material prevents the full number of guns and howitzers being issued at present.

2. Organization of Foot Artillery.
Four companies of foot artillery are in process of organization, to serve in the fortified areas of Warsaw, Wilno, Brzesc-nad-Bugiem, and Przemysl. Each company (which is equivalent to a group in other branches of the artillery) consists of 3 batteries. The armament is very varied.

3. Organization of a Heavy (Heaviest) Artillery Regiment.
A regiment of heavy field artillery consists of regimental headquarters, signal platoon, sound ranging section (in heavy regiments only), and three.groups. A group of heavy artillery consists of group headquarters, 3 batteries, 1 of two 105 mm. guns, and 2 of four 155 mm. Schneider howitzers each, and, on mobilization, an ammunition column. Batteries have only 2 guns (howitzers) horsed in peace. Some regiments have only two groups at present. Guns (and howitzers) are drawn by teams of 8 horses.

The regiment of heaviest artillery has three groups of 3 batteries of 120 mm. guns, which in peace have 2 guns each, but on mobilization will have 4. The guns are mounted on carriages with caterpillar wheels, and are drawn by teams of 8 horses.

The peace establishment of the regiment, for heavy and heaviest artillery, is 28 officers and 422 other ranks.

4. Organization of Foot Artillery Company.

The company is commanded by a major and his headquarters include a signal section, administrative staff, and 8 pairs of draught horses.

The establishment is :—

Headquarters :—4 officers, 51 other ranks, 23 horses, 2 carts. In this are included signal detachment of 1 W/T patrol and 4 signal patrols on foot, with 2 carts, administrative personnel and tradesmen.

Battery :—2 officers, 27 other ranks, 3 riding horses, and 2 guns.

5. Organization of Heavy and Heaviest Batteries.

The battery is commanded by a captain. A battery of 105 mm. guns has 2 guns only, those of 120 mm. guns and 155 mm. howitzers have 4 pieces. The ammunition is carried in transport wagons, the number of which varies according to the weapon. The battery has also 2 carts for machine guns, 2 telephone carts, a wagon for technical stores, a field kitchen, and 4 transport wagons.

6. Ammunition Columns.

The group ammunition column of a heavy group is divided into three sections, one carrying 105 mm. shell, and the other two 155 mm. shell, the total number of wagons available for carrying shell being 60. The first section (of 10 wagons) carries 160—105 mm. shell, the other two (of 25 wagons each) carry 175—155 mm. shell each, these amounts representing about 2 days' supply per gun.

7. Regimental Transport.

As for field artillery regiments, except that the supply column consists of two sections of 33 wagons each.

8. Regimental Specialists.

As in field batteries.

The personnel of the sound ranging section are trained at the Sound Ranging Section of the Artillery School at Torun.

9. Personnel.

As in the field artillery.

10. The Heavy Field Howitzer.

This is a 155 mm. French Schneider howitzer, 1917 pattern of which the principal details are given in the Appendix at the end of this chapter.

11. The Heavy Gun.

(*a*) 105 mm. French gun, 1913 pattern.
(*b*) 120 mm. French gun, 1898 pattern, on caterpillar wheels.

THE POLISH ARMY

12. Ammunition.

The ammunition carried in a heavy artillery regiment is :—
- Per battery 105 mm. guns, 80 rounds per gun, or 2 days' supply.
- Per battery 155 mm. howitzers, 49 rounds per howitzer, or 2 days' supply.
- Per ammunition column, 160—105 mm. shell, and 350—155 mm. shell, or roughly 2 days' supply per gun or howitzer.

The types of shell include high explosive, and gas shell, and a small proportion of shrapnel.

D.—Mountain Artillery.

1. Organization of the Branch.

The mountain artillery is organized in one regiment, which is not allotted to divisions, but is army artillery. It consists of regimental headquarters, signal platoon, one group of 3 batteries of 4 guns each, and one group of 3 batteries of 4 howitzers each. Shortage of equipment prevents the full complement of guns and howitzers being issued.

The establishments of regimental and group headquarters, and of the signal platoon, is the same as those of the field artillery.

2. Organization of a Battery.

Batteries are commanded by captains, and consist of 4 guns or howitzers.

In the gun batteries the gun is carried on two small two-wheeled carts, from which it can be taken and put on pack saddles. These carts are drawn by 2 horses each (harnessed tandem). With each gun are 4 other one-horsed carts for ammunition (which can also be taken from them and put on pack saddles), and 1 two-horsed transport wagon.

In the howitzer batteries the howitzer is carried on 3 two-wheeled carts pulled by 2 horses in tandem, and is accompanied by 4 one-horsed carts and 3 two-horsed transport wagons for ammunition. The weapon and ammunition can also be taken from the carts and put on pack saddles.

The detachments are composed of gun commander and ammunition N.C.O. (both mounted) and 6 men for working the gun or howitzer, exclusive of the drivers, of whom there is one for every horse harnessed to the carts, and one for the two-horsed transport wagons for ammunition. The gun sub-section therefore amounts to 17 men, 12 horses, 6 carts and 1 wagon, and the howitzer sub-section to 21 men, 18 horses, 7 carts and 3 wagons.

The battery staff is the same as that of a field battery, *i.e.*, includes 2 officers, 3 scouts, 4 telephonists, armourer, saddler, 2 shoeing smiths and other personnel. Only one section per battery is horsed in peace.

The peace establishments of batteries are :—

	Officers.	Other Ranks.	Horses.	Vehicles.
Gun battery	3	94	45	33
Howitzer battery	3	106	57	45

3. Transport.

As in field batteries each battery has 2 carts for machine guns, 2 telephone carts, a cart for battery stores, a field kitchen, and 4 transport wagons.

4. Regimental Specialists.

As in the field artillery.

5. Personnel.

As in the field artillery.

6. The Mountain Gun (Howitzer).

The mountain gun is a 67 mm. French mountain gun, 1906 pattern.

The howitzer is a 100 mm. Skoda howitzer, 1916 pattern, details of which are given in the Appendix at the end of this chapter. The three loads into which it is divided are : (*a*) howitzer and cradle ; (*b*) shield and axle ; (*c*) trail with wheels and travelling axle.

E.—Trench Mortars.

There are no trench mortar units in the Polish Army.

F.—Close Range Batteries.

There are no close range batteries in the Polish Army.

G.—Ammunition Supply.

1. Front Line Ammunition Supply.

The immediate requirements of the fighting line, cavalry, infantry, or artillery, in ammunition are supplied from regimental reserves, carried in wagons belonging, in the cavalry or infantry, to the regiment, and in the artillery to the ammunition column of the group. These vehicles are at the entire disposal of the regimental or artillery group commander, and it is the duty of these officers to warn their immediate chiefs, *i.e.*, the commander of the divisional infantry or the artillery regimental commander, when they need refilling. These latter officers report their requirements to the chief of the divisional artillery, who arranges to fill up the regimental wagons at a rendezvous which he fixes, from the reserves at his disposal.

2. Ammunition Transport Columns.

The next echelon in the ammunition supply is formed by the transport columns of the division (or cavalry division). Each division has 8 of these columns, and they are not permanently allotted to the transport of a definite load, but can be used according to the plans of the army or corps commander, who regulates the proportion of ammunition or supplies carried, according to the requirements of the situation. For instance, if a battle is imminent, a larger number would be allotted for ammunition, but if the division is on the march with no immediate prospect of a fight, then the majority would carry supplies. The only proviso that regulations lay down is that never less than two must be allotted for ammunition. In exceptional cases the decision as to the proportion of ammunition to supplies carried is left to the divisional commander.

THE POLISH ARMY

Each of these columns consists of 60 wagons of the usual country pattern, available for transport of ammunition with a few additional wagons for the use of the columns, *vide* Chapter XVII, D.

Each column is capable of carrying either half a day's supplies for an infantry division, one day's expenditure of S.A.A., or one day's expenditure of gun ammunition, and normally 4 would be allotted to supplies and 4 to S.A.A. In a cavalry division a column carries either a half day's ration, 2 days' S.A.A. for the division, or 2 days' ammunition for the horse artillery group (3 batteries). When a battle is imminent, and it is desired to assure a plentiful supply of ammunition, the division orders a certain number of the columns carrying food to dump their supplies in suitable places and to assist in bringing up ammunition. Generally some columns would be detailed for S.A.A. and others for artillery ammunition.

3. Ammunition Tractors.

There are no special motor units allotted to the transport of ammunition, but if required, the army commander may detail any of his own transport units, horse or motor, for that duty. *See* below.

4. Chain of Ammunition Supply.

The Ministry of War is responsible for preparing reserves of ammunition in peace, holding them in magazines of the armament service, some of which are put at the disposal of the Commander-in-Chief on mobilization. These magazines are located according to strategical requirements, and at the outbreak of war are classed as either main reserve magazines, in the home area, or magazines of the regulating commissar (*vide* Chapter VIII, 16), in the Front Area.

The regulating commissar has direct disposal of the ammunition magazines in his area, and supplies the army direct from them. Their capacity is fixed by the Commander-in-Chief. He is responsible for keeping them filled, and for this purpose credits are allotted him in the main magazines of the Home Area. For all duties connected with these ammunition magazines he has on his staff a director of armament services, and units known as army park platoons are attached.

When the units of an army require fresh supplies of ammunition the army commander informs the regulating commissar of the quantity required for each division, or cavalry brigade, and for army troops. He arranges with him an ammunition railhead, and the time at which formations will draw their ammunition there. The regulating commissar is then responsible for delivering the ammunition at the railhead at the time agreed upon. Should the formation of the army be so far from a railway that they cannot draw their ammunition themselves, the army commander arranges a refilling centre for that formation within its reach, and arranges to transport the ammunition from railhead to this centre by the means of transportation at his disposal (horse transport, motor transport, light railway, etc.). Advanced depots of ammunition may also be formed by the army not closer to the front than 10 kilometres.

The orders regarding ammunition supply are included in Part II Orders of the army, issued by the IV Bureau of the Staff, and are drawn up in conjunction with the regulating commissar and the head of the armament service (commander of the army artillery).

The orders include :—
- (a) Location of railhead, advanced depots, and refilling centre.
- (b) Times at which different formations draw ammunition.
- (c) Quantity to be issued to each formation.
- (d) Routes to be followed by transport columns.
- (e) Means of transportation from railhead to advanced depots or refilling centres.

For carrying out the various duties connected with the supply of ammunition each army possesses an army armament park, which keeps a reserve of guns, gun stores, and small arms, and has a repair shop.

Divisions (and independent cavalry brigades) demand from the army their requirements in ammunition *en bloc*, and receive them at the above-mentioned railheads or refilling points. From these points the ammunition is carried forward, by the transport columns of the division, to divisional refilling points, where it is received by group ammunition columns of artillery and regimental S.A.A. wagons of other arms. In a similar manner as for the army, divisional Part II Orders allot the refilling points for different units, times at which units refill, quantity to be taken, routes to be followed by columns and regimental wagons, and indicate the location of the divisional armament park.

The divisional armament park keeps a reserve of small arms only, and has a workshop for carrying out minor artillery repairs. That of an independent cavalry brigade has no workshop.

In the artillery, each group commander fixes the locality where his batteries may fill up from the group ammunition column, which is divided into as many sections as there are batteries in the group.

5. Expenditure of Ammunition.

The average rate of expenditure of ammunition (1 day's supply) is as follows :—

S.A.A.—
- 40 rounds per rifle.
- 2,000 rounds per light machine gun.
- 4,800 rounds per heavy machine gun.

Shell—
- 60 rounds per 75 mm. gun.
- 40 rounds per 100 mm. howitzer.
- 60 rounds per 3-inch horse artillery gun.
- 60 rounds per 65 mm. mountain gun.
- 40 rounds per 100 mm. mountain howitzer.
- 40 rounds per 105 mm. gun.
- 40 rounds per 120 mm. gun.
- 24 rounds per 155 mm. howitzer.

6. Ammunition Trains.

One day's supply for a division (gun and rifle ammunition) is reckoned as being a load for 6 railway wagons. In the course of an action, on the calculation that a division actually fighting will expend on an average 2 days' supply, it is reckoned that an ammunition train of normal composition (55 wagons) can bring up fresh supplies of ammunition for 4 divisions.

APPENDIX TO CHAPTER XII.
ARMAMENT OF POLISH ARTILLERY.

	75 mm. Field Gun.	100 mm. Field Howitzer.	3 in. Horse Artillery Gun.	65 mm. Mountain Gun.	100 mm. Mountain Howitzer.	105 mm. Gun.	155 mm. Howitzer.
Provenance or type	French 1897 pattern	Skoda type 14	Russian 1902 field gun	French 1906 pattern	Skoda 1916 pattern	French 1913 pattern	French 155 mm. Schneider 1917 pattern
Material	Steel	Steel/bronze	Steel	—	Steel	—	Steel
Calibre	2·95 in.	3·9 in.	3 in. 7·62 mm.	2½ in.	3·9 in.	4 in.	6 in.
Weight with carriage and limber.	38 cwt. full	45½ cwt. full	38 cwt. full	900 lb. gun & carriage alone	28 cwt. full	52 cwt.	73 cwt.
Weight of wagon and limber.	21 cwt. empty	43 cwt. full	38 cwt. full	—	—	—	—
Breech action	Wedge block with lever	Screw thread block	Block with interrupted screw threads	—	Block with interrupted screw threads	—	Screw threaded block with obturating pad
Control of recoil	Hydraulic buffer and compressed air	Hydraulic buffer and spring	Hydraulic buffer and springs	—	Hydraulic buffer and spring	—	Hydraulic buffer with compressed gas
Shield	Bullet-proof at 200 yds.	Steel 19 in. thick	·2 in. thick	—	4·7 mm. thick	—	—
Greatest range	12,500 yds.	—	7,000 yds.	—	—	—	—
Weight of shrapnel shell	16 lb.	29 lb.	14·3 lb.	9 lb.	29 lb.	37½ lb.	90 lb.

Armament of Polish Artillery—*continued.*

	75 mm. Field Gun.	100 mm. Field Howitzer.	3 in. Horse Artillery Gun.	65 mm. Mountain Gun.	100 mm. Mountain Howitzer.	100 mm. Gun.	155 mm. Howitzer.
Weight of H.E. shell ..	A. 12¼ lb. B. 13¾ lb. C. 17½ lb. D. 14¾ lb.	A. 35¼ lb. B. 30¾ lb. C. *29¾ lb.	A. 14½ lb. B. 13·6 lb.	—	35 lb.	A. 34½ lb.	A. 95 lb. B. 96 lb.
Bursting charge ..	A. 1⅔ lb. B. 1½ lb. C. 1½ lb.	—	A. ⅘ lb. melinite B. 1 lb. trotyl	—	—	5 lb.	A. 22½ lb. B. 10 lb.
Limits of elevation ..	−11° +18°	− 8° +48°	− 6° +16° 40′	—	− 8° +48°	—	− 0° +42° 20′
Limits of traverse ..	3° each way	2° 49 R. 2° 32 L.	2° 45 each way	—	5° 21′	—	3° each way
Propellant charge or charges.	1·3 lb. or 1·4 lb.	6 varying from ·4 lb. to 1·2 lb.	1·85 lb.	—	—	—	7 charges varying from 7¾ lb. to 18¼ lb.
Initial velocity ..	A. 1804 f.s. B. 1918 f.s. C. 1656 f.s. D. 1810 f.s.	—	1928 f.s.	—	—	—	Varying from 1476 f.s. to 754 f.s.

* This is a combined shrapnel and high explosive shell.

CHAPTER XIII.
TECHNICAL TROOPS (ENGINEERS).

1. General.
The engineer troops of the Polish Army consist in peace of :—
- 10 sapper regiments.
- 1 electro-technical battalion.
- 1 bridging battalion.

These troops are administered by Department V (Engineers) of the Ministry of War.

The Engineer Corps totals in peace some 692 officers (with 779 reserve officers) and about 9,000 men.

2. Personnel.
The officers are recruited from young men who, after passing through the first year's general course at the Podchorąży School at Warsaw, are then sent to the Officers' Engineer School, also at Warsaw, for a further 3 years' course, after the second year of which they become 2nd lieutenants.

The professional non-commissioned officers are selected from among suitable men of the annual contingent, who go through a regimental N.C.O's. school before being allowed to extend their service and become professional non-commissioned officers.

The rank and file (and junior N.C.Os.) are taken from the annual contingent. Only a part of these is tradesmen.

Officers are armed with sword and pistol, N.C.Os. (senior) with sword and pistol, or pistol only, others with carbine and bayonet.

3. Sapper Regiments.
Each military district should have normally 1 sapper regiment, organized in 3 battalions, the battalions bearing numbers corresponding to the divisions in the military district, which they join on mobilization. For convenience of training, however, the regiments are not always located in their correct district, and the locations are :—

1st Regiment	Modlin.
2nd ,,	Pulawy.
3rd ,,	Wilno.
4th ,,	Sandomierz.
5th ,,	Krakow.
6th ,,	Przemysl.
7th ,,	Poznan.
8th ,,	Torun.
9th ,,	Brzesc-nad-Bugiem.
10th ,,	Przemysl.

Each battalion should consist of headquarters and 2 companies. As a measure of economy, however, the third battalion headquarters has been abolished, and its two companies added to the other two battalions.

Each regiment also has a reserve battalion cadre.

The peace establishment of a regiment is :—

	Officers.	Other Ranks.	Horses.	Vehicles.
Regimental headquarters	7	51	30	12
2 Battalion headquarters (each)	3	10	2	—
6 Companies (each)	3	100	2	1
Total regiment	21	671	46	18

In war the regimental organization is broken up, and the battalions join the divisions bearing a corresponding number, a new battalion headquarters being formed from regimental headquarters to replace the missing one for the third division. Each of these battalions then has 2 companies. A divisional sapper column is formed on mobilization, and becomes part of the divisional sapper battalion; the full war establishment being :—

	Officers.	Other Ranks.	Horses.	Vehicles.
Battalion headquarters	5	45	43	19
Signal section	—	25	2	2
Two companies	8	440	66	36
Sapper column	4	140	140	63
Total battalion	17	650	250	120

Each company has 2 machine guns.

The transport of the companies is as follows: 3 vehicles for machine guns and S.A.A., 1 field kitchen, 1 cook's wagon, 1 baggage wagon, and 12 wagons for R.E. stores, namely, 4 tool wagons, 3 wagons with explosives and mine stores, 3 wagons with bridging equipment, 1 forge, and 1 wagon with topographical, photographical and similar technical stores.

The sapper column has a field kitchen, cook's wagon, 2 forage wagons, and 59 vehicles for R.E. stores, namely :—

    8 wagons for entrenching tools, 1,280 shovels and 280 picks.
    2 wagons for ammunition, grenades, pistols.
    2 wagons for assault stores for infantry, with flame-throwers, wire-cutters, etc.
    9 wagons for bridging material.
    3 wagons for carpenters' tools.
    3 wagons for joiners' tools.
    2 wagons for sandbags.
   17 wagons for barbed wire, pickets, and stores for wire entanglement.
    3 wagons for ironmongery.
    3 wagons for forges.
    3 wagons for explosives (240 kilogrammes per wagon).
    1 wagon for miners' and masons' tools.
    1 wagon for lighting equipment.
    2 wagons for miscellaneous articles.

4. Electro-Technical Battalion (Bataljon Elektrotechniczny).

The electro-technical battalion is stationed in Nowy Dwor, a suburb of Modlin. It consists of :—
>Battalion headquarters.
>2 companies searchlights, Nos. 1 and 2.
>2 companies electro-technical, Nos. 3 and 4.
>Searchlight school.
>Electro-technical school.
>Workshops.
>Reserve cadre.

The duties of the battalion are :—
> (a) To train personnel for searchlight and electric lighting detachments.
> (b) To hold and maintain equipment for the above units.
> (c) To carry out certain works in peace, such as operation of Modlin power station and water works.

The recruits are all selected from young men employed in electrical works and engine shops, where they have already become familiar with the technical equipment. In the battalion they are given theoretical instruction until they are capable of operating the equipment themselves. The best of the recruits are given further training (in one of the two branches, searchlights or electric lighting plant) and from these again are selected those to become professional non-commissioned officers, if they so wish. The officers are interchangeable with other engineer units.

The battalion possesses well-equipped workshops, with its own power station which, however, is kept in reserve, power being generally obtained from the Modlin power station. It has a variety of searchlights of various types mostly taken from the occupying armies, and a number of engines (petrol or steam) of various sizes. The whole of the equipment has been repaired and put in order by the unit, and the workshops and power plant erected by them.

For field use, the searchlights adopted are :—
> (a) 110 cm. diameter, Siemens Schuchert, 180 ampères. The equipment is carried on 4 wagons :—
>> (1) For the lamp,
>> (2) For the motor,
>> (3) For cable,
>> (4) For petrol and stores.
>
> The first two wagons are drawn by 6 horses, the last two by 4 horses.
> The range is 5–6 kilometres.
>
> (b) 60 cm. mountain searchlight, Siemens Schuchert, 60 ampères. It is carried on 7 one-horsed carts, the loads being :—
>> (1) Light,
>> (2) Stand,
>> (3) Cable,
>> (4) Motor,
>> (5) Petrol,
>> (6) ⎱ Tools and spare parts.
>> (7) ⎰
>
> The range is 3–4 kilometres.

A searchlight company consists of 3 platoons, of which 2 have one 110 cm. searchlight each, while the third has two 60 cm. searchlights. During the summer, training is carried on in conjunction with anti-aircraft units, but hitherto only against balloons. Training against aeroplanes is to be introduced this year.

The electric lighting plant comprises :—

> (a) 25 kilowatt set, consisting of 4 cylinder engine, water-cooled, and switchboard, made at Schenectady, U.S.A. This is to be used for lighting army and general headquarters. There are at least 12 such sets in possession of the battalion.
>
> (b) 5 kilowatt set, also made in America. It is said that the battalion has 140 such sets. A platoon, with 2 sets, would be allotted to a division.

The whole of this equipment was bought from the American army stocks in France, and when bought was in bad order. The battalion has repaired the whole.

The means of transport varies. Two railway wagons are kept fitted up ready for use, the one containing two of the larger sets, the other one large and two small sets. The smaller sets would be mounted on horsed wagons or motor lorries according to circumstances.

The battalion breaks up into companies on mobilization, which are allotted to armies as required. The war establishments of units formed from it are :—

Unit.	Officers.	Other Ranks.	Horses.	Vehicles.	Motor Vehicles.
Electro-technical company (for lighting Army H.Q.) ..	4	96	51	26	—
Searchlight company (for co-operation with A.A. Artillery) ..	3	106	57	29	—
Motor searchlight platoon ..	1	27	—	—	3

5. Bridging Battalion (Baon Mostowy).

This unit is also stationed at Modlin. It is composed of :—

> Battalion headquarters,
> 2 bridging companies,
> 1 mining and water transport company,
> Workshops,
> School,
> Reserve cadre.

Its objects are :—

> (a) To train its own personnel in heavy bridging.
> (b) To give N.C.Os. of other sapper units training in bridging of a more advanced type than they can get in their units.
> (c) To train personnel in mining.
> (d) To hold mining and bridging stores.

In war time it also breaks up into independent companies, whose establishments are:—

Unit.	Officers.	Other Ranks.	Horses.	Vehicles.	Motor Vehicles.
Pontoon company (headquarters and 3 platoons) ..	4	243	300	59	—

Each platoon can make a bridge 53 metres long, with material carried on 14 wagons, namely: 2 pontoon wagons, each with 2 sections of pontoon, 4 trestle wagons, each with 1 section of pontoon and 2 trestles, and 8 other wagons, each with 1 section of pontoon and riband, chesses, etc.

Bridging company	4	230	73	29	4
River mining platoon	1	84	31	15	—
Water transport company	4	232	188	24	1

The transport of the water transport company includes 9 wagons with motor boats and 9 wagons with technical stores.

The majority of the bridging material is of the Wagner type, formerly in use in both the Austrian and Russian armies, with slight modifications. It is made in Poland.

6. Units formed on Mobilization.

(*a*) *Army Engineer Company* (3 platoons and machine gun section).—War establishment: 4 officers, 227 other ranks, 37 horses and 20 vehicles, including 12 for technical stores, and 8 for machine gun section.

(*b*) *Army Engineer Park* (3 platoons).—War establishment: 3 officers, 170 other ranks, 130 horses, 61 vehicles. Each platoon has 18 vehicles, which carry entrenching and carpenters' tools, pontoons and timber, explosives and other engineer stores and tools.

(*c*) *L. of C. Engineer Store.*—War establishment: 3 officers, 65 other ranks, 16 horses, 8 vehicles.

(*d*) *Engineer Store on Section of L. of C.*—War establishment: 11 other ranks, 6 horses, 3 vehicles.

(*e*) *Headquarters R.E. Services on L. of C.*—War establishment: 6 officers, 20 other ranks, 4 horses, 1 vehicle.

('*f*) *Headquarters R.E. Services on Section of L. of C.*—War establishment: 4 officers, 11 other ranks, 2 horses, 1 vehicle.

(*g*) *Labour Company.*—War establishment: 2 officers, 88 other ranks, 27 horses, 12 vehicles.

(*h*) *Hydrotechnical Platoon.*—War establishment: 1 officer, 40 other ranks, 30 horses, 14 vehicles.

(*i*) *Boring Platoon.*—War establishment: 1 officer, 50 other ranks, 30 horses, 14 vehicles.

Chemical Warfare.

1. General.

The Polish Army has had no experience in chemical warfare, and has very little equipment. It is, however, occupying the attention of the authorities, and a school of gas warfare has been established in the suburbs of Warsaw, where laboratory experiments are carried out, and which is endeavouring to diffuse a knowledge of anti-gas protection throughout the army.

For the present, the general policy as regards gas warfare is confined to :—

(a) Providing anti-gas protection by gas masks and neutralizers.
(b) Building up a supply of gas shell for the artillery and gas bombs for the aviation service.

There are various types of gas mask in the army, but the French type is being adopted throughout, and all other patterns excluded.

2. Chemical Warfare Units.

The Central Gas School is located in the village of Marymont, in the northern outskirts of Warsaw. The staff consists of a commandant, chief instructor and three other officer instructors, but civilian chemists are also employed as instructors and in the laboratory. The objects of the school are :—

(a) To train regimental officers to become anti-gas instructors in units. The course lasts 1 month.
(b) To train senior regimental officers and medical officers in the theory of gas warfare and anti-gas defence.
(c) To train selected officers to fit themselves to become technical experts in anti-gas defence. This course lasts 7 months.

The instructional chemical company is also located at Marymont. Its establishment is 4 officers and 100 other ranks, and its equipment includes Stokes mortars, Livens mortars, and gas cylinders.

The Gas Warfare Research Institute is located in Warsaw.

3. Manufacturing Establishments and Depots.

No factories are definitely known to be producing gas for military purposes, but there are a large number of chemical works in Poland and, in view of the attention paid by the authorities to gas warfare it is probable that some, at any rate, of these factories are in a position to supply the army with gas-producing substances if required.

Among the principal chemical works are :—

Przemysl Chemiczny w Polsce (Polish chemical industry) at Zgierz, near Lodz: produces dyes, sulphuric, nitric and muriatic acids, chlorides of zinc and tin.

Pabjanickie Towarzystwo Akcyjne Przemyslu Chemicznego (Pabjanice Chemical Industry Company) at Pabjanice, near Lodz: produces aniline dyes, formic acid.

Panstwowa Fabryka Związków Azotowych (State Factory of Nitrogen Compounds) at Chorzow, Upper Silesia.

Malopolskie Towarzystwo Akcyjne Dla Przemyslu Chemicznego (Chemical Industry Company of Little Poland—Galicia) at Zniesienie near Lwow: mineral and bone phosphates.

THE POLISH ARMY

Towarzystwo Akcyjne Fabryk Przetworow Chemicznych (Company of Factories of Chemical Products) " Redziny " at Rudniki, near Częstochowa : mineral superphosphates, sulphuric, nitric, and muriatic acids.

" Azot " at Bory, near Jaworzno, in Eastern Galicia : potassium and sodium ferrocyanides.

Kijewski Scholtze & Co., Warsaw : mineral superphosphates, sulphuric acid, muriatic acid.

" Grodzisk " at Grodzisk : chloroform, muriatic acid.

" Protekta " at Radom : gas masks.

Belonging to the Army there are :—
 (1) Mask factory at Zegrze,
 (2) Central Gas Store, Zegrze,
 (3) Central Gas Store, Krakow.

4. Gas Shell in the Artillery.

It is believed that no serious steps are being taken to prepare for the employment of gas in war by means of instruments producing gas clouds.

On the other hand various indications point to the fact that it is intended to employ gas shell in all natures of artillery, and that supplies of gas shell are being steadily built up. At the present moment these are almost entirely of French manufacture, but there is every reason to believe that the local shell factories will shortly be, if they are not already, in a position to fill their own shell with gas producing mixture, thus carrying out the policy of being independent of foreign supply.

Gas shell seem to be distinguished by being painted blue.

CHAPTER XIV.

TANKS AND ARMOURED CARS.

1. Organization.

The Polish Tank Corps is a branch of the infantry, and as such is administered through Department I of the Ministry of War.

At the present moment the corps consists of one regiment only, with depot, stationed at Zurawica, near Przemysl, but the formation of a second regiment is projected.

The first regiment consists of three battalions, but it is believed that this organization is not definite, and is merely adopted to conform with the number of tanks in possession, which is about 120 of all sorts, serviceable and unserviceable. Each battalion is to be organized into two companies, which in peace time have from 12 to 16 tanks.

The first regiment has French light Renault tanks dating from the end of the Great War. Many of them are in bad condition. It is probable that the second regiment to be formed will be equipped with a newer type of light Renault tanks.

The corps is as yet only in the initial stages of development, owing to lack of equipment, therefore the organization is only provisional, and will probably be changed when more tanks arrive.

2. Tank Depots.

The depot is at Zurawica, but it does not appear to be capable of anything but small repairs, as heavy repairs are carried out at the central motor transport workshops at Warsaw.

3. Armoured Car Units.

The units of armoured cars are the " dywizjon," or group, and the squadron. Both contain 3 platoons, of either 4 light cars or 3 heavy cars each.

The groups have hitherto been organized with old pattern vehicles dating from the war, and have been attached to the mechanical transport column of the military district in which they happen to be stationed, and are unallotted to formations. Since the army manœuvres of 1925, five new squadrons have been formed, allotted one to each cavalry division and to the 5th Cavalry Brigade, and equipped with Citroen-Kegresse or Peugeot cars, officered by cavalry officers seconded for this duty. Each of these squadrons consists of 3 platoons of 4 cars each. The establishment is not known, except that 4 officers are appointed to the squadron.

4. Tank Units.

The war organization of the Tank Corps is by battalions, which consist of battalion headquarters and 3 companies.

The war establishment is :—

	Battalion Headquarters.	Company.
Officers	3	5
Other ranks	6	117
Motor cars	1	1
Lorries	—	5
Tractors	—	1
Trailers	—	2
Motor cycles	—	1
Tanks	—	22
37 mm. guns	—	14
Machine guns	—	8

The company has 3 platoons, each of 5 tanks, of which 2 are armed with a machine gun, and 3 with a 37 mm. gun.

The platoon is an indivisible fighting unit. Company headquarters has 7 tanks, namely, C.O.'s tank, wireless tank, and a "transport" platoon of 5 tanks in reserve, with 1 touring car, 3 lorries, 1 petrol lorry, 1 tractor and 2 trailers. Company headquarters also has a repair platoon with 1 workshop lorry.

5. Personnel.

Officers are taken from all arms of the service, and after passing through the required training and tests are transferred to the infantry.

The non-commissioned officers and men are specially selected and taken from other arms as required.

The uniform is the same as that of the infantry, but a badge, *vide* Chapter XXIX, para. 2, is worn on the left sleeve above the elbow.

THE POLISH ARMY

The arms and equipment are the same as in the infantry; except that a carbine replaces the rifle.

6. Description of Tank.

The tank now in use is an old pattern light Renault dating from the end of the Great War. It is armed with either 1 machine gun or one 37 mm. gun, carries 2 men (driver and gunner), and is capable of speed up to 7 kilometres per hour. Its length overall is 4·1 metres with 1·7 metres, height 2·1 metres, and weighs 6·5 or 6·7 tons, with armour 16 mm. thick. It carries either 4,800 rounds S.A.A. for the machine gun or 227 rounds for the 37 mm. gun.

There are a few old tanks of a heavier type but these are very unreliable.

It is believed that in addition to the new light Renault tanks to be bought in France (*see* para. 1), it is intended also to buy a number of a heavier type, but no decision has been arrived at as to what type shall be obtained.

7. Description of Armoured Car.

The Citroen-Kegresse armoured car is a small car with 11 h.p. engine. The framework is supported on an axle in front with two ordinary rubber-tyred wheels, but the rear is supported on an undercarriage fitted with a continuous track running on two large wheels and under four small rollers. The body of the car alone is armoured and 1 machine gun is carried in a conical turret projecting above the body. Its speed is about 10 miles per hour maximum on good ground. The Peugeot 30 h.p. is an old car, very heavy and slow, with a similar track arrangement instead of the rear wheels.

It is recognized that the weight of both types is too great for the engine, and no more are to be bought, but a newer and improved type, capable of greater speed and with fuller protection, is being looked for.

CHAPTER XV.
SIGNAL SERVICE.
A.—Peace.

1. Organization.

The Signal Service (Wojska Łącznosci, troops of communication) consists of :—
> One signal regiment (pułk łączności) and 3 independent battalions (telegraph and telephone).
> One wireless regiment (pułk radiotelegraficzny).

The signal regiment is stationed at Zegrze ; the independent battalions are at Krakow, Poznan, and Brzesc respectively, and the wireless regiment at Warsaw with 1 battalion at Benjaminow.

The signal regiments each consist of regimental headquarters, 5 battalions and 1 duty company. Each battalion consists of 3 companies. The first company of the first battalion is a mounted company, trained for use with cavalry formations.

The wireless telegraphy regiment consists of regimental headquarters, 2 battalions and a duty wireless company. Each battalion consists of 4 companies. The first company of the first battalion is a mounted company, trained for use with cavalry.

Regimental headquarters and battalion staffs are peace time organizations only, designed to supervize the instruction of the units and make mobilization arrangements.

B.—War.

In war the regimental and battalion organization disappears, and companies or platoons become the unit and are detailed to G.H.Q., Army Headquarters, divisions, cavalry divisions and cavalry brigades as required.

Below divisional headquarters all signals are in the hands of the regimental communication sections, forming an integral part of the unit.

The general scheme of war signal organization is as follows :—

G.H.Q.	A chief signal officer with 1 heavy signal and 1 W/T platoon.
Army H.Q.	A signal officer with 2 heavy companies, 1 W/T company, 2 pigeon sections, and 1 signal park.
Divisional H.Q.	A signal officer with 1 signal company and 1 W/T platoon.
Cavalry division or brigade	A cavalry signal company and 1 cavalry W/T platoon.

The officers on regimental and battalion staffs, and in certain headquarter offices which cease to function on mobilization, are available for these appointments as signal officer to formations during war, and many of them are definitely detailed for such appointments beforehand in peace.

The signal parks are formed on mobilization and have no place in peace organization.

2. Signal Units.

The peace establishments of signal units (telegraph or wireless telegraph) are :—

	Regimental H.Q.		Battalion H.Q.	Dis-mounted Company.	Mounted Company.
	C.O.'s Staff.	Admin. Staff.			
Officers.					
O.C.	1	—	1	1	1
Second-in-command	1	—	—	—	—
Regimental officers	—	—	—	3	3
Adjutant	1	—	1	—	—
Quartermaster (major)	—	1	—	—	—
Officer for personnel	—	1	—	—	—
Officer for materiel	—	2	—	—	—
Paymaster	—	1	—	—	—
Supply officer	—	1	—	—	—
Stores officer	—	1	—	—	—
Other ranks	46 (43)	66	3	114	114
Horses	36 (30)	—	1	—	105
Vehicles	22 (15)	—	—	—	—

The total establishment of a signal regiment is 79 officers, 1,837 other ranks and 146 horses; of a wireless regiment 45 officers, 1,027 other ranks and 137 horses.

THE POLISH ARMY

3. Regimental Communication Detachments.

In peace the headquarters of an infantry regiment contains a communication platoon in which all the signallers of the regiment are collected and trained. For field operations the personnel of this platoon are distributed to headquarters, battalions, and companies, according to requirements. A cavalry regimental headquarters also contains a communication troop, and an artillery regiment (or independent group) has a signal platoon, while batteries have also a few men trained in signal duties.

Normally 4 men, *i.e.*, an N.C.O. in command who carries the telephone, a pole man, a " glove " man, and a drum man, form a communication patrol, to which is added, if a special cart is provided for carrying the equipment, a driver and a horse.

The normal means of communication within regiments is by telephone, but visual signalling is taught and employed in addition.

4. Telegraph Units.

At war strength a signal company which forms part of a division is organized, in 4 platoons, each under an officer and supplied with all necessary signal stores so that it can be detached from the company. The strength of the company is 5 officers, 190 other ranks, 49 horses, and 18 vehicles, of which 15 are technical wagons of the first echelon of the fighting transport, and 3 are of the second echelon, namely, field kitchen, cook's wagon and baggage wagon.

The means of communication include field telegraphy, field telephone, visual (lamps and flags), cyclists and 1 motor cyclist, mounted orderlies, runners, rocket and Very lights.

The heavy signal company which is allotted to army and general headquarters has a similar organization in 4 platoons, but with more apparatus and greater length of cable, and is not provided with visual signalling appliances. Its war establishment is 5 officers and 208 other ranks, horses and vehicles unknown.

A cavalry signal company has 4 or 3 platoons, according to whether it is allotted to a cavalry division or independent cavalry brigade. The establishment is 6 officers, 150 other ranks, 150 horses and 18 vehicles, or 14 officers, 100 other ranks, 100 horses and 14 vehicles, which figures include the wireless platoons (*vide* para. 6 below).

5. Telephone Units.

There are none in the Polish Army.

6. Wireless Telegraph Units.

The war establishments of various units are :—

	Officers.	Other Ranks.	Horses.	Vehicles.
W/T platoon with infantry division	1	30	13	5
W/T company with army	3	65	?	?
W/T platoon with G.H.Q.	2	25	?	?

Wireless platoons are also included in the composition of cavalry signal companies, *see* above.

7. Wireless Telephone Units.

These units do not exist in the Polish Army.

8. Listening Set Units.

There are no special units of this type.

It is believed that there are a few listening instruments taken over from the old armies, which might be issued to signal units if required. Their use is taught in the signal school.

9. Messenger Dog Units.

The use of dogs is provided for, but in actual practice there are none.

10. Carrier Pigeon Units.

Carrier pigeon lofts are part of the equipment of each signal regiment and are the object of much attention. Lofts are allotted to headquarters of formations when required.

11. Despatch Riding.

In each signal or wireless company there are a dozen or so bicycles, and one or two motor cycles. Men can be mounted on them for use as despatch riders, if necessary supplemented by mounted men or dismounted men of telegraph patrols not actually working.

12. Signal Parks and Depots.

Signal parks do not exist in peace, they are formed on mobilization and allotted to army headquarters. The war strength of a signal park is 3 officers and 75 other ranks. Its transport is not known.

At each district headquarters there is either an independent signal battalion or a cadre battalion with depot of signal stores. This cadre contains all the mobilization stores of the signal battalion which will be allotted to the troops of the district in question. On mobilization, therefore, the personnel for signal battalions of these districts which have not got their signal battalions permanently with them will have to be sent from the regimental peace station to the district headquarters and be completed with stores at the latter place. This is not a satisfactory arrangement, and it is expected that eventually the system of having a signal battalion at each district headquarters will be extended throughout the army.

In places where there is a cadre battalion, this also contains a small instructional cadre, which trains selected regimental signallers to become signal instructors in their unit. Its strength in peace is 4 officers and 38 other ranks, with 2 wagons and 8 horses.

13. Army Wireless Stations.

Permanent (or semi-permanent) W/T stations directly under the Ministry of War are at Warsaw, Wilno, Lwow, and Torun (the latter under the Navy Department).

The Warsaw station is equipped with a Telefunken apparatus, built by the Germans. Its power is 5 kilowatts, it is capable of communicating with Paris (under favourable

THE POLISH ARMY

conditions at night), wave length 650–1,000 metres, with two masts 75 metres high, and an oil engine, generating 220 volts, magnified by a transformator into 9,000–10,000 volts. It has a second apparatus, of the type selected for general headquarters, similar to the Marconi Z.C.2 (*see* para. 19 below).

The other three stations are equipped with field type sets, but on semi-permanent mountings. The apparatus has a power of 100 watts, with a water-cooled petrol engine, Aster type, and a single mast 30 metres in height. These sets were made by Radiopo (the Polish Marconi Company).

There are other army stations in various places on the frontier, such as Rowno, Baranowice, etc., where they are employed in keeping touch with frontier garrisons and guards; and also instructional stations in each military district, between which wireless telegraph communication is kept up as practice for the wireless operators, under the control of the main station at Warsaw.

14. Army Wireless Telephone Stations.

There are no army wireless telephone stations.

15. Personnel.

The officers are taken from those cadets who, after their first year's training at the Podchorąży School at Ostrow, proceed to the engineer course at the Engineer School at Warsaw for 2 years, after which they do 8 months' special signal training at the signal school at Zegrze.

The other ranks are taken from the annual contingent as it is called up, by specially selecting, as far as possible, men of better education, or with technical knowledge (*i.e.*, of electricity) which would be useful in the signal service. They are for the first 3 months trained in general duties, with the rudiments of signalling, and afterwards are divided into 3 categories: telegraphists, constructors, and general duties, and their further training is of a more specialised character according to their categories.

Officers and men are armed as in the engineers.

The distinguishing collar patch on the uniform of the signal troops is black (officers black velvet) with blue edge.

16. Technical Equipment (Telegraph and Telephone).

The telegraph and telephone equipment of the signal service is at present heterogeneous. Material formerly used in the Russian, Austrian, or German armies, or bought (principally in France) since 1918, is used as available. But all this is being gradually replaced by telegraph instruments, and combined buzzer and induction telephones made at the State Telegraph and Telephone factory at Warsaw.

17. Listening Sets.

The further use of these instruments is now under consideration, but at the present time no special pattern has been decided upon.

18. Technical Equipment (Wireless Sets).

Here again such material as was obtained from the armies of the partitioning Powers is at present in use, mostly of German manufacture.

The Polish staff, however, attach great importance to the development of wireless communication, owing to the difficulty of arranging any other form in the Eastern districts in the case of a war in this theatre. They have therefore adopted the following programme :—

(*a*) *For G.H.Q. and Armies.*—A station similar to the Y.B. Marconi type, of which over 50 sets have been ordered, will be introduced for the use of army headquarters and other higher staffs. It is on the continuous wave principle, power $\frac{1}{2}$ kilowatt, with a Douglas $2\frac{3}{4}$ h.p. engine, capable of transmitting to a distance of 500 kilometres, and with a wave length 600 to 1,200 metres. It has two masts, each 20 metres high. It is carried on two light lorries. It is said that sufficient have already been received to supply requirements.

(*b*) *For Divisions, Cavalry Divisions and Brigades.*—A smaller station, similar to the Marconi Z.C.2 set, has been adopted for these formations and a large quantity has been ordered, many parts being bought in England and assembled by the Polish Marconi Company. It is on the continuous wave principle, power 100 watts, Douglas $2\frac{3}{4}$ h.p. engine, capable of transmitting to a distance of 250 kilometres, with a wavelength 200–600 metres. It is carried on two-horsed vehicles. Enough have already been produced to supply one to each division.

(*c*) *Regiments (Cavalry and Infantry).*—For the present one set will be allotted to a regiment, but as more become available battalions will also be furnished with a set.

The type has not been finally decided, but trials are being made with a British pattern Marconi Z.A.1 set, manufactured by the Polish Radio Company, which will probably be adopted. The advantage of this set is that the power is supplied by hand, with the help of dry cells and without accumulators. It has a valve station, a power of 20 watts, a radius of 35 kilometres, and two light wooden masts 15 feet high.

19. Wireless Telephone Sets.

There are a few French wireless telephone sets, T.P.S. type, in possession of the army, the use of which is taught at the signal school, and it is proposed that such sets shall be issued eventually to signal companies.

20. Signal Lamps.

Signal lamps are part of the signalling equipment of divisional signal companies.

21. Signal Flags.

The signal flags used consist of a square flag, red on one side and white on the other, stretched on a light frame hinged so as to be capable of folding along the diagonal.

The signals are made by the Morse code by showing the white side of the flag, and obscuring it by folding it along the diagonal so that the red side covers the white, and therefore is no longer visible.

22. Very Lights.

Very lights are used for intercommunication between companies in front line and battalion headquarters, and also by aeroplanes working with infantry and artillery.

23. Message Throwers and Projectiles.
These are not in use.

24. Signal Horns.
There is no provision for the use of these instruments.

CHAPTER XVI.
MAPPING AND SURVEY.

1. Military Geographical Institute.
The Military Geographical Institute is stationed at Warsaw and contains 87 officers of all ranks belonging to the Corps of Military Topographers. It works under the orders of the Chief of Staff, through the IV Bureau of the General Staff.

The institute is divided into :—
- (a) Administration.
- (b) Three sections
   - (1) Triangulation.
   - (2) Topographical.
   - (3) Cartographical.
- (c) Map store.

Attached to it are :—
(1) The Officers' Topographical School, which trains officers of the Topographical Corps and also provides courses in topography for officers of other corps.
(2) The School of Draughtsmen, which takes boys aged from 14 to 18, for a 4 years' course, after which they are bound to serve for 6 years in the topographical service of the army.

2. Organization of Surveying in the Field.
Surveying detachments are composed of officers of the Corps of Topographers with a few soldiers for purely manual duties. A detachment may consist of 6 to 8 officers, one of whom is in charge, and contains geodesists (triangulators), topographers (for filling in the detail), and cartographers (for plotting the results and making up the map). The first two categories work on the ground, the last in an office.

It is with detachments such as these, with the assistance of aviators taking photographs, that the eastern frontier has been defined and mapped.

Similar detachments are at present working over the territory of the Republic, revising and completing old maps, and laying the basis of a fresh triangulation.

3. Organization and Duties of Surveying Detachments.
Field topographical sections are provided for in the establishment to be allotted to headquarters of armies. Their establishment is 24 officers, 97 other ranks, 49 horses, and 14 vehicles. These sections provide detachments as described above.

4. Survey Units with Artillery.
Establishments and regulations refer to units, forming part of heavy artillery regiments, known as the company of artillery measurements. The personnel of this unit belongs to the artillery.

THE POLISH ARMY

The company is divided into platoons, for visual ranging and sound ranging.

The visual ranging platoons seek out and locate enemy batteries by means of establishing a number of posts, equipped with very accurate optical instruments, and connected with a central co-ordinating station where the results of the observations of the posts are mapped. Three to four posts are considered sufficient to watch over a sector 5 to 10 kilometres long. A platoon can commence work 6 hours after arriving on the ground.

Sound ranging platoons work on the same lines, but with acoustical instruments (microphones). In theory, three acoustical posts are sufficient to locate accurately a hostile battery, but in practice a fourth is employed as a check. Four posts can watch over a sector 6 to 8 kilometres in length. The time required to install a platoon varies from 6 to 24 hours.

There exists a school of artillery ranging, attached to the artillery instructional camp at Torun, where the personnel of these ranging units are trained.

In the anti-aircraft artillery regiments there is also a listening platoon, details of which are not known.

5. Types and Scales of Maps in Use.

At the beginning of her existence Poland was dependent on the maps made by the partitioning Powers of the districts occupied by them, and on maps made during the course of the Great War. These maps cannot be made to correspond exactly; for instance, between Russian and Austrian maps there was a difference of 8 minutes.

At first, photographic reproductions of existing maps were made for use during the Bolshevik war, but in 1921 a beginning was made to produce Polish maps with Polish orthography. There now exist the following maps :—

(a) 1 : 25,000. Either adapted by photography from old German maps, uncoloured, or freshly compiled in four colours. These maps only cover certain important districts, and fortified areas such as Wilno. Contoured.

(b) 1 : 100,000. Tactical map. Originally photographic reproductions of Austrian 1 : 75,000 maps (hachured), Russian 1 : 84,000 maps (hachured), and German maps 1 : 100,000. On this basis the maps have been corrected, redrawn, and printed in four colours, with contour lines.

(c) 1 : 300,000. Operations map. The first edition was merely a reproduction in four colours of old German and Austrian maps, with heights shown by shading. A new edition with additions and corrections is being produced, with contour lines.

(d) 1 : 750,000. Political map. Showing the administrative divisions of the country and main communications. In five colours.

There are no large-scale maps for artillery purposes except the 1 : 25,000 map, which covers certain training camps and practice grounds. This map is divided up into kilometre squares, which are numbered in each area from a local reference point.

6. Meteorological Service.

The meteorological service is part of the aviation corps, there being a station with each regiment in peace.

CHAPTER XVII.

TRANSPORTATION.

A.—General.

1. General Notes on the Transportation Service.

All the various means of communication in Poland are in the hands of the State. The railways are under a special ministry, which also looks after civil aviation. Roads and waterways are under the Ministry of Public Works, and the post and telegraph services, after having been under a ministry of their own, are now under a branch of the same ministry.

Under these circumstances the work of co-ordinating their use to meet the requirements of the State in war is greatly simplified.

The responsibility for the working of the different methods of communication in war rests with the IV Bureau of the General Staff.

This bureau is divided into three sections, namely : (1) Supplies (of all kinds), (2) Lines of Communication (étapes) and (3) Transportation.

In peace it deals with the current requirements and movements of the army, but its principal work is the organization and preparation of all the administrative services for their work in war. To that end, through its first section, it carries out the preliminary organization of the different étapes or lines of movement from the home area to the zone of the armies. This section fixes the routes to be followed, localities at which depots and stores of all kinds, food, munitions, engineer stores, etc., are to be situated, their contents, and how much is to be maintained in peace, arranges halting places, supplies troops en route, locates prisoners' camps, and arranges for the security of these establishments (by the military gendarmerie).

The second section arranges for the provision (purchase, requisition) of the stores required, which, however, does not come under the heading of transportation.

The third section prepares for the movement of troops and stores. It draws up the train arrangements for mobilization and concentration, and organizes the further employment of the railways during operations. It also organizes the use of the roads, waterways, civil telegraphs, telephone and postal services in accordance with the requirements of the army.

To assist in adapting the various means of communication to the needs of the army, representatives of the latter are appointed to work in conjunction with them, namely, a Military Commissar General for Railways at the Railway Ministry, and military commissars of waterways, roads, posts, signals (telegraph and telephone), and aviation at the corresponding department of the ministry concerned.

B.—Railways.

1. General Organization and Administration of the Service.

The IV Bureau of the General Staff keeps in touch with the Railway Ministry in peace by means of the Military Commissar General of Railways (a colonel of the general staff) who works with the Vice-Minister of Railways.

The State railways are divided into 8 district administrations, namely: Warsaw, Wilno, Radom, Krakow, Stanislawow, Lwow, Poznan and Gdansk, and at each of these there is a district representative of the military commissar general who works with the president of the district administration. These district representatives work for 6 months of the year in their district, and for 6 months at headquarters for co-ordinating the whole work.

By means of this organization the time-table in detail of all the railway movements required on mobilization, and for the concentration of the troops according to the plan of operation, is worked out and arrangements made for its immediate execution. On the representations of the general staff, made through the commissar general, preparations are made in peace, such as provision of stores of coal, of material for repair of line and bridges, construction of suitable platforms, sidings, and so forth, and for distribution of rolling stock so that whatever is required is available at once.

2. Railway Personnel and Units.

The railway directing staff consists of the officers and their staffs mentioned in the previous paragraph, who function both in peace and war.

The administration of railway troops is carried out by the third section of No. VI (Technical Troops) Department of the Ministry of War.

The railway troops consist in peace of 2 regiments, stationed at Krakow and Jablonna (near Warsaw) respectively, each of 3 battalions of 2 companies. The 2nd Regiment has in addition a company of railway motor vehicles.

The establishments are :—

	Officers.	Other Ranks.
Railway company	5	198
Battalion	12	399
Railway motor company	5	227

The personnel are armed and equipped as dismounted men of the Engineers. The distinguishing patch on the collar is of black, with no edging, and a winged wheel is worn as a badge on the left sleeve.

Railway troops are employed on the following duties :—
- (*a*) Maintenance of permanent way and railway plant.
- (*b*) Repair and construction of bridges (iron girder and timber).
- (*c*) Construction of short lengths of normal gauge, or of narrow gauge railways.
- (*d*) Operation of sections of normal gauge railways that may be allotted to them, or of narrow gauge light field railways.
- (*e*) Training of personnel for armoured trains and maintenance of the latter.

3. Organization of Traffic.

The whole of the railway traffic in war time, serving the needs of the armies in the field, is kept in the hands of the IV Bureau on the Staff of the Commander-in-Chief of the Armies (General Headquarters). This bureau continues as in peace to work through the Military Commissar General of the Railway Ministry.

This railway traffic is of two kinds, the first, between the depots of the Commander-in-Chief and the regulating station (*see* Chapter VIII, 15), and the second, between the regulating station and the railheads. Traffic on the first of these is arranged by the IV Bureau of General Headquarters, through the military commissars at the Railway Ministry or railway directorates, and on the second by the regulating commissar at the regulating station behind each army. Trains of the first category are known as "Type" (typowy) trains and carry a definite load of a certain article or class of articles. Trains of the second category are known as supply trains (whether for food supplies, or ammunition, or stores) and are so constituted as to take a given quantity of requirements for formations (*e.g.*, 1 day's supplies for 2 divisions).

The timing and frequency of the latter are entirely controlled by the regulating commissar, according to requirements. In the former category certain definite train arrangements, that is to say, a certain number of Type trains on a definite march-route, are allotted to him for use if he requires them.

Traffic between the front area and the home area direct, *e.g.*, transport of reinforcements, sick and wounded, is arranged by the IV Bureau of General Headquarters direct with the Railway Ministry through the military commissars.

Traffic between the centres of production and the main depots of the Commander-in-Chief is arranged by the IV Bureau of the War Ministry with the Railway Ministry. In this case the composition of trains varies according to requirements.

There are a number of light railways in Poland, connecting up the smaller towns which are not on the normal gauge railways. In Eastern Poland there are also many light railway lines laid down by the German Army in 1917 and 1918, for the purpose either of communication with the front line, or for exploiting the timber, of which they cut down a large quantity. Some of these light railways are still in use.

4. Movement of Troops.

The number of trains required to move an infantry division is 42, of which 4 are required for each infantry regiment (1 per battalion and 1 for regimental headquarters), 13 for the artillery (1 per battery or ammunition column and 1 for regimental headquarters), 2 each for divisional cavalry and divisional engineers, 1 for each horse transport column, and 1 for divisional headquarters, 1 for signal units, and 2 for medical units and minor units (armament and intendance parks), and 1 spare.

A cavalry division requires 58 trains, and an independent cavalry brigade requires 31 trains.

A standard military train contains 55 railway vehicles, namely, 36 covered goods wagons, 17 platform trucks, 1 passenger carriage and 1 guard's van. Its speed is reckoned at from 20–25 kilometres per hour.

The time taken for entraining into or detraining from a standard military train is reckoned at 3 hours. A division, therefore, using 3 entraining stations, requires 2 days to be set in movement and 2 days to be collected at the end of its journey.

As no railway station in Poland is provided with a raised passenger platform from which animals or vehicles can be loaded on to railway wagons, entrainment and detrainment must normally take place at stations provided with the necessary special platforms, or else these must be built for the occasion. There are, however, in possession of the railway authorities, portable detraining platforms, as used formerly in Russia, by which horses and vehicles can be detrained anywhere along the line.

C.—Mechanical Transport.

1. General Organization and Administration.

The mechanical transport service is administered by the M.T. Branch of No. VI (Technical Troops) Department of the Ministry of War.

In peace a M.T. column is allotted to each military district. It consists of :—

2 instructional columns, 1 for mechanical transport and 1 for armoured cars.
2 transport columns, 1 of motor cars and ambulances and 1 of lorries.
1 depot.
1 reserve cadre.
1 workshop.

The establishments differ, as the number of motor cars and lorries allowed by peace establishment to the different districts varies from over 200 vehicles in Warsaw to about 60 at Lodz.

There is at Warsaw a central M.T. repair shop, employing 800 mechanics, where all kinds of heavy repairs are carried out, not only to mechanical transport but also to tanks and armoured cars. This is a very well organized establishment, on American lines, and produces really good results very economically.

2. Organization in the Field.

Motor transport units are allotted to armies, not to divisions, except on special occasions when M.T. columns may be lent to them temporarily.

The motor transport service is under a director of motor transport at general headquarters.

There is no fixed allotment of M.T. columns to armies, as their use depends on the number of roads available.

3. Motor Transport Columns.

The peace transport columns expand on mobilization and form :—

(a) Motor transport columns, each consisting of 20 lorries.
(b) Motor ambulance columns, each of 20 ambulances, capable of taking 4 lying or 12 sitting cases.

The war establishment of motor transport units is :—

	Officers.	Other Ranks.	Motor Vehicles.
Motor transport column	2	65	21
Motor ambulance column	2	65	22 (20 motor ambulances).
Army M.T. park	13	230	39 (6 cars, 3 tank lorries, 25 lorries, 5 ambulances).

The motor transport columns are capable of carrying alternatively :—

1 days' rations for a division (cavalry or infantry).
2 days' expenditure of S.A.A. for an infantry division.
2 days' expenditure of shell for an infantry division.

THE POLISH ARMY

4. Allotment of Motor Cars.

Motor cars are allotted for the personal use of senior officers of the Ministry of War, including heads of departments, and a small number to each military district headquarters, army inspectors, chiefs of certain establishments and schools, and so forth.

In each district motor cars allotted for the above are borne on the strength of the district M.T. column.

5. Mechanical Transport Troops.

The personnel of the M.T. service is recruited in the normal way from the annual contingent. It is said that it takes 8 months to teach an ordinary country recruit to be an efficient motor driver. A large number of the mechanics are men who take on for a long service engagement after going through a course of instruction, either in units or at the M.T. school at Warsaw.

Polish M.T. drivers are almost invariably bad. Their main object is to go as fast as the machine will go, and they never think of going slowly over bad roads. Consequently the repair bill is very heavy. Most motor vehicles, except those of senior officers, suffer from neglect.

The officers are taken from young men who, after 1 year's instruction at the Podchorazy School at Ostrow in company with cadets entering other arms of the service, proceed for a 2 years' course to the Officers' Engineer School at Warsaw, at the conclusion of which they are appointed 2nd lieutenant. They then do an M.T. course at the M.T. Instructional Camp at Warsaw.

6. Motor Reserve.

The State is authorized by law to register in peace all types of motor vehicles and motor cycles, and to purchase them by requisition in time of war.

The number of vehicles available, however, is not large, and they are principally to be found in Western Poland and in large towns. In Eastern Poland there are practically none, except a few light vans and motor cars belonging to well-to-do people.

The types of these vehicles are very diverse. There is as yet no motor manufacturing industry in Poland, consequently all have been imported. A factory, named " Ursus," has, however, been established at Warsaw, which is to execute an order of the War Ministry for 1,050 motor vehicles, of types (*a*) Spa 25C. Polonia light lorry, and (*b*) Berliet C.B.A. heavy lorry.

7. Types of Military Motor Vehicles.

These lorries may be taken as the future standard type for the Polish Army, but at present various types are in use, also a number of Ford vans and Ford motor ambulances.

8. Motor Cars.

Are of various types, American Cadillacs predominating.

9. Caterpillars.

None.

10. Steam Lorries.

None.

11. Petrol Stores and Supplies.

Poland possesses oil wells in Eastern Galicia and consequently has no lack of petrol. But supplies are only kept in large towns and in the west of Poland. In Eastern Poland no large stocks are kept.

12. Motor Lorries on Rails.

The railway units own a few dressines driven by petrol engines, which is the only form of petrol-driven railway transport in Poland.

13. Traffic Regulations.

The rule of the road is " keep to the right." It is very badly observed, especially by peasants driving carts in the country districts.

D.—Horse Transport.

1. General Organization and Administration.

The horse transport service is administered by the H.T. Branch of No. II (Cavalry) Department of the Ministry of War.

In peace time there is 1 horse transport squadron (Szwadron Taboru) allotted to each military district. It serves both for local transport of district headquarters, where it is stationed, and as a training unit for the personnel of the service. Its peace strength is 11 officers, 310 other ranks and 180 horses, and is divided into squadron headquarters, 2 training columns and 1 duty column.

It is also the cadre which mobilizes the horse transport columns required from the district on mobilization, together with all the wagons, horses and drivers required for units which are formed on mobilization, or which have no transport in peace, such as field hospitals, medical companies and so forth, excluding, however, technical units, *e.g.*, sapper companies, artillery ammunition columns, which keep their mobilization transport in their own stores in peace.

2. Organization in the Field.

Horse transport columns are allotted to formations on mobilization as under :—

    8 for each division (infantry or cavalry) belonging to the district,
    4 for each independent cavalry brigade in the district,

while armies have in addition 2 transport columns for every division or cavalry division comprised in the army, together with an army transport park.

Transport workshops are allotted one to each division, cavalry division or cavalry brigade.

A horse transport park is an army troops unit.

3. Horse Transport Columns.

A horse transport column, as stated above, consists of 71 vehicles, of which 60 are " useful." These 60 are divided into three sections of 20 each. The establishment of a column is 1 officer, 112 other ranks, and 156 horses.

The column is capable of carrying alternatively :—
  $\frac{1}{2}$ day's rations (meat excepted) for a division or cavalry division.
  1 day's S.A.A. for the infantry of a division.
  1 day's ammunition supply for the artillery of a division.
  2 days' S.A.A. for the cavalry of a cavalry division.
  3 days' ammunition supply for a horse artillery (3 batteries) group.
  2 days' ammunition supply for a heavy artillery group.
  180 sick, lying.
  300 sick, sitting.

A horse transport park and workshops with an army has a war establishment of 4 officers, 73 other ranks, 45 horses and 21 vehicles.

A horse transport workshop consists of 1 officer, 26 other ranks, 19 horses and 9 vehicles.

4. Transport Vehicles.

The transport wagon in general use is similar to the wagon used by all the peasantry, and has undoubtedly been evolved as the most suitable pattern.

It is a long low wagon, with sides sloping inwards to the bottom, on four wheels, the rear two on a rigid axle, the front two on a rotating under-carriage giving it greater flexibility in turning (the peasants' carts often have the front axle also rigid). It is supplied with a central draught pole, and has no brakes or springs. The wheels are about 3 feet 6 inches in diameter and the track is about 4 feet. The peasants generally have the sides of their wagons composed of a row of vertical rails held together top and bottom by a longitudinal pole, but the military pattern has solid sides of planks and is bound with iron. The tailboard is removable. The vehicle, with 2 horses, is capable of carrying 400 kilogrammes and its own weight is about 350 kilogrammes.

Another type is in possession of regiments in Poznania, having been taken from the Germans. It is the German pattern G.S. wagon, high up off the ground, the front wheels on a rotating under-carriage which enables the wheel to go under the wagon at sharp turns, and carrying about 2 tons. It is, however, only suitable for use in Poznania and Pomorze, where the roads are good.

5. Colour of Army Vehicles.

These are generally unpainted, and from continued exposure to weather and from never being washed down, are often a dirty mud colour. There is usually a wooden board, 12 inches by 9 inches, attached to the side near the front, on which is painted the name of the unit, the number of the vehicle, and, sometimes, its allotment.

E.—Water Transport Service.

There is very little water transport in Poland. The rivers are shallow except after the melting of the snows, in spring, and they are much impeded by shifting sandbanks.

A few barges navigate the principal rivers, Bug, Warta, Niemen, Vistula, and the Vistula-Notec Canal running west from Bydgosc. and a few small passenger steamers the Vistula.

There is no possibility of sending troops by sea on an expedition, as Poland has at present no port of her own and very few sea-going ships. The port of Danzig, however, is well equipped with docks and wharfage accommodation, but could only be used for embarking Polish troops if the League of Nations sanctioned such a measure.

CHAPTER XVIII.

INTENDANCE AND SUPPLY.

1. General Peace Organization and Strength.

The peace strength of the Intendance Corps (Sluzba Intendantury) is approximately 1,400 officers, 1,000 N.C.Os. and 1,700 privates. The officers are divided into two branches, that of General Direction and Control (Intendantura) and the executive branch Administration and Management (Administracyno-Gospodarczy), there being about 100 of the former and 1,300 of the latter. In regiments, etc., supply duties are carried out by officers of the unit.

The duties of the corps are :—

(a) Provision of funds for payment of troops, and troop movements.

(b) Supply of rations, fuel, light, uniform, equipment, bedding, barrack furniture, field kitchens, field bakeries, office requirements, and financial operations connected with these articles.

(c) Accountancy and control, through the management committees of units, of State funds and property.

(d) Paymaster's duties in units that do not have their own administrative personnel.

(e) Administration and payment of civil personnel employed by the army.

It is organized into an Intendance Detachment, which, like a combatant unit, has to prepare in peace registers of personnel (active and reserve), arrangements for mobilization, and to supervise training. It will probably in future develop into an Intendance Regiment.

2. Personnel.

The intendance personnel is all employed on administrative duties, that is to say, in arranging for the purchase of, or requisition of supplies and equipment as specified above, and for its distribution to the troops. The actual transport of the material is not in their hands, but is carried out by the transport columns, or by the regimental second line transport.

The intendants are those officers who have passed through a course, either in the Polish Army or in one of the former armies.

The officers of the Administrative and Management branch are at present those who have been selected for service by reason of their suitability, but they will be recruited in future from young men who go through the usual one year course at the Podchorąży School at Ostrow, and then through a course at the Central Administration School at Krakow. This school also gives courses of instruction for officers of units employed in administrative duties in their units.

Professional N.C.Os. of the intendance service will also be those who pass through an N.C.O.s' class at the Central Administration School, and who are on long service engagements.

3. Supply Service.

The intendance service is under Department VII (Intendance) of the Ministry of War, at the head of which is a brigadier-general.

Immediately under Department VII are the Higher Intendance School, closely connected with the Supreme War School (Staff College), the Central School of Administration, and a Bureau of Technical Investigation. This bureau carries out researches into the nutritive value of different articles of food, their analyses and preservation, into the suitability of various patterns of uniform, equipment, etc., and into designs for barracks, and so forth, and fixes the regulation patterns. Apart from these three institutions there are no other establishments or stores immediately under Department VII, all depots, etc., being under the control of the intendance branch of staffs of military districts.

The intendance staff at district headquarters has assigned to it a credit from the yearly budget, a certain personnel, and a number of stores and depots. The districts are divided into three regions for intendance purposes, each under its own chief.

In each district there is one district supply depot, and one district equipment depot, generally located at the headquarters of the district.

The district supply depot (Okręgowy Zakład Gospodarczy or O.Z.G.) consists of :—

Headquarters, with management committee,
Store,
Bakery,
Butchery,
School for supply N.C.Os.,
Cadre of supply personnel of the district.

Any of these depots may be enlarged to contain in addition a central reserve of war material at the direct disposal of the Ministry of War.

The duties of the depot are :—
- (a) The collection, and eventually the production, and maintenance of supplies of food, fuel and light, both for current use and as reserve stocks in the event of war.
- (b) Despatch of articles to recipients.
- (c) Maintenance of " regional " stores.

The district equipment depot (Okręgowy Zakład Mundurowy or O.Z.M.) consists of a store and a tailors' shop, and its duties are :—

    (a) The collection, and eventually the manufacture, and maintenance of supplies of clothing, equipment, tailors', shoemakers' and saddlers' tools, bedding, barrack stores, office equipment, both for current use and as reserve stocks.

    (b) Selection and despatch to recipients.

In each "region" is the chief of the intendance service of the region, who is responsible for the supply of intendance stores to each unit. Within his region he has to :—

    (a) Keep ration strength for all units.
    (b) Take charge of all intendance stores.
    (c) Report to district headquarters on the resources of the region.
    (d) Make contracts with private purveyors for supply of requirements.
    (e) Carry out first inspection of ledgers of units.
    (f) Administer and supervise stores required for setting up field depots.

While in practice the regions coincide with divisional areas, the chief intendance officer of the region is not subordinated to the divisional commander, except in regard to field depots forming part of the organization of the division. On the other hand he is in direct touch with the civil administration. To him are allotted by the chief intendant of the military district certain sums for carrying out his duties, and he has a staff of subordinates in the depots under his charge.

In each region there is one regional depot (Rejonowy Zaklad Gospodarczy), with bakery and butchery, except when the region headquarters is in the same town as district headquarters. The duties of these regional depots are analogous to those of districts depots, and in addition they hold stores for forming field depots on mobilization. Regional depots may set up branch depots, by detaching a portion of their personnel, in cases where the accommodation at headquarters is insufficient.

The location of stores is as follows :—

Military District.	District Supply Depot.	District Equipment Depot.	Regional Supply Depots.
I	Warsaw	Warsaw	Dęblin, Modlin, Lomza.
II	Lublin	Lublin	Chelm, Kowel, Rowno.
III	Grodno	Grodno, with branch at Suwalki.	Grodno, Wilno, Lida.
IV	Lodz	Lodz	Lodz, Częstochowa, Skierniewice.
V	Krakow	Krakow, with branch at Tarnow.	Bielsko Biala, Myslowice, Tarnow.
VI	Lwow	Lwow	Lwow, Tarnopol, Stanislawow.
VII	Poznan	Poznan	Poznan, Gniezno, Kalisz.
VIII	Torun	Torun	Torun, Grudziądz, Bydgosc.
IX	Brzesc	Brzesc	Brzesc, Siedlce, Baranowice.
X	Przemysl	Przemysl	Kielce, Jaroslaw, Stryj.

4. Engineer Services.

The duties of the engineer services are :—

(1) The building and maintenance of fortifications, barracks, training grounds, and military railways, waterways and bridges.

(2) Supply to the troops of engineer material, building material and explosives.

(3) The purchase and sale of land and buildings on behalf of the army.

The engineer service consists of special technical personnel, namely :—

(a) Officers of the Engineer Corps.

(b) Warrant officer sappers as assistants.

(c) Sappers on the establishment of the engineer service.

In a similar way to the distribution of the intendance service, the engineer service has :—

(a) At headquarters the administration of the service with central depot.

(b) In each district, the district administration and district depot.

(c) In sub-divisions of each district, called regions, local administrations and local depots.

The " regions," however, are not coterminous with the intendance " regions."

The central engineer store is at Warsaw, subordinate for technical questions to the Ministry of War (Department VI), but for discipline to the Warsaw military district.

It consists of :—

(a) Headquarters.

(b) Technical office.

(c) School for engineer artificers.

(d) Stores for—

(i) land service,

(ii) water service,

(iii) mining service.

(e) Workshops.

In each military district the chief of the engineer services has at his disposal credits for carrying out his duties and the necessary personnel, and maintains a district store.

The military district is divided into 2 or 3 engineer regions, at the head of which is a district engineer, whose duties include :—

(a) Keeping a register of all buildings, land, fortifications, railways, waterways and bridges, and maintaining them in good order.

(b) Supervision of work.

(c) Contracts for work.

(d) Repair and maintenance, and also new construction, of systems of drainage, water supply, heating and lighting.

(e) Maintenance of stores.

(f) Fortification plans.

Region engineer staffs are arranged in two classifications, in the first of which the element of fortification prevails, in regions where fortified areas exist, while the second is mainly for barracks.

Each unit appoints an officer or N.C.O. to be in charge of the buildings which it occupies, and if the building contains special apparatus (pumps, electric power, etc.) may employ civil personnel to look after it.

The division into regions, and location of depots is as follows :—

Military District.	District Depot.	Regions.
I	Warsaw	Warsaw, Dęblin, Modlin.
II	Lublin	Lublin, Rowne, Kowel.
III	Grodno	Grodno, Lida, Wilno.
IV	Lodz	Lodz, Częstochowa.
V	Krakow	Krakow, Tarnow, Katowice.
VI	Lwow	Lwow, Stanislawow, Tarnopol.
VII	Poznan	Poznan, Kalisz.
VIII	Torun	Torun, Grudziądz, Bydgosc.
IX	Brzesc	Brzesc, Baranowice, Pinsk.
X	Przemysl	Przemysl, Rzeszow, Kielce.

5. Organization of Intendance and Supply in the Field.

The provision of the supplies of food, fuel, clothing, and other intendance stores is the duty of the IV Branch of the General Staff, working through the intendance service as its administrative organ, *vide* Chapter VIII, para. 6.

The Chief of the Intendance Service at General Headquarters carries out the orders of the IV Bureau, in peace, as regards the preparation of intendance depots, and, in war, as regards their replenishment. Certain central depots are under his control.

In armies, the chief of the army intendance maintains field depots for his army, replenishing them by demands on G.H.Q. Intendance, addressed to the Regulating Commissar, *vide* Chapter VIII, para. 16. He also fixes railhead and rendezvous (these may be one and the same) where supplies are delivered to divisions. He is responsible for exploiting local resources, within limits laid down by G.H.Q.

Divisional intendance officers are responsible for maintaining the reserve of supplies held in divisional transport columns, and for the divisional intendance park, and, when ordered, for exploiting local resources.

6. Arrangements for Feeding Troops in Battle.

The unexpended portion of the current day's ration is carried, part on the soldier (oats on the horse) and the remainder in the field kitchens.

The next day's rations for man and horse are carried in the company cook's wagon.

The regimental supply column (Tabor Zywniosciowy) carries a further 2 days' rations for men (less meat) and horses.

A divisional transport column can carry ½ day's rations (less meat) for the troops and horses of a division. Under normal circumstances four of these columns carry rations.

Four days' beef on the hoof accompanies the division. For the distribution of this the divisional intendance park includes a field butchery. If beef on the hoof is not provided, divisional meat columns of 14 horsed wagons or 8 lorries, carrying 1 day's meat for the division, are substituted.

Thus the division itself carries altogether 6 days' food for man and beast.

Army headquarters fix for each subordinate division a place (and a time) as the divisional railhead (Stacja Zaopatrzenia) for the next day, communicating these in daily orders. Army also orders what is to be delivered (normally 1 day's supplies with or without meat) and what units are to find the loading parties (generally divisions are ordered to find their own loading parties). In the same orders army also indicates what places are likely to be the railheads for the following day. Orders also include how the division obtains its fresh meat, either from its own cattle column or from the railhead, and other intendance supplies. If corps headquarters are interpolated between army and divisions, army headquarters continue to fix railheads for divisions; corps headquarters only receive from army headquarters orders regarding railhead for itself and corps troops.

The supplies are brought to the railhead by the army, railhead being a suitable small station within reach of the division. A day's supplies for a division requires about 10 to 12 railway wagons.

If divisions are out of reach of railhead, as might happen in a war in the East, army fixes a rendezvous at which divisions will take over the supplies, which would be brought there from railhead by auxiliary transport (probably requisitioned peasant wagons) under army arrangements.

The supplies are taken over at the railhead (or rendezvous) by the horse transport columns of the division. In normal circumstances on any given day two columns would be proceeding from their combined bivouac to railhead to fill up, while the other two would be moving forward to deliver to the regimental supply columns. All are supposed to return at night to a concentration bivouac or billet. If the distance from the railhead to regiments is not more than 20 kilometres, regimental supply columns would refill direct at railhead, cutting out the divisional transport columns.

7. Depot Supply Parks.

Each division contains an intendance park, which consists of butchery, with herd of cattle, a detachment for exploiting local resources, and a small transport column for carrying meat. This intendance park may, if the circumstances admit, set up a small semi-permanent supply depot for the division.

Each army arranges supply depots in suitable locality, generally on railways, from which the supply trains (or horse or motor transport columns) take the supplies up to within reach of divisions, as described in para. 6 above.

Establishments.—

	Officers.	Other Ranks.	Horses.	Vehicles.	Motor Vehicles
Divisional intendance park (cavalry and infantry divisions), army troops intendance park including herd of cattle	2	94	28	13	—
Supply store	5	280	25	12	2
Field bakery	1	137	48	12	—
Field butchery (army cattle herd)	2	88	36	18	2
Railhead intendance office	3	18	4	1	—
Railhead supply detachment	1	54	—	—	—
L. of C. supply store	3	50	10	5	—
Reserve intendance group	3	81	16	6	—

8. Field Bakeries.

As previously stated, the peace organization of the intendance service allows for bakeries (and butcheries) to be set up at district headquarters and in intendance regions, which organize field bakeries (and butcheries) to take the field. There should be one for every division, equipped with Weiss ovens. These are under army headquarters.

9. Field Butcheries.

Similar arrangements hold good with regard to field butcheries. There would be normally a field butchery for every division, accompanied by a herd of cattle.

10. Scales of Rations.

The peace ration scale of a soldier is :—

Bread	1,000 grammes.
Meat	250 ,,
Fats	50 ,,
Potatoes	700 ,,
Fresh vegetables	200 ,,
Dried Vegetables	150 ,,
Salt	25 ,,
Onion	$12\frac{1}{2}$,,
Coffee mixture	50 ,,
Flour for cooking	10 ,,

with a small quantity of vinegar and spices.

The reserve ration consists of 300 grammes biscuit, 200 grammes preserved meat, and 50 grammes coffee mixture.

The diet of the soldier includes a first breakfast of hot soup with bread, a mid-day dinner of soup, meat, potatoes, vegetables and a final course of pastry or something similar, and an evening supper of soup and bread.

An increased ration is given to recruits during their first 3 months' service, and to all ranks during camping and manœuvre periods and during war. Officers and professional N.C.Os. do not receive a free issue of rations, but may draw them on repayment. In war they get rations but a portion of their pay is deducted on this account. Married families get no rations.

11. Forage Rations.

Arm.	Peace.			War.			Reserve Rations.
	Oats.	Hay.	Straw.	Oats.	Hay.	Straw.	Oats.
	Weight in kilogrammes.						
Riding and artillery—							
Light draught	4·5	4	1·5	6	4	1·5	4
Heavy draught	4	6	1·5	5	6	1·5	4
Light draught (train) and pack ..	3	4	1·5	4	5	1·5	3
Mules	3	5	1·5	4	5	1·5	2·5
Donkeys	2	4	1·5	3	4	1·5	2

The peace ration is given in war time to animals not in the field armies. The war ration is given also during manœuvres. The reserve ration is calculated at the least ration required to maintain an animal for a short period when full rations are not available, and is carried in units as a reserve for exceptional circumstances and is not used without orders.

12. Requisitions.

Laws have been passed authorizing the requisitioning on mobilization of motor transport vehicles, and of horses, mules and carts. Among the latter, thoroughbred horses, registered and certified mares and stallions approved by the Ministry of Agriculture, and certain other draught animals and vehicles approved by the same ministry are exempted from requisition.

The requisition of animals is carried out by the civil authorities, but they can call on the army to help. In peace all animals and vehicles have to be registered, by orders of the Ministries of War and Interior in conjunction, and are liable to inspection by local commissions of inspection, composed of the civil head of the district and two assistants, a military member and a veterinary officer, of military status if possible. The decision as to the fitness of any animal for military service rests entirely with the military member, advised by the veterinary officer. On mobilization the same commission becomes a commission of enrolment, and takes the animals and vehicles required.

The number of animals and vehicles required is fixed by the Ministry of War who, with the Ministry of the Interior, divide this number among the Wojewodstwos, whose quota is further divided by the civil authorities among the Powiats and Communes.

The requisitioning of animals and vehicles is ordered by the combined order of the Ministries of War and Interior and can operate over the whole State or any part of it, and for all or any specified class of animals and carts. Owners must then produce the animals and vehicles previously earmarked by the commission of inspection at the place and at the time fixed by the civil authorities where they are to be taken over.

Payment is made at once, at the place of requisition, according to a fixed price list.

Similar arrangements are made for requisitioning motor vehicles, but the requisitioning districts vary greatly in size, as in certain parts of Poland no motor transport is used.

13. Billeting.

The normal procedure when troops are away from barracks is for them to be billetted. Troops in the so-called summer training camps, when these are not on ground owned by the military and previously prepared to receive troops, are billeted among the neighbouring villages, using sheds, barns and outbuildings largely for the men, and large buildings, even schools and so on, for the officers. The owner of the billet provides nothing but the locality; all food and covering, and light, when given, is provided by the army.

In war, when accommodation is limited, cavalry are given preference over the infantry.

14. Travelling Kitchens.

The travelling kitchen consists of a limbered wagon, the limber being a receptacle for supplies of food and cooking utensils, the rear part consisting of a fireplace and three large cauldrons, constructed so as to be served by the fire.

15. Design and Care of Barracks.

Barracks vary very greatly; including large, airy, clean, well built, well kept, and comparatively artistic structures set up by the Germans; solid, square, ugly and badly kept Russian barracks; Austrian barracks somewhere between the two, and in many places temporary wooden huts of various designs. New barracks are being built in some places to a Polish design, of which the main feature is small rooms for 10 or 12 men, where the peasant recruit feels more at his ease than in a great bare, badly heated barrack room for 100 men or more, such as are to be found in many Russian barracks.

German barracks are well found with kitchens, bathhouses, latrines, and so on, which are often neglected in Russian barracks.

Barracks in general are very badly cared for. In Western Poland, which was untouched by the war after 1915, the barracks are generally in good repair, principally owing to the excellent condition in which they were taken over by the Poles. In Eastern Poland, however, the reverse is the case. Much intentional damage was done by the Bolshevik invaders in 1920, and the military budget has not yet been able to afford capital repairs to barracks that are in need of them. Barracks have been patched up as occasion offers, and in one block it may be that material from one half-destroyed building has been used to repair a neighbouring one.

One effect of the shortage of funds is to throw the duty of rendering barracks habitable and comfortable on the officers and men of the unit, and it is noticeable how they have often used great ingenuity in obtaining material and carrying out repairs. In this the characteristics of the officers in charge show themselves; one believes in cleanliness, and scrapes up tubing, and bores holes in it, and arranges shower baths under which every man passes at reveillé; while another devotes his greatest energy to equipping a men's dining room with crockery, cutlery and decorating it with pictures and so on.

The stables are in similar conditions, excellent in the west and dilapidated in the east.

16. Water Supply.

Whereas most barracks have water laid on, even in ex-Russian barracks; there are cases where water has to be carried in carts, for instance at Rowno, where regiments are supplied with carts that have to go to a public water supply and take their turn with the civil population to fill up and bring the water back to barracks.

17. Army Postal Service.

The arrangements for the postal service are organized by the IV Bureau of the General Staff, through a military postal commissar attached to the Department of Posts in the Ministry of Posts and Telegraphs.

CHAPTER XIX.
MEDICAL SERVICES.

1. Peace Organization and Strength of Medical Service.

The strength of the medical corps in peace is as follows:—

Officers	1,264 (Army List, 1924).
Other ranks	3,000 (approximately).
Officers of reserve	3,933 (Army List, 1924).

The officers are divided into five categories, as under:—

	Regular.	Reserve.	Rank.
Doctors	627	2,425	Lieutenant to colonel.
Under-doctors	282	779	Captains and subalterns.
Pharmacists	102	504	Lieutenant to colonel.
Dentists	15	92	Lieutenant to colonel.
Administrative	238	133	2/Lt. to Lt.-Colonel.

The medical corps is organized in peace into:—

A.—Central Establishments.

(a) Military Medical Institute, comprising a technical scientific section and the Military Medical School.
(b) Central Medical Store.

B.—District Establishments and Units.

10 Medical battalions.
10 District hospitals (600 beds, except Warsaw, 1,400).
30 Regional hospitals (300 beds).

C.—*Medical Personnel Serving in Army Units.*

Officers and N.C.Os. of the medical service are attached to units, but borne on the establishment of the medical battalions under B. above.

A medical battalion consists of :—
> Battalion headquarters,
> 3 companies (of 4 platoons each),
> Medical workshop,
> Cadre of reserve battalion ;

but of the 4 platoons in each company, 2 are detached to provide the hospital personnel at the district and regional hospitals.

2. Administration of the Medical Services in Peace.

(*a*) The medical service is administered by Department VIII of the Ministry of War, at the head of which is a brigadier-general, with a staff of some 20 other officers. This department is divided into 2 branches, namely :—
> (1) Organization of medical services and provision of stores.
> (2) Hygiene and technical.

For expert advice a Military Medical Council, consisting of both military and civil experts, may be consulted. It is not a permanent institution, but meets when required.

In the military districts the medical establishments are directly under the chief of medical services of the district, to whom is allotted a certain sum of money from the yearly budget.

(*b*) The duties of the Chief of Department VIII are :—
> (*i*) To look after the health of the army.
> (*ii*) To train officers and men of the medical corps.
> (*iii*) To supply all medical equipment.
> (*iv*) To inculcate the principles of hygiene.
> (*v*) To look after the welfare of invalid soldiers.

He is allotted each year a sum of money from the Army Budget, out of which he makes a grant to heads of medical services of districts.

(*c*) The duties of district heads of medical services are analogous, and in addition they are responsible for supervising the mobilization arrangements, whereby units not existing in peace are formed on mobilization by the district medical battalion.

(*d*) Medical officers with troops are responsible for maintaining a small regimental hospital for minor ailments, and are the technical advisers in medical matters of the regimental commander, to whom they are directly subordinated. They are charged with the duties of training the regimental stretcher bearers and supervising the sanitary arrangements of the unit. They are assisted by a small staff of N.C.Os. of the medical service and by soldiers of the unit trained as sanitary men or stretcher bearers.

(e) The personnel of the medical services is obtained as follows :—

(i) *Officers*.—Candidates for the medical service must go through a course of training at the Military Medical School at Warsaw. To enter this school a young man must be between the ages of 17 and 24, and must have reached a standard of education authorizing him to enter the medical branch of a university, and he must sign a declaration that he will serve in the army for a period twice as long as the time he spends at the school. The school is in close contact with the medical branch of Warsaw University, and the students attend lectures and demonstrations with the students of the University. But as the instructional year at the Medical School is longer, and begins earlier than the University medical course, the pupil spends the preliminary time as follows :—

Newly enrolled	Recruits' drill.
1st and 2nd classes	Military service in a unit.
3rd class	Preparation for examination at the end of the medical Podchorąży course (*see* below).
4th and 5th classes	Military service with a unit during training season or manœuvres.
6th class (doctors)	Preparations for the final examinations giving the medical degree.

The training lasts 6 years in two courses. The junior course, called the "School of Medical Podchorążys," lasts for 3 years and corresponds to the first 3 years (or classes) of the university course; the senior course, called the "School of Application," corresponds to the fourth, fifth and sixth years of the university course.

The pupils will number 300, but the school has only been in existence 3 years, and the first three courses number actually 136 pupils.

The school is organized as a military unit (battalion) under a commandant, assisted by a director of studies, a battalion commander, and an administrator, with a staff of teachers, company officers and N.C.Os. The pupils receive rations, uniform and equipment, and are housed similarly to cadet schools of other arms, in barracks attached to the Warsaw district hospital. The pupils receive their instruction in medicine, surgery and hygiene at the Warsaw University in company with civilian students. In their own military school they are taught the application of these in the army and also military organization and administration.

After successfully passing the examination at the end of the third year the pupils are promoted serjeant, and at the end of the sixth class are appointed second-lieutenant.

(ii) *Other Ranks*.—The rank and file of the medical service are obtained from the yearly contingent. They are first posted to medical battalions, where they do their training during 1 year, after which they are sent as medical personnel to different units.

Professional N.C.Os. are taken from those men of the contingent who are sent to a 5 months' course at the Central School for N.C.Os. of the Medical Service at Przemysl.

(iii) *Reserve Medical Officers*.—These are young men who have passed the medical course at a university, on the completion of which they are called up for their military service, *vide* Chapter VI. They do 3 months' service with a combatant unit, then 6 months in a school for Podchorążys of Reserve, and are sent to finish their colour service in a military hospital.

3. Nursing Service.

There are about 500 nursing sisters employed in the hospitals, included in the establishment of civil personnel employed by the army. There are no special regulations for this service; their employment is governed by the rules for State employees in general.

There is at present no organization corresponding to our Voluntary Aid Detachments. The Red Cross, however, during the Bolshevik war provided many helpers, men and women, to work in military hospitals, to run buffets at railway stations, and similar work, and would do so again in the event of necessity.

The women's sections of the various patriotic societies (*vide* Chapter XXI) would also supply a number of women with some degree of training to help in hospitals.

But the whole question of the employment of women in general is not yet regulated, though a women's committee has been formed to take up the question with the Ministry of War.

4. Medical Organization in the Zone of Operations.

(*a*) The medical services of the armies are administered by the Head of the Medical Department at General Headquarters, through his representatives on the staffs of armies, divisions, and line of communication districts.

In the home area the medical establishments are subordinate to the Chief of the Medical Department of the Ministry of War.

The different medical units are therefore divided into two classes, those in the zone of the armies comprising :—

Army Medical Units.

    Evacuation hospital.
    Field hospitals (100 beds) ⎫
    Motor ambulance columns ⎭ 1 per division forming part of the army.
    Ambulance trains.
    Army medical park (including bacteriological laboratory).
    Convalescent depot (300 cases).
    Bath and disinfecting columns.
    Bath and laundry train.
    Line of communication hospitals.
    Reserve medical company.

Some of the above are directly under the orders of the line of communication commandant.

Divisional Medical Units.

    Medical company.
    Field hospital (100 beds).
    Field dentistry.
    Motor or horse ambulance column (lent on occasions by the army).
    Motor advanced operating theatre (part of evacuation hospital).
    Disinfecting column (part of bath and disinfecting column).

Cavalry Divisional Medical Units.
    Medical company.
    Field hospital (100 beds).
Cavalry Brigade Medical Units.
    Medical platoon.
    Field hospital (100 beds).

(*b*) Regimental medical duties are carried out by the regimental medical officer and his assistants, with a few N.C.Os. of the medical service and some men of the unit specially trained in medical, sanitary and stretcher bearer duties. In an infantry regiment the allotment is 2 stretcher bearer sections (6 men) per company; 1 medical officer and 1 N.C.O. of the medical service, 1 stretcher bearer section and 2 ambulance wagons per battalion; and the same (but with 1 ambulance only) per regimental headquarters.

During an action one or two advanced dressing stations are established in the neighbourhood of regimental headquarters, where the wounded are collected by the stretcher bearers and given first aid. They are taken from these by regimental ambulance wagons to main divisional dressing stations, which should be out of reach of artillery fire.

(*c*) Divisional medical companies consist of 3 platoons. Each platoon contains 10 ambulance wagons, with field kitchen, baggage and store wagons, while the headquarters carries equipment for equipping the main divisional dressing station for urgent treatment. At this station the most necessary alleviation is given to urgent cases before they are sent back in the company ambulance wagons to the divisional field hospital.

War establishment: 7 officers, 210 other ranks, 117 horses, 53 vehicles.

(*d*) A divisional field hospital is equipped to take 100 cases. The staff consists of 7 officers, which includes 3 medical officers, a chemist, and a chaplain, with a few nursing sisters. It only retains cases which it would be dangerous to move any further, and light cases requiring a few days' treatment. The others are sent further to the rear in motor or horse ambulance columns or ambulance trains.

War establishment: 7 officers, 107 other ranks, 5 sisters, 63 horses, 29 vehicles.

(*e*) An evacuation hospital consists of 3 branches, namely, patients' branch, operating branch, and evacuation branch, with store and distributing station. Each branch is divided into sections, the number of sections in each branch being the same as the number of divisions in the army. The patients' section has 100 beds.

War establishment (with 6 sections): 50 officers, 506 other ranks, 26 horses, 14 vehicles, 12 motor vehicles (operating theatres).

(*f*) An army medical park contains a bacteriological laboratory, a workshop, and a delousing station.

War establishment: 9 officers, 101 other ranks, 20 horses, 9 vehicles.

(*g*) A bath and disinfecting column contains bath and disinfecting section, bacteriological section, and water purifying section.

War establishment: 5 officers, 74 other ranks, 52 horses, 22 vehicles.

(h) A reserve medical company, consisting of headquarters and 3 platoons, has a war establishment of 4 officers, 177 other ranks, 12 horses, 5 vehicles.

(i) A mobile disinfecting column, detached if required from the bath and disinfecting column, has a war establishment of 2 officers, 37 other ranks, 30 horses, 12 vehicles.

(j) Motor operating theatres, detached if required from evacuation hospitals (*see* above), have a war establishment of 2 officers, 15 other ranks, and 2 motor vehicles.

5. Medical Organization on the Line of Communication.

As the so-called etape (line of communication) area behind each army is controlled by the army commander, all the medical establishments contained in it are under his orders and are enumerated above. The following establishments are generally located in the line of communication area :—

Line of communication hospitals, which are of various sizes, from 300 to 2,000 beds, organized in sections of 100 beds.

Convalescent depots, for 300 cases. War establishment : 6 officers, 86 other ranks, 8 horses, 4 vehicles.

Disinfecting and bath trains. War establishment : 1 officer, 29 other ranks.

6. Medical Organization in Home Territory.

In the home territory the peace time district and regional hospitals continue to work, after being expanded to increased capacity. Civilian hospitals may be taken over wholly or in part, and convalescent camps organized. These all come under the head of the medical services of the military district.

7. Transport of Wounded and Sick.

Horsed Ambulance Transport.—There are no special horsed ambulance columns, but the horse transport columns of divisions and armies returning empty to railhead or refilling point are used when required.

Motor Ambulance Columns.—These columns consist of 20 motor ambulances and are used when the roads permit. War establishment : 2 officers, 65 other ranks, 22 motor vehicles.

Ambulance Trains.—These are of two types, one for 336 lying cases, the other for 250 cases part lying, part sitting. War establishment of medical personnel : 2 officers, 40 other ranks.

Hospital Ships.—None exist.

8. Hospitals.

In most towns of Poland there are State hospitals, some of them, in the bigger towns, being well equipped and efficient. These, or sections of them, would be used as base hospitals.

Certain big towns have isolation hospitals also.

Red Cross and voluntary aid hospitals do not exist and would hardly be created in war. The personnel of the Polish Red Cross would rather be employed in the existing hospitals.

9. Inoculation and Vaccination.

All Polish citizens are obliged by law to be vaccinated twice during their life, the first time within a year of birth. This law is well carried out, except in the eastern districts, where it is difficult to get hold of people living in out of the way districts. In addition every recruit is vaccinated afresh when he joins the army.

In peace also all soldiers are inoculated every 6 months with a serum protecting against typhoid and paratyphoid. In war all soldiers are in addition inoculated against cholera.

10. Dentistry.

The officers of the medical corps include a number of dentists, who are on the staff of the various peace time hospitals. In war dentistry units are attached to various field hospitals in the army zone, in the étape zone, and in the home area.

Field dentistry units are of three types: 3 officers and 11 other ranks; 2 officers and 8 other ranks; and 1 officer and 7 other ranks.

11. Travelling Laboratories.

Bacteriological laboratories form part of certain army units, namely, the army medical park, bath and disinfecting column.

12. Red Cross Brassard.

The Red Cross brassard is worn, during war time only, by all officers and men of the medical corps, and also by men of other arms, definitely appointed for medical duties; such as soldiers of regiments employed as stretcher bearers or as sanitary orderlies, transport personnel of mobile medical units, and so on. The brassard has to be stamped with the stamp of the unit to which the soldier belongs.

CHAPTER XX.

VETERINARY SERVICE.

1. Organization and Strength.

The veterinary service is composed of :—

Officers	Veterinary officers with diplomas.
Other ranks ..	Veterinary soldiers.
	Master farriers.
	Shoeing smiths.

The whole of this personnel is employed in veterinary units and establishments with the exception of certain veterinary officers attached to mounted units.

The service is administered by the Veterinary Branch of II Department (Cavalry) of the Ministry of War. Subordinate to this, in military districts, there is a senior veterinary officer, with a staff of two other officers, who directs the service in the district and keeps in touch with the civil veterinary profession.

The soldiers of the veterinary service are obtained in the normal way from among the annual contingent, and are trained in minor veterinary duties in the establishment to which they are posted. Selected men are given more advanced instruction at special courses, to which also are sent N.C.Os. of mounted units selected for veterinary duties. Farriers are trained in the district veterinary establishments, and a Central Shoeing School at Warsaw gives further instruction to senior farriers on long service engagements.

Veterinary officers are appointed from young men who have been so trained in civil life. From time to time they are sent through refresher courses at the Cavalry School at Grudziądz.

2. Veterinary Duties with Troops.

Veterinary duties with troops are carried out by :—
  (a) Officers of the Veterinary Corps attached to the unit.
  (b) N.C.Os. and men of the unit specially trained in veterinary duties.
  (c) Farriers and shoeing smiths belonging to the unit.

Regiments of cavalry and artillery have usually 1 veterinary officer and 3 regimental N.C.Os. for veterinary duties on regimental headquarters, while farriers and shoeing smiths are distributed among squadrons, batteries and other equivalent mounted units. The veterinary officer is borne on the establishment of the veterinary service.

In each unit where there is a veterinary officer a small horse hospital for the unit's sick horses is established.

The regimental veterinary and farriery personnel are given their initial training in the regiment, but selected men are sent to veterinary and shoeing courses at the district veterinary establishments and to the central shoeing school at Warsaw.

3. Veterinary Hospitals and other Establishments.

Directly under Department II are three central establishments, viz. :—
  (1) Serological and Bacteriological Institute.
  (2) Central Veterinary Pharmacy.
  (3) Central Shoeing School (Warsaw).

In each military district there is one district veterinary hospital for 100 horses, which is a part of the horse transport column of the district.

This district veterinary hospital is the unit on the strength of which is borne all the veterinary personnel employed in the district in question ; it is an instructional establishment for the lower ranks (veterinary soldiers and shoeing smiths) ; it is also the unit which mobilizes all the veterinary establishments required in war ; and finally is the establishment where all horses of units which do not possess regimental horse sick lines are treated.

On mobilization the district veterinary hospital expands and forms :—

  (a) *In the District.*
    1 district veterinary pharmacy.
    1 district veterinary hospital (500 horses).

THE POLISH ARMY

(b) *In the Zone of the Armies.*

Field veterinary hospitals.

Evacuation veterinary hospitals (1 per army), including 2 hospital sections each for 200 horses, 2 feeding up sections each for 200 horses, and 2 evacuation detachments.

The war establishments of the various veterinary units are as follows (provisional only) :—

	Officers.	Other Ranks.	Horses.	Vehicles.
District veterinary hospital	9	305	13	26
Field veterinary hospital	9	230	67	30
Evacuation veterinary hospital	12	400	53	25

4. Stables.

The barracks that were erected by the Germans in German Poland before 1914 contained well-built modern stables, with good light, air and drainage. But in the Austrian and Russian districts the stables are not so good, especially the standings, and the drainage is poor. Many of these are also in bad repair, and owing to lack of funds cannot be greatly improved at present.

5. Remount Services.

The remount service is under the Remount Branch of II (Cavalry) Department of the Ministry of War. At each district headquarters is a branch office of the remount service under a senior officer, who is also in charge of horse-mastership in all units of the command. This officer has also to collate the results of the registration of horses in his district, prepare plans for calling up the selected horses on mobilization, and for collecting them and handing them over to units. He has to keep in close touch with local horse breeders and the civil administration.

All horses required by the Polish Army are bought direct from owners and breeders by remount purchasing commissions.

There are four of these commissions and they divide the whole country between them. It is hoped eventually to buy all the horses required in Poland, but at present some horses are bought abroad, Hungary and Great Britain being the most favoured markets. Some 7,000, or 10 per cent. of the peace establishment, are required yearly.

Horses are bought at 4 years old, and are issued to units as soon as possible. As the purchasing commissions are at work all the year, and hand over the horses as soon as possible to the units indicated by the Remount Department, there is no necessity to take temporary charge of the young horses in remount depots. Only 3 remount depots, at Góra Kalwarija (near Warsaw), Wyrzysk (Pomerania), and at Zamosc exist, to which are sent well bred young horses, specially bought at 3 years old for officers' chargers. They are kept at these depots for a year, running loose in paddocks throughout the whole period, and are then issued to units.

Besides the above purchasing commissions, registration commissions are periodically appointed, composed of an officer of a mounted unit, a military veterinary officer, and a representative of the civil power, to carry out the registration of horses within a given district. Orders are issued for all horse owners to produce their animals at a given time and place before these commissions, who inspect them, classify them, and note down those that will be required on mobilization. They work under the district remount officer.

In war time there is a remount officer on the staff of each army, with a number of remount depots at his disposal. The war establishment of a remount depot is as follows:

	Officers.	Other Ranks.	Horses.	Vehicles.
Headquarters	4	27	5	2
Section (for 100 horses)	—	39	4	2

The depot consists of a variable number of sections.

6. Horse Breeding Establishments.

The breeding of horses is a matter of private enterprise entirely. The State, through the Department of Agriculture, assists, with the object of improving the type of horse, by providing good stallions whose service the peasant breeders can obtain at a nominal fee (3 zloty or 1s. 6d.). These stallions are kept in stud farms in various parts of the country, namely:—

    Janow (near Brzesc-nad-Bugiem).
    Lonsk (near Płock).
    Boguslawice (near Piotrkow).
    Sadowa Wisznia (near (Lwow).
    Krakow.
    Gniezno.
    Sierakow (in Poznania).
    Starogard (in the Danzig Corridor).

There are 1,370 stallions altogether in these 8 farms, which serve on an average 50 mares yearly, producing 70,000 good foals annually.

The Government (Ministry of Agriculture), however, in addition to the above has two small breeding establishments, namely, at Janow and at Kozienice (opposite Dęblin on the Vistula); at the former half-bred horses, and at the latter thoroughbred horses, are bred.

Many private landowners have studs of varying size with many thoroughbred and half-blood horses, but the majority of horse breeding is in the hands of the peasantry.

THE POLISH ARMY

Most studs in Poland (except German Poland) were ruined during the war, the best horses being requisitioned without thought of the future, and are now only being started again under considerable difficulties.

7. Statistics.

It is stated that there are now (1924) a total of four million horses in the whole of Poland. Of these there is a high proportion of mares, and about 50 per cent. of these latter are stated to be suitable for the breeding of horses for the army (*i.e.*, over 1·55 metres in height).

There is no attempt made to produce a special type of light draught horse suitable for field artillery. The same type of horse is considered suitable for all arms, the more sturdy ones being allotted as draught horses. The flat country with its absence of good roads, and its network of sandy or muddy tracks, has developed a type of small light horse which the peasant uses for all purposes.

It is the pick of these horses, being gradually improved by careful feeding, and by breeding from the State stallions, that form the greater part of the horses in the Polish Army at the present time, and although they appear light and small in comparison with British army horses, they are undoubtedly the most suitable for Poland.

It is said that by giving oats to the local peasant horses, as an extra to their normal feed of hay, straw chaff, and grazing, in one generation the height of the horse is increased from 5 to 8 centimetres.

CHAPTER XXI.

AUXILIARY UNITS AND SEMI-MILITARY FORCES.

1. General.

In addition to the regular army the armed forces of the State include :—
   (1) The Customs Guard. (Straż Celna.)
   (2) The Frontier Guard Corps. (Korpus Obrony Pogranicza Panstwa, K.O.P.P.)
   (3) Patriotic League and Clubs patronized by the Government.

2. The Customs Guard.

The frontier of Poland is guarded by two independent bodies working together. The first of these bodies, for the preservation of order, or the prevention of crossing the frontier by unauthorised persons or goods, is either the Police or the Corps of Frontier Guards. Neither has any duties in connection with customs whatever. The inspection of merchandise coming across the frontier, its detention, confiscation, valuation and taxation, etc., is in the hands of a special body of men under the orders of the Ministry of Finance, the Customs Guard (Straż Celna). They wear a uniform similar to the Army, but of dark green colour, and are armed with rifle and bayonet. They are all paid functionaries of the State (not conscripts) and service in the Guard is not reckoned as military service. They number some 6,000 all ranks, under an inspector, a retired general, in the Ministry of Finance.

3. The Frontier Guard Corps.

The duty of guarding the frontier against illegal attempts to cross or to bring in goods is the function, on the German and Czecho-Slovak frontiers, of the State Police, but on the Lithuanian and Russian frontiers a different system is necessary.

Lithuania is in a state of war (without active operations) with Poland, and the disturbed state of Russia, the peculiar laws prevailing there, the constant threats by her leaders to Poland's security, and the hostile attitude of the army and officials, rendered it necessary in the autumn of 1924 to organize a special armed force, called the Corps of Frontier Guards, to maintain order and repel raids from beyond the frontier.

This Frontier Guard Corps has its headquarters in Warsaw, as a branch of the Ministry of the Interior, under whose orders the force is placed, and which is responsible for its whole administration, discipline, organization and employment. The force is, however, subject to the same military laws and regulations as the army. Its total strength was originally intended to be 30 battalions and 30 squadrons, but 24 battalions and 20 squadrons have been found sufficient. These have been formed in three batches, the first batch by November, 1924, the second batch by April, 1925, and the third batch by the end of 1925. The first batch took over the eastern frontiers of the provinces of Wilno, Nowogrodek, and Wolhynia ; the second batch the eastern frontier of Polesia and Tarnopol ; and the third batch the Lithuanian and Latvian frontiers.

It is recruited as follows :—

(a) Officers. Enough officers have volunteered to serve in this corps, both from the active army and the reserve, to complete the first two batches.

(b) Professional N.C.Os. A large number have been obtained from volunteers both from the active army and the reserve, and the remainder of the requirements of the first batch have been obtained by detailing N.C.Os. from active regiments.

(c) Non-professional rank and file are taken from the annual conscript contingents. When the men of the yearly class which has just become liable to military service are allotted to units at the " pobor " in the spring of the year, a certain number are allotted to the Corps of Frontier Guards. As regards the infantrymen, these are sent, when the time of joining arrives, to a line infantry regiment for their recruit's training for a period of 6 months, after which they are sent to join their appointed battalion of Frontier Guards. Each battalion of Frontier Guards is linked with two line regiments, each of which has always to have 110 men under training for the Frontier Guards. This figure represents one-sixth of the conscript establishment of a Frontier Guard battalion. As this number has to be formed by two regiments every 6 months, and as the soldier has another 18 months to serve to complete his 2 years, the strength of the battalion is assured. As regards the cavalry, the recruits for each cavalry squadron are sent to a linked cavalry regiment for 1 year's training, after which they join *en bloc* the Frontier Guard squadron, replacing the whole of the conscript personnel of it. As a cavalryman has to serve 25 months, the squadron has 1 month during which the two contingents serve side by side, and the new contingent learns its duties.

THE POLISH ARMY

The Frontier Guard Corps is organized into 6 brigades, 1 for the eastern frontier of each of the provinces bordering on Russia, and 1 for the Lithuanian and Latvian frontiers. The strength of each brigade varies from 4 to 6 battalions and squadrons, according to the extent of the sector of the frontier allotted.

Battalions are all in the front line, each having its own section of the frontier, but it is desired, if the money is forthcoming, to have an extra battalion in reserve in each brigade area, thus making up the total of 30 battalions, which was intended originally.

The following is the establishment of a battalion :—

	Officers	O.R.	Horses.	Remarks.
Battalion Headquarters	8	53	20	
Signal platoon	1	50	7	
Machine gun platoon	1	18	4	2 machine guns.
4 companies at	4	171	10	12 machine guns.
Total	26	805	71	2 heavy and 48 light machine guns.

Battalions on the Lithuanian frontier have a reduced establishment of 24 officers and 711 other ranks only.

Posts are being built along the frontier to be occupied by these troops. Each post is to hold half a platoon, or an N.C.O. and 26 men, with or without an officer. The posts consist of wooden buildings, with an observation tower in the centre, with barrack rooms, rooms for N.C.O. and officer, kitchen, store, bath house, etc., surrounded by an earth rampart, the latter being again surrounded by a barbed wire entanglement. These posts are at a distance of about 4–5 kilometres from one another.

In each province the brigade allotted to it is directly under the orders of the civil authorities, i.e., the Wojewode or governor of the province, in the same manner as the police and other administrative organisations. The commander of the corps merely fulfils the role of technical administrative head and has no control over the employment of the corps. His headquarters contains 7 general staff officers for organization, training and intelligence, and 11 administrative officers for the administrative services of the corps. Brigade staffs also include officers for operations and intelligence, and even battalions will have an intelligence officer. These intelligence staff and other officers are to co-operate closely with the civil police.

The assumption of duty by this corps has already effected a great improvement in the eastern districts, and security of life and property is now well established. Raids from across the Russian frontier have entirely ceased.

4. Rifle Clubs and Similar Organizations.

When Poland was under the domination of the partitioning Powers the national aspirations of the people led to the formation of a number of societies which, carefully camouflaged under the guise of sport, musical, educational or agricultural societies, served to keep alive a spirit of nationality, while some of them took more active steps to prepare the younger generation for the eventual struggle for liberation, both by giving physical and, when possible, military training. Such were the Sokol Gymnastic Society and Pilsudski's organizations in Galicia, *vide* Chapter I.

When Poland's independence was restored a further number of societies sprang up, of a similar conspiratorial nature, to maintain Poland's rights in territory she was occupying, though her claim had not been formally admitted, and for winning back still wider lands over which Poland had ruled in the past. These societies included in Wilno the Związek Bezpieczenstwa Kraju (League of Security of the Land) which has now been incorporated into the Związek Strzelecki; in Upper Silesia the Rebel Organization which has now become the Związek Powstancow Gorno-Sląskich (League of Upper Silesian Rebels), and others.

At the same time, the open situation of Poland's frontiers and the experience of the World War induced the educational authorities to improve the physical standard of the nation by introducing physical training in all schools, and to encourage the formation of school military training detachments (Hufiec Szkolny).

Thus, at the present time, physical and military training is given to the younger generation both in schools and by various patriotic societies, but as there is no controlling hand to guide the activities of all to a common end and on a common programme, the Government has drawn up a bill to legislate for :—

(a) Physical training in all schools, of whatever degree, for both sexes.

(b) Military training in all educational establishments (schools and universities) for boys and young men over 16 years of age.

(c) The encouragement of physical and military training in certain approved societies.

(d) The establishment of government control over the whole.

This bill is to be laid before the legislature, but in the meantime some of its provisions are being put into force by administrative decrees.

Here it must be mentioned that there is another object for establishing control over the work of the various societies, and that is to keep an eye on their activities and frustrate any attempt to use them as political forces. Unfortunately many of these societies started with a distinctly political colouring, and those like the Sokol that were, at their inception, quite aloof from politics, have been drawn into the net.

The Związek Strzelecki, for instance, which is the descendant of Pilsudski's rifle clubs in Galicia before 1914, is suspected of having taken part in the Krakow riots of 1923, and certainly took a large share on Pilsudski's side during the *coup-d'état* of May, 1926, when rifles were issued to it in large numbers from army stores. Former Governments have, therefore, forbidden them to possess arms.

It is probable, however, that all of them have secret stores of arms, and it has been openly stated by persons in authority, that a society in Poznan for organizing defence against possible German agression has armed and organized the villagers for this purpose.

THE POLISH ARMY

The 7 associations authorized to give physical and military training are :—
(1) Sokol Gymnastic Society.
(2) Związek Strzelecki (Rifle League).
(3) Związek Harcerstwo Polskiego (League of Polish Boy Scouts).
(4) Stowarzyszenie Bywszych Powstanców Górno-Sląskich (Association of former Upper Silesian Rebels).
(5) Zjednoczenie Młodźiezy Polskiej (Union of Polish Youth).
(6) Związek Młodźiezy Wiejskiej (League of Rural Youth).
(7) Związek Straźy Poźarnych (League of Fire Brigades).

The first three have branches all over Poland and are by far the most influential societies.

The organization and supervision of physical and military training in all these societies is effected by a newly-created Council of Physical Training and Military Preparation (see Chapter XXVII, 8), which works under the Ministry of Education. This council also includes representatives of the army, of the Ministry of Public Works, and of the above-mentioned societies. It draws up the general programme and co-ordinates the work of the various Government departments concerned.

In the execution of this, the chief army organ is the section for physical training and military preparation (wychowanie fizyczne i przysposobienie wojskowe, or, shortly, w.f. i p.w.). This section used to belong to the 1st Department (Infantry) of the Ministry of War, but owing to the greater attention that is now being paid to the whole subject it is to be included in the General Staff (III Bureau) of the Inspectorate General. Subordinate to this are sections for w.f. i p.w. in military districts, who are responsible for organizing the work in the districts in general, and for preparing camps, competitions, and for keeping touch with the local authorities and the organisations. Below them divisions have a staff officer for w.f. i p.w., who is the technical adviser of the divisional commander, but has not much executive authority. The executive organ throughout the country is the regimental cadre for w.f. i p.w. The whole country is divided into 90 territorial districts, each of which is affiliated to an infantry regiment stationed in it or in its neighbourhood. The regimental cadre for w.f. i p.w. is responsible for the actual instruction carried out in the district among the societies, and also in schools (see Chapter XXVII, 8). A major is in charge of the cadre, and he is assisted by a number of officers and N.C.O.s, which varies according to the population of the district and the strength of the organizations and schools in it. The principle in general is that there should be one officer for the Sokol, one for the Rifle League, one for schools, and, if necessary, one for other organizations whose strength in the district may warrant it. This cadre is directly under the commanding officer of the regiment, and acts with his authority and under his supervision, thus keeping the regiment in the closest touch with the district. The officers of the cadre are permanently in their district, and have to organize, through the heads of local branches of the organizations (and the school authorities), the training assemblies. They are empowered to fix the hours and places for these assemblies (generally the evenings, and, as regards country districts, not during the season when the peasants are busy on the land), but the bringing of the members to the meeting place is the duty of the head of the local branch of the organization in question. Discipline is within the organization, except during the actual carrying out of the training, when the members are under the p.w. officer. These cadres also supply the staff for the summer camps that are organized, and make the arrangements for rifle meetings, sports meetings, and so on, in their district.

In consequence of this organization, which has been developed during the year 1926, though the foundations were laid during the time General Sikorski was Minister of War, the infantry regiments are brought in close contact with the members of the organizations. These have therefore been organized in platoons, companies, and battalions, and consider themselves as affiliated to their regiment.

The programme of military training in the organization includes musketry, bombing, bayonet fighting, elementary field operations, hygiene, and field engineering and, when the conditions allow of it, courses in signalling, wireless, etc., are also arranged.

As far as possible the organizations provide their own instructors, and prefer to do so. The regimental p.w. cadre are always available to give instruction themselves if asked to do so, but their duties are generally limited to supervision, co-ordination, and criticism, and to training the instructors. For this purpose summer camps and winter courses are arranged by the military authorities, and are staffed by the p.w. cadres, to which the associations send selected members with a view to their becoming instructors for the general body of members. The organizations also send members to the Central Musketry School at Torun, where regular courses for such young men are held, and to the Central School of Gymnastics and Sport at Poznan, or to other physical training courses which are arranged by the Ministry of Education from time to time pending the creation of the Central Institute of Physical Training.

The regimental cadres also keep a stock of rifles, which are issued out for training purposes. They are not allowed to be kept by the organization, but have to be returned at the end of the day's work to the officer or military representative who supervised the exercise.

At present the personnel of the cadre is found from suitable officers of the regiment, but it is intended in future that all of them shall have special preparation for it by passing through a course of instruction, which will include physical training.

To those young men who go through the course of w.f. i p.w. in these organizations (and in schools also, *vide* Chapter XXVII, 8) certain privileges as regards carrying out military service are granted, provided they pass the necessary qualifying tests. These privileges are :—

> To those who pass the first p.w. test (individual training) is given the right to choose the arm of the service, regiment and garrison within the competence of the Recruiting Commission before which they have to appear. They obtain no reduction of service.
>
> Those who pass the second p.w. test (training within the section) have the same choice as above, and in addition have their service shortened by 2 months (the time of individual training of the recruit), and join 2 months later than the rest of the contingent, *i.e.*, in the beginning of December.
>
> Those who pass the third p.w. test (training within the *groupe de combat*) receive the same privilges as to choice, and have their service reduced by 6 months, joining the colours in March. If they wish to become reserve officers, they also have their period of training in the School of Podchorązy's of Reserve reduced by 3 months (*see* Chapter VI, 4 (*c*)).

5. The Związek Strzelecki (Rifle League).

The Rifle League is the descendant of Pilsudski's military organizations in Galicia, but has now been extended all over Poland. It numbers 200,000 active members, mostly young men between 17 and 21, and includes the Związek Legjonistów (League of Legionaries), *i.e.*, veterans of Pilsudski's Legions that took the field in 1914. Of the members 75 per cent. are peasants and 25 per cent. town-dwellers, the latter portion including 5 per cent. of intelligentsia.

It is organized in Okręgi (districts) co-terminous with military districts, Odwody (regions) co-terminous with P.K.U's., and detachments, of which there are some 1,000. There are 5 women's detachments with 600 women members. The subscription is 10 grosze (1*d*.) per month, being low because in general young countrymen have no money of their own and if required to subscribe more would be apt to sell their parents' property. On the other hand they subscribe produce, rye, potatoes, etc., which the League sells. Other funds are subscribed by "sympathisers" or persons too old to undergo any training. The total budget is some 400,000 zlotys (£16,000) a year. The League has about 6,000 instructors at the present time, *i.e.*, members who have been through the summer camps mentioned above, ex-officers, ex-Legionaries, and voluntary helpers, and it aims at having 12,000. These instructors provide the staffs at headquarters in the districts and regions, as well as the actual teaching personnel in the detachments. The instruction given in the detachments includes football, athletics, marching, musketry, and in certain centres where the appliances have been obtained, telegraphy, electricity, and so on. The teaching is intended to improve the young man physically and morally and to prepare him for his term of military service.

The Związek Strzelecki is closely connected with Marshal Pilsudski, and is a powerful weapon in his hands, as was shown by the events of May 1926. It had previously, when Pilsudski was living in retirement, maintained an attitude aloof from politics, but now it is clear that this outward attitude only concealed its inner activities. It is also in close touch with the P.O.W. (formerly Polska Organizacja Wojskowa, Polish Military Organization, now Polska Organizacja Wolności, Polish Organization of Freedom), which was formed by Pilsudski out of his legionaries when the legions were disbanded by the Germans in 1927. The Związek used to receive no aid from the Government, but now that Pilsudski is in power it is in a privileged position.

The members wear a semi-military uniform, consisting of a tunic of military pattern with metal buttons carrying the Polish eagle, and cap also similar to that of the army and also carrying the military cap badge (eagle) in front. Breeches and footwear are less uniform in appearance. Badges of rank in the organization are worn on the collar of the tunic, *e.g.*, officers have crossed carbines and a number of stars varying according to rank, and the distinctive badge of the organization, a crimson shield bearing a white eagle, is worn on the left arm.

6. The Sokol Society.

The Sokol (Falcon) is a gymnastic society that has been in existence for 30 years. Formerly in Russian Poland it was a secret organization, only in Austrian Poland was it tolerated by the authorities. Its members are of both sexes, organized in nests (gniazdo), of which there are 1,300 in all Poland, circles (okręgy), and districts (dzielnica), of which the latter corresponds to the territory of a Wojewodstwo. In addition there are 200,000 Polish Sokols in America, 65 nests in France, and a few in Belgium and in England. All sokols are under the presidency of Count Adam Zamoyski, M.C., former A.D.C. to the Tsar. The sokols carry out principally gymnastic and athletic training, but are beginning to take up military training more seriously, and aim at preparing every young member so that when his term of military service arrives he shall be capable of becoming a junior N.C.O. at once and instructing the other recruits. Training is carried out by their own members, sometimes under the supervision of "liaison officers" appointed by the military authorities, and rifles are loaned from the nearest barracks or stores of arms. Mounted detachments of sokols are also formed and trained as cavalry. The organization is stated to be non-political, but it is generally considered to be in sympathy with the Right as opposed to the Radicals and Socialists. It arranges summer camps for its members, and also sends many of them to the summer camps organized in military districts.

Its funds are obtained by small subscriptions from all members and by larger ones and gifts from those in a position to afford them.

Sokols wear a kind of uniform, of which the principal feature is a feather in the cap, grey coat with braid of the same colour, and often a red shirt and collar in one piece, without tie. National costumes are also worn.

The Sokol is one of the societies that have been affiliated to the League of Mutual Societies of the Polish Republic (also under the presidency of Count Zamoyski), together with the League of Ex-soldiers of Dowbow-Musnicki's Troops (Dowborczyk), Haller's Army (Hallerczyk), League of Reserve Officers, League of Veterans of 1863, and others, all more or less in political sympathy with the Right.

7. The Scout Movement.

The Scout movement is guided by a Chief Inspector in the Ministry of Religion and Public Instruction, and numbers 31,000 Boy Scouts, mostly 14 to 15 years old but including boys up to 18, and 19,000 Girl Guides of similar ages, organized in detachments all over Poland. These detachments were formed into a League of Polish Scouts (Związek Harcerstwa Polskiego) under the presidency of General Josef Haller, and the League was officially recognized by the Government in 1920. The League contains four classes: (1) Patrols of Scouts and Guides; (2) Clubs of Old Scouts and Guides; (3) Scouts' Friends; and (4) Instructors and Chiefs. The 4th class and delegates from (2) and (3) form a Supreme Council, who appoint an executive committee to carry on the work. Under the Supreme Council are district councils. In 1923 a combing out was ordered, which resulted in the removal of inefficient members and reduced the total membership, improving the quality.

The local detachments carry out meetings and field exercises on the same principle as in England, while district councils arrange summer camps, at which all attendance is voluntary. At these exercises and camps the instruction has as its object the improvement of the physical qualities and moral character of the youths, based on the principles of the Roman Catholic form of the Christian religion, at the same time teaching them useful tasks of daily life, and games. Military instruction as such is not given, but many former Scouts, now reserve officers, give their services as instructors, and this tends to foster a military spirit. On the other hand, many Scouts join the summer training camps organized in military districts, where military instruction forms part of the programme. Scout detachments are often organized in the gymnasiums, or middle schools.

The funds of the League are mainly obtained from voluntary subscription by members of the class of Scouts' Friends. The Government grants a small subsidy, and gives material help in the form of camping material, etc.

The usual uniform of the Scout has been adopted and detachments have their own distinguishing badge as in England, but a Polish four-cornered hat is often substituted for the usual slouch hat. The majority of the Scouts are the children of intelligentsia, though 30 per cent. are children of workmen and artisans, and 15 per cent. of peasants.

8. Women's Organizations.

During the Bolshevik war women's battalions were formed and some of them actually took part in the fighting. Other women were taken into offices and on to staffs and dressed in uniform. But now all these organizations have been dissolved and there is no peace preparation for the employment of women in war.

The League of Polish Women, Koło Polek, however, aims at organizing the female population and at inculcating patriotism and improving the position of women in Poland, and could probably organize some branches of women's work, on behalf of the military authorities, if called upon to do so.

Women's sections of the various societies mentioned above also aim at preparing women to take over auxiliary duties in war time, and a Committee of Women has lately been established to co-ordinate the work of the various societies and to supervise it. It is also getting in touch with the Ministry of War, to obtain its help and guidance.

CHAPTER XXII.
POLICE AND GENDARMERIE.

1. The Civil Police.
A.—Organization.

The civil police force is under the Department of Public Safety in the Ministry of the Interior, in which there is a Police Headquarters charged with the organization, instruction, recruiting, promotion and other personal questions affecting the police force. For the first two years of its existence it had the benefit of the help of a British Police Mission, which came to Poland to assist and advise in its organization.

Subordinate to the Police Headquarters are the inspectors, one to each Wojewodstwo (and to the City of Warsaw) who are under the orders of the Wojewode. Below the inspectors are commissars, of which there is one to each Starostwo into which the Wojewodstwos are divided. These commissariats are the smallest police units to which a police officer is appointed. Below the commissars are non-commissioned officers appointed to command police posts in communes or grouped communes.

The police force is, however, not organized into units of fixed establishment. Each Wojewodstwo, Starostwo, etc., has the number of police considered necessary according to local conditions. Small organized bodies of police, platoons or companies, can, however, be formed in case of disturbances. The police stationed in each Wojewode are grouped together in a detachment, bearing a distinguishing number.

The police carry out their duties on foot, but in every Wojewodstwo there are mounted police of varying numbers, for instance in Warsaw City there are 150 mounted police.

The police force is divided into the "external" police (foot and mounted) who carry out their duties in uniform, and the criminal and political police, who work in mufti, but both branches are combined in one for the purposes of organization and administration.

The unmarried police and the police reserves (*see* below) are housed in barracks, if available; but married police are permitted to live in their own houses.

B.—Personnel.

(*a*) Police officers of Wojewodstwos are graded as follows :—
    Commandant General of Police,
    Assistant Commandant General,
    Chief Inspectors,
    Inspectors, and
    Sub-Inspectors.

These ranks correspond to army officers of field rank.

Police officers of Starostwos as :—
    Chief Commissars,
    Commissars, and
    Aspirants.

These ranks correspond to captains and subalterns in the army.

The rank of Commissar is given to police officers of Starostwos. Aspirants may be appointed to Starostwos, but are usually appointed to the more important Communes or Grouped Communes.

Police officers include a few who served in the police of the partitioning powers. Some are former officers, who are transferred direct into the police with officer's rank; but the normal way to become a police officer is to join the ranks of the police. Those with the requisite educational qualifications (to have finished a middle school) and considered siutable are sent to the Police Officers' Training School at Warsaw for a five-months' course, at the close of which they are appointed Aspirants with 6 months' probation before being confirmed in that rank. Promotion is given partly by seniority and partly by selection to fill vacancies.

The pay of all ranks is calculated according to the table given on page 134, the Commandant General being graded as Category IV, an Aspirant in Category IX, and a constable in Category XIII.

(b) *Non-commissioned Officers.*—There are only two ranks of non-commissioned officers, serjeant and senior serjeant, and these ranks are given to those in charge of communal police posts.

Non-commissioned officers may be those of the former police forces of the partitioning powers, but are now being obtained by training selected constables at the N.C.Os'. training schools, where the course lasts 6 months. There are 6 such schools in Poland.

(c) *Constables.*—A few of the constables come from the former police forces of the partitioning Powers, but the majority are ex-soldiers and volunteers. All constables must have passed through an elementary school, and be between the ages of 25 and 42 on enrolment. They sign no contract, but can be discharged or resign freely. After a certain number of years' service they have the right to a pension. On joining a man is sent to a recruits' school for a 6 weeks' course, after which he is posted for duty to a detachment. There are two grades, constable and senior constable.

C.—Duties.

The police force carries out its duties under the orders of the Department of Public Safety, of the Wojewode or of the Starosta, according to its distribution. These functionaries alone are empowered to give orders on this subject.

The external police is charged with securing the safety and security of the inhabitants of the State, with the regulation of traffic, the prevention of crime, and the arresting of malefactors, and is responsible for the custody of the latter. The policemen may be posted singly or in patrols of 2 or more, but the present tendency is to reduce the number of single posts. In the country districts patrol duty is performed on horseback. The hours of duty are 8 hours daily.

In each Wojewodstwo a part of the police force is kept as a police reserve in areas where such reserves are considered necessary. These reserves are composed of specially selected bachelor constables, and can be sent rapidly to any area where their presence is required. When the situation is quiet they take their turn of patrol duty with the remainder of the police force.

The criminal police force is charged with the duty of discovering and hunting down criminals.

The political police keep surveillance over the political tendencies of the population.

D.—Relations with the Army.

The police may only arrest an army officer if armed with a special order from the military authorities or in a case of *flagrante delicto*. They can arrest soldiers, but must hand them over as soon as possible to the military authorities.

In case of public disturbances the police have to restore order, and may then act in formed bodies like regular troops. If they are not able with their own resources to restore peace, the civil authorities may request the military authorities to put a body of troops at the disposal of the police authorities. In cases of extreme gravity the civil power may pass into the hands of the military authorities.

In case of mobilization of the army the police force continues to carry out its duties, and the men are not required to join the army.

E.—Numbers.

The establishment of the police force is approximately 32,000 men, to which must be added 400 officials and 573 civil employees.

The following table shows the distribution of ranks:—

Establishment of Police Force.

Rank.	Category for Pay.	Total.
Commandant general	IV	1
Chief inspectors	V b	1
Inspectors	V	23
Sub-inspectors	VI	26
Chief commissars	VII c	107
Commissars	VII	193
Sub-commissars	VIII	277
Aspirants	IX	272
Total Officers		900
Senior police sergeants	X	2,180
Police sergeants	XI	3,849
Senior constables	XII	5,260
Constables	XIII	19,838
Total other ranks		31,127

F.—Uniform.

The uniform of the police consists of a coat, trousers or breeches, cap and greatcoat of military pattern and of navy blue cloth, with pipings of light blue. On the collar of the coat and greatcoat is a patch of light blue cloth. A number in white metal is worn by constables on the collar. In addition the number of the detachment, allotted to each Wojewodstwo, is worn on the shoulder strap in roman numerals of white metal.

THE POLISH ARMY

The badges of rank are as follows :—

Rank.	On Blue Collar Patch.	On Sleeve.
Constable	Number in white metal	Nothing.
Senior constable	Do. do.	One blue chevron.
Serjeant	Do. do.	One silver chevron.
Senior serjeant	Do. do.	Two silver chevrons.
Aspirant	One silver stripe and silver palm branch	Nothing.
Sub-commissar	Do. do. do. do.	One silver stripe.
Commissar	Do. do. do. do.	Two silver stripes.
Sub-inspector	Two silver stripes and double palm branches	One silver stripe, with curl.
Inspector	Do. do. do. do.	Two silver stripes, upper one with curl.
Chief inspector	Do. do. do. do.	Three silver stripes, upper one with curl.
Assistant commandant	Three silver stripes and treble palm branches	One broad silver stripe with curl.
Commandant General	Do. do. do. do.	One broad silver stripe with treble curl.

The armament of constables of the uniformed foot police consists of rifle, bayonet and pistol. Constables of the mounted police have carbine, sword and pistol. All ranks above that of constable, both foot and mounted, have sword and pistol.

2. The Military Gendarmerie.

Under the Ministry of War, Department I (Infantry) is a sub-branch for the administration of the military gendarmerie.

This corps is organized into divisions, of which there is one with each military district, the strength of each division varying, in peace, according to the requirements for each district.

It is recruited by voluntary engagement of soldiers of good character and qualifications, after they have completed their period of colour service.

The duties of the gendarmerie are two-fold—(1) to guard certain military establishments of special importance and military treasuries, and (2) to perform the duties of the civil police in connection with officers and soldiers. The civil police can only arrest an officer or soldier when they are observed in the act of committing a crime. All other disciplinary measures against soldiers are taken by the gendarmerie.

In war time detachments of gendarmerie are allotted to headquarters of divisions, cavalry brigades and higher formations, where they act, in addition to the duties mentioned above, as Intelligence Police.

The strength of the military gendarmerie is, in peace, about 200 officers and 2,000 other ranks.

3. The Provost Service.

In peace, at all places where troops are quartered, the senior officer, in addition to his duties as the commander of his unit, is also commandant of the town (in large garrisons an officer, who may be a brigadier-general, is specially appointed to this office and has no other duties). At the headquarters of the garrison is an officer specially appointed for provost marshal's duties, seconded from his unit. If there is a detachment of gendarmerie in the town, under an officer of suitable rank, this officer may be appointed to this duty, but otherwise an officer of another arm of the service is appointed.

In war time a similar organization prevails in the home area, but in the zone of the armies, the officer commanding the unit of gendarmerie with a formation is the provost marshal of that formation.

CHAPTER XXIII.
PAY, ALLOWANCES, GRATUITIES AND PENSIONS.

1. Pay of Officers and Professional N.C.Os.

By a law of 9th October, 1923, a new system and scale of pay was introduced for government officials and for officers and men of the Armed Forces. The fundamental principle of the law is that all the above-mentioned public servants are divided into 16 categories, that each category has its monthly pay fixed in a unit termed " points " and that these points are multiplied by a variable multiplier in order to arrive at the sum due in Polish zloty. The multiplier is fixed by the Cabinet on the 20th of every month, for reckoning the pay of the following month, which is payable on the first day of the month. In fixing the multiplier the Cabinet are guided by the increase (or decrease) in the cost of living during the period that has elapsed since the last definition.

The table fixing the monthly pay of the different categories of public servants is as follows :—

Category.	Ranks in Army and Navy.	(a)	(b)	(c)	(d)	(e)	(f)	(g)
1	Marshal	2,600	—	—	—	—	—	—
2	General / Admiral	2,200	2,300	2,400	—	—	—	—
3	General of division / Vice-admiral	1,800	1,900	2,000	2,100	—	—	—
4	General of brigade / Rear-admiral	1,400	1,500	1,600	1,700	1,800	—	—
5	Colonel / Captain	1,100	1,200	1,300	1,400	1,500	1,600	—
6	Lieutenant-colonel / Major / Commander	800	875	950	1,025	1,100	1,175	—
7	Captain / Lieutenant-commander	600	660	720	780	840	900	—
8	Lieutenant	480	520	560	600	640	680	—
9	Second-lieutenant / Sub-lieutenant	390	420	450	480	510	540	—
10	Senior serjeant-major / Senior artificer / Senior boatswain	330	350	370	390	410	430	450
11	Serjeant-major / Artificer boatswain	270	290	310	330	350	370	390
12	Serjeant / Junior artificer / Boatswain's mate	240	255	270	285	300	315	330
13	Corporal / Mate / Tradesman	210	225	240	255	270	285	300
14	Senior sailor	180	195	210	225	240	255	270
15	—	150	165	180	195	210	225	240
16	—	130	140	150	160	170	180	190

Note.—Lieutenant-colonels receive pay as for Category 6, but with an addition of **75 points**.

THE POLISH ARMY

The public servants whose pay is fixed by this table, besides the Army and Navy, include civil servants, government clerks, police, railway employees on the establishment, postal, telegraph and telephone employees, and teachers in all State schools.

The primary rate of pay of any category is that given in column (a). After each period of 3 years' service in that category the rate of pay is advanced one column to the right.

The period of compulsory military service (2 years), periods spent on leave without pay, under arrest, or on the non-active list due to sickness not incurred owing to military duties, are not reckoned in these periods of 3 years for obtaining increase of pay.

Over and above the rates given in the table additions are granted until the financial conditions are stablized. These are :—

(a) Special (regulation) addition of 70 points.
(b) Economic addition for those who are the support of their family of 45 points per dependant, for not more than 5 dependants.

Dependants are (a) wives, provided that they are not accommodated in any State institution, or (b) children and step-children up to 18 years of age, or, in certain cases, up to 24 years of age.

When the Cabinet decides that the re-habilitation of the finances has sufficiently progressed, the special addition will be reduced by 10 points every half year, and the economic addition by 1 point monthly.

In the autumn of 1926 two Cabinet decrees were published granting to all professional officers and non-commissioned officers an addition to their pay, in the form of a " dodatek służbowy " or charge pay. The monthly rates of charge pay are as follows.

Category	Post.	Rate of Points.
I	(a) Inspector general	5,000
	(b) Minister of War	2,500
II	Vice-Minister of War, Chief of Staff Inspectors	1,500
III	(a) Commanders of military districts	1,200
	(b) Other equivalent posts	1,000
IV	(a) Divisional commanders, Sub-Chief of Staff	900
	(b) Others	800
V	Brigade commanders	700
VI	(a) Regimental commanders	600
	(b) Other colonels	500
VII	Battalion commanders, lt.-colonels, majors	350
VIII	Company commanders, captains	250
IX	Platoon commanders, lieutenants, 2nd lieutenants	150
X	Ensigns	90
XI	Sergeant-majors	80
XII	Staff-sergeants	70
XIII	Sergeants	50
XIV	Corporals	30

Note.—The categories have no connection with the categories in the table given above.

The multiplier for the month of November, 1926, having been fixed at 43 grosze, the monthly pay of certain ranks works out at (according to the present rate of exchange) £1 = 43·6 zloty.

	£	s.	d.
Inspector General (Marshal)	76	0	0
Major, O.C. Battalion	11	10	0
2nd Lieutenant, on joining	5	8	0
Corporal	2	8	0

exclusive of special and economic additions.

The above rates of pay are inclusive, and on them the officers and N.C.Os. are supposed to live, finding their own accommodation, fuel, light and food. If they live in quarters provided by the State, a deduction is made from their pay.

Non-professional (reserve) officers called up for reserve training, or for military service, receive pay at the rate of one-thirtieth of the monthly pay of their rank for every day of service. If called up on mobilization they receive pay as for regular officers, that is to say, monthly pay in advance on the first day of the month, at the lowest rate of pay prescribed for their rank. If the individual called up for mobilization is in Government service and his military pay is less than what he has been receiving, the civil branch of the administration to which he belongs has to make up the difference. Married reserve officers called up for active service at a place other than their home receive a separation allowance in addition.

2. **Pay of Other Ranks.**

Non-professional soldiers, *i.e.*, the rank and file and junior N.C.Os. carrying out their compulsory period of military training, are not paid according to the rules given in para. 1, but according to the following monthly scale of points (which are multiplied by the multiplier referred to above) :—

Senior serjeant-major	7 points.
Serjeant-major, mate-volunteer	6 ,,
Serjeant, senior sailor-volunteer	5 ,,
Corporal, sailor-volunteer	4 ,,
Senior private, senior sailor-conscript	2·5 ,,
Private, sailor-conscript	2 ,,

For the month of March, 1925, the pay of a senior serjeant-major, if doing his 2 years' compulsory service, works out at about 3s., and of a private at about 8d.

The conscript receives in addition to the above free lodging, fuel and light in barracks, clothing and equipment and food; but in certain cases he can draw money allowance in lieu of the latter.

The conscript's monthly pay is divided into three equal portions, payable on the 1st, 11th and 21st of each month.

Conscripts called up for training or military service receive daily pay at the rate of one-tenth of the decadial instalments for each day's service.

Conscripts called up on mobilization receive pay as for conscripts doing their period of colour service, that is to say, three decadial instalments per month.

3. Pay of Air Service.

The basic pay of all ranks of the Air Force is the same as that given in paras. 1 and 2 above, but special Air Force pay and bonuses are given, for which *see* Chapter XXVII.

4. System of Issue of Pay.

Pay according to the scale shown in para. 1 is issued in advance on the first day of each month, or if this happens to be a holiday, on the preceding day. It is issued in the form of cash to each individual officer and professional soldier by the paymaster of the unit or organization to which the recipient belongs.

The same paymaster issues his pay to the conscript according to the scale shown in para. 2.

5. Pay Books.

Officers and professional N.C.Os. paid according to the system described in para. 1 are provided with pay books, in which is noted down the pay issued each month, against the signature of the officer, or N.C.O.

Men doing their period of military service whose pay is as described in para. 2 are not provided with such a pay book. Their issues of pay are recorded on a nominal roll kept by the company or corresponding unit, and furnished to the pay officer of the management committee.

6. Gratuities.

Gratuities are given to professional officers and soldiers who are transferred to the reserve, or to the Stan Spoczynku (which is equivalent to the retired list) without pay, that is to say, with no right to pensions.

According to the law of universal service a professional officer or soldier can only be placed in the reserve by order of the President of the Republic, under the following conditions :—

    (*a*) At his own request.
    (*b*) After being twice unfavourably reported on.
    (*c*) On account of ill-health, certified by a medical board.

The reserve includes all men subject to the law of universal service and fit for service who are not professional officers or soldiers.

The rate of gratuities is as follows :—

(a) Officers, after from 2 to 5 years' service in the Polish Army, 6 months' pay. After more than 5 years' service in the Polish Army, 12 months' pay.

(b) Other ranks, after more than 12 years' service in the Polish Army, 18 months' pay. After more than 10 years' service, 12 months' pay. After more than 6 years' service, 6 months' pay. After more than 3 years' service, 2 months' pay. After more than 1 year's service, 1 month's pay.

These gratuities, however, are not given to officers and soldiers :—

(a) Placed on the non-active list (for which *see* para. 8).
(b) Given immediate employment under the State or local State service.
(c) To officers placed in the reserve at their own request (for which *see* para. 7).
(d) To other ranks who lose the privilege of being professional soldiers owing to disciplinary measures.
(e) Sentenced by a civil court.

When officers and men are called up for active service from the reserve on partial or total mobilization, on demobilization they receive a gratuity as follows :—

Officers.
After less than 1 year's active service : 1 month's pay.
After less than 2 years' active service : 2 months' pay.
After more than 2 years' active service : 3 months' pay.

Other Ranks.
After less than 1 year's active service : 10 days' pay.
After less than 2 years' active service : 20 days' pay.
After more than 2 years' active service : 30 days' pay.

7. Pensions.

The law regarding pensions dated 11th December, 1923, like the law regarding pay is applicable to all State employees, whether civil or military, but includes special provisions applicable to military personnel only, from the special nature of their duties.

Pensions are in all cases calculated on the basis of the pay drawn by the recipient at the moment of leaving the service, including the special addition but excluding the economic addition (*vide* para. 1), taken at the rate for a bachelor on the following principle : the pension for an individual with service up to 10 years is 40 per cent. of his last rate of pay, and for every additional year's service he adds 2·4 per cent., provided the total never exceeds 100 per cent. of his last rate of full pay. For instance, after 15 years' service the pension is 40 plus 5 by 2·4 per cent., *i.e.*, 52 per cent. of the last rate of full pay at the rate for a bachelor.

To this rate of pension additions may be made for certain reasons, and its grant is governed by certain conditions. Pensioners who are the only support of their family receive in addition, as long as it lasts, the whole of the economic addition mentioned in para. 1.

THE POLISH ARMY

A.—Retired Professional Officers and Soldiers.

Pensions, calculated as above, are granted to professional officers and soldiers having at least 10 years' service if they are put on the retired list (Stan Spoczynku) for any of the following reasons :—

A.—*At their own request.*
  (1) Irrespective of age, if by reason of failing health or mental powers they are unfit for further service.
  (2) After attaining the age of 55 years.
  (3) If they have earned the right to full pension.
  (4) Irrespective of health, after 30 years' service for an officer or 20 years' service for a soldier.

B.—*By order of the authorities.*
  (5) If they have reached the age limits laid down in the military service law.
  (6) If they have been on the non-active list longer than the specified time.
  (7) If they are unfit for service.
  (8) On reduction of establishment.

If the earning power of the pensioner has been reduced by 95 per cent. or over, he is entitled to add the percentage for 10 years (*i.e.*, 24 per cent.) to the coefficient for calculating his pension.

If a professional officer or soldier applies to be transferred to the reserve without fulfilling any of the above conditions he has no right to a pension, but reverts to the same footing as every other citizen, and is liable to military service either as an officer of the reserve or as a soldier, according to his qualifications.

Pensions are granted as exceptional cases :—
  (*a*) Irrespective of length of service, if the claimant becomes permanently unfit for service on account of an accident suffered on duty, or during military operations, or owing to having contracted an epidemic disease at his permanent station.
  (*b*) After 5 years' uninterrupted service, if the claimant is rendered permanently unfit for service by reason of becoming crippled or ill, not from his own fault.

In the case of (*a*) the pension as calculated above may be increased if his earning capacity is reduced.

Aviators rendered unfit for service on account of a flying accident are entitled to add their flying pay to their normal pay for the purpose of calculating their pension.

Time spent on active service, between the dates of beginning of military operations and the conclusion of an armistice preceding peace, counts double towards calculation of pensions, as does also service in mobilized formations, the Ministry of War, or in General Headquarters if the mobilization is only partial.

Personnel of the aviation service count as double periods of service during which they are actually employed in duties that include actual flying. Similarly for the Navy, or soldiers employed in ships, each month actually spent on a cruise is reckoned as 40 days.

B.—Widows and Orphans.

Pensions for widows, apart from any pension they may have earned by their own service in State employ, and orphans, are only granted to those whose husband or father was entitled to a pension. They are calculated on the basis of the pension, or of the last rate of pay of the deceased, counted as a bachelor (*i.e.*, without the economic addition granted to married men).

The pension of the widow of a man having a right to a pension is 50 per cent. of his pension, but a widow of an officer or soldier killed or dying in the course of military operations is 50 per cent. of his pay.

Children who have lost their father draw pensions varying between one-quarter and two-thirds of a widow's pension, according to circumstances.

Children can also draw a pension based on the service of their mothers, if State employees, but cannot draw both pensions at the same time. They have the right to draw whichever is the greater.

A widow of a professional officer or soldier who dies while on the active list without having obtained the right to a pension receives a gratuity at the rate of one-half of his yearly pay. This gratuity is also given, if the mother is dead, to the surviving children under 18 years of age.

In addition to pensions or gratuities mentioned above in this paragraph, an additional gratuity of 3 months' pay is granted to dependants of the deceased (widows or orphans) for doctor's fees and funeral expenses, or, in the absence of such dependants, the actual cost of medical attendance and funeral up to a sum not exceeding 3 months' pay is refunded to the nearest relatives.

If a Musalman professional officer or soldier has more than one wife, a pension is granted at his death at the rate for only one widow, but is divided equally among them.

C.—Temporary Provisions.

Pensioners of the old German, Russian or Austrian armies, now qualified Polish citizens, may obtain a pension from the Polish State up to 75 per cent. of the pension that they would be entitled to if their qualifying service had been in the Polish Forces. Widows and orphans of deceased pensioners of the old partitioning Powers, if of Polish citizenship, may obtain pensions similar to that to which they would be entitled if the deceased had been in the Polish State service. The right to a pension must have been originally granted in Germany and Austria before 1st November, 1918, and in Russia before 1st November, 1917, in order to be valid in these two cases.

Men who served in the armies of the former partitioning Powers, or in the Polish military formations that existed before the present Polish Army was formed, may reckon such service, under certain conditions, as qualifying for a pension from the Polish State, or in the event of not being able to comply with the conditions for a pension they may obtain a generous gratuity.

Persons who, while in the service of the former partitioning Powers, rendered special services to the Polish nation may, by special order of the Cabinet, receive an increased pension.

8. Half Pay and similar Payments to Officers and Professional N.C.Os.

Officers and professional N.C.Os. may be placed on the non-active list (Stan Nieczynny), which means that while they are still reckoned as serving officers or N.C.Os., they are temporarily not employed. It corresponds to the "Half Pay List."

Note.—An officer can be put on the non-active list by the Minister of War under the following conditions:—

(a) At his own request, for long leave.
(b) Temporary ill-health, certified by a medical board.
(c) Reduction of establishment.
(d) Made a prisoner of war or reported missing in war.
(d) Elected member of the Sejm or Senate.

When an officer or professional N.C.O. is transferred to the non-active list by the grant of indefinite leave, he at once ceases to draw pay, if he has served less than 15 years. If, however, he has more than 15 years' service to his credit he receives 6 months' full pay.

When an officer or professional N.C.O. is placed on the non-active list on account of temporary unfitness for service, certified by a medical board, he receives full pay for the first half year, and subsequently pay at the rate of the pension he would receive if the unfitness was permanent. If such an officer or N.C.O. has not qualified for a pension his pay after the first 6 months is reckoned at the rate of the lowest pension he would get. If, however, the unfitness is due to causes produced by military service, the officer or N.C.O. draws full pay for the whole period of unfitness.

Officers and professional N.C.Os. transferred to the non-active list on account of reduction of establishment receive full pay for the first 3 years, and afterwards no pay at all. Those elected members of the Sejm or Senate cease to draw pay.

A professional soldier given indefinite leave during the concluding period of his engagement with a view to fitting himself for employment, whether under the State or not, receives pay as though on the active list, but for not more than 6 months.

9. Prisoners of War or those Reported Missing during Military Operations.

An officer, professional N.C.O. or soldier who is taken prisoner or reported missing, if a bachelor or childless widower, loses all pay. If he has dependants the dependants draw half of his last rate of pay, provided that the circumstances attending his capture indicate that it was not due to his own fault, in which case the dependants draw nothing at all.

On return from captivity, if it is established that his capture was not due to his own fault, he receives for the whole period of his captivity his full pay, less any sums that may have been paid to his dependants.

If an officer or soldier is still missing a year after the declaration of peace, his dependants lose all right to further pay, but receive temporary pensions at the rate mentioned in para. 7 (B), for a period of $2\frac{1}{2}$ years after the armistice. Before the expiry of this period they must obtain from a court of justice a decree of "presumption of death" and with this apply for a permanent pension.

10. Allowances.

An officer or professional N.C.O. has the right to the following allowances:—

(a) Allowances when absent on a mission, travelling on duty, or on transfer.
(b) Medical assistance for himself and family.
(c) For uniform and equipment.

The allowances of officers and men when travelling on duty or when being transferred to a new station are given in " points " varying from 65 points daily for categories 1 and 2 to 15 points for category 9 and 4 points for private soldiers. Allowances given when officers and men are seconded on temporary duty away from their station are : for married men 50 per cent. and for bachelors 25 per cent. of these " points."

The uniform and equipment allowance is as follows :—

On appointment as second-lieutenant	1,500 points.
After every 2 years	700 ,,

Officers of the reserve on mobilization are also given an equipment grant of 700 points.

Officers and professional soldiers obtain free education for their children in the State schools ; and under certain conditions, if they are unable to place the children in State middle schools, may obtain a grant towards the cost of education in a private middle school, not exceeding the average cost of educating each child in the State middle schools.

There are no allowances such as lodging, fuel and light, ration allowances, etc., as the consolidated monthly pay of officers and professional N.C.Os. is supposed to cover such items, while conscripts receive housing, food, etc., at government expense, and may only draw money in lieu in exceptional cases.

Extra allowances are also given to officers and soldiers stationed in places where the cost of living is high, or where the conditions are bad. For instance, for those stationed in Warsaw an increase of 20 per cent. and in Upper Silesia of 40 per cent. is given on account of the former reason, and to those in the eastern districts an increase of 20 per cent. is given as a compensation for the latter reason.

Extra allowance is also given to officers and professional soldiers during manœuvres away from their permanent station, for officers and professional soldiers of technical troops during training, for privates on probation of gendarmerie, and working pay for soldiers employed on heavy labour.

During war there is granted a daily battle allowance for actual participation in battle of 16 points for junior officers, captains and lieutenants, 8 points for professional soldiers and 4 points for soldiers, or alternatively a daily field allowance for being in the area of operations of 30 points for generals, 16 points for field officers, 8 points for junior officers, 4 points for professional soldiers and 2 points for soldiers.

Allowances are also given to active officers who possess higher educational qualifications. If an officer has passed the prescribed course at a university, or corresponding institution, he draws pay at one rate higher than the normal for his category and length of service, that is to say a second-lieutenant on joining, who has passed the university, draws 420 points monthly instead of 390, and continues to draw pay increased above the normal throughout his service in similar fashion.

The educational establishments which grant the right to this increase are the universities, polytechnics (engineering universities), schools of agriculture, mining, commerce, veterinary academy, art academy and a number of theological colleges now existing in Poland, together with a number of educational establishments of the former partitioning Powers and foreign countries, amongst which are the English universities of Oxford, Cambridge, Bristol, Edinburgh and others.

CHAPTER XXIV.

DISCIPLINE.

1. **Military Penal Code.** (*See* note at end of paragraph.)

(*a*) *General.*—Poland has not yet had time to formulate her own civil penal code. The penal codes of the old partitioning Powers are still in force in the respective areas formerly subject to them, and similarly the military penal codes of these Powers still hold good in these three parts of the State. These respective civil codes are the Russian code of 1903, the Austrian of 1852, and the German of 1871.

The system of procedure, however, has been unified, and regulations, which are those of the old Austrian Rules of Procedure of 5th July, 1912, with certain omissions and amendments, have been published.

Polish citizens are, in peace, liable to account under military law for offences specified in the military codes, when they are :—

(i) Doing their period of colour service, or deserters from it.
(ii) Military invalids in State hospitals, and prisoners under military guard.
(iii) Men who, after having received the order to join their unit, do not join it.

After a mobilization, or when a state of war is imminent, the Council of Ministers may extend the application of the military codes to other persons.

In giving effect to the codes, there exists a special Corps of Officers of Justice (Korpus Sądowy, K.S.) composed of men who have completed the study of law, and who have also done at least one year's service as officers. This corps is divided into two sections, the Judges' section and the Procurators' (Prosecutors') section. The Judges' section includes both judges (in the ordinary sense of the English word) who try cases and award punishments and so-called "enquiring judges," who, like a French *juge d'instruction*, make the preliminary investigation and prepare the case for submission to the Court.

Note.—The provisions of the military code apply equally to the Navy, except that the nomenclature of certain tribunals are given naval names in naval stations.

(*b*) *Support of Civil Power.*—Troops can be called out to aid the civil power, when the latter is unable to deal with the situation unaided, in cases of :—

(i) Natural disasters, for preventive and rescue work.
(ii) Acts of violence, threatening the State, or life and property.
(iii) In cases provided for by law.

The request for the aid of troops must be made by the proper Authority of the civil power, or his representative, preferably in writing, to the commanding officer of the nearest garrison.

This officer refers the request, with his comments, to the commander of the military district, who will authorize or refuse the employment of troops. If, however, the situation demands immediate action, the garrison commander may act at once on his own responsibility.

The military commander alone is responsible for deciding the strength of the troops used, and their method of action. The civil authorities are responsible for bringing the troops to the scene of action, informing the commander of the situation and of the objects to be attained.

Before the troops make use of their arms, the representatives of the civil power must first of all appeal to the crowd to desist from violence, warning them that if they do not, the troops will be obliged to use their weapons—and before they do so, the trumpet is to be blown three times. However, if the situation admits of no delay, the appeal and the trumpet may be dispensed with. It is strictly forbidden for the troops to hold any parley with the crowd, or to come to any mutual agreement with them—once arms are used, the end must be the complete dispersal of the crowd and the arrest of the leaders.

In anticipation of riots, troops may be moved to localities where there is no garrison, and the civil power may request that troops should be confined to barracks in readiness to take action. They may, however, not be used until the civil power, realizing its inability to control events, makes the demand for assistance in the proper form.

2. **Courts Martial.**

(a) There are three types of military court :—
    (i) Regional (or Garrison) Courts Martial.
    (ii) Courts Martial of Military Districts.
    (iii) The Supreme Military Court.

These courts are all permanent institutions, appointed by the Minister of War, and composed of a varying number of officers of the Corps of Justice.

A regional (or garrison) court (Sąd Rejonowy or Zalogowy) consists of the regional (or garrison) judge and a number of officers of the Corps of Justice; the district court consists of the Chief of the Court and a number of military judges. These do not sit in their entirety to try a case, but form judging tribunals for trying cases, as follows :—

When a trial takes place the judging tribunal is formed of one or two officers of the Corps of Justice on the strength of the court martial (regional or district), and a number of officers or non-commissioned officers of the army appointed for the trial by the garrison or district commander. The tribunal is then called the voting tribunal, as every one has the right of vote at the end of the trial, beginning with the junior in rank.

The voting tribunal in the case of a regional court consists of an officer of the Corps of Justice as president and two assessors, of which one is an officer and the other a non-commissioned officer.

In the case of a district court, if the offence is punishable by death or long term imprisonment, the voting tribunal consists of two officers of the Corps of Justice, and as assessors, three officers not of junior rank to the officer accused.

If the accused is a soldier two non-commissioned officers take the place of two of the assessor officers. If the crime is punishable by a lesser punishment than stated above one of the officers of the Corps of Justice sitting on the tribunal is replaced by a regimental officer.

THE POLISH ARMY

The only qualifications required of an assessor are that he must be of good character, free from any accusation, and able to read and write.

The competence of regional courts is as follows, for soldiers only :—

(a) Military offences not punishable with more than 1 year's imprisonment, or for offences punishable with not more than 3 years when in view of extenuating circumstances the punishment is not expected to exceed 1 year.

(b) Civil offences. Misdemeanours and civil crimes with proviso similar to (a) above—but which vary in details with the code under which they are judged.

The competence of district courts includes all offences not within the competence of the regional courts, including all offences committed by officers and appeals against the sentence of garrison courts.

Whenever a trial takes place, there must be present a prosecutor (procurator) or his representative, and a recording official (protokulant).

The Supreme Military Court sits at Warsaw, and is composed of a President (a General of the Corps of Justice), one or more Vice-Presidents, and Judges of the Supreme Military Court. Its competence is to examine, from a legal point of view, the proceedings of any other court martial, when an appeal against the verdict and sentence is made, and it may either confirm the proceedings, verdict, and sentence or annul them, and order a new trial by the original court. It does not itself try cases, and is like a French *Cour de Cassation*. Its composition is therefore entirely of officers of the Corps of Justice with legal training.

(b) *Summary Courts Martial.* (Sądy Doraźne).—In addition to the normal organization as outlined above, summary military courts may be set up to deal with crimes such as violence, espionage, when there is a special prevalence of such offences among the troops. A proclamation has to be made by the Government that such courts will be established, specifying the class of offences that will be tried by them. The convening of these summary military courts is entrusted to commanders of military districts. The courts may be held at any suitable place, even in the open air, and are of the same composition as district courts martial. They have the right of inflicting any penalty, including death, which is carried out within 24 hours of the sentence being given. Their verdicts have to be reported at once by telegraph to the Minister of War.

(c) *Field Courts Martial.* (Sądy Wojskowe w Polu).—Field courts martial are, like courts martial in peace, permanent institutions, attached to the headquarters of divisions and higher formations, and appointed by the Commander-in-Chief. There is only one type of court, which is competent to try any offence committed by any individual subject to military law, from civilian employee to General. There is no appeal against its verdict, but the Commander-in-Chief is empowered to reduce or mitigate the punishment awarded. The court sits at divisional (or other) headquarters.

The court is of the same composition as district courts in peace, but the voting committee is always composed of one officer of the Corps of Justice and four other officers as assessors (never soldiers) whose rank varies with the rank of the accused. The assessors are appointed by the commander of the formation to which the court belongs.

(d) *Field Summary Courts Martial.* (Sądy Doraźne w Polu).—When crimes which have a dangerous influence on the course of military operations are frequent, such as desertion, espionage, parleying with the enemy, or when other crimes are prevalent, the Commander-in-Chief may issue a proclamation that such named crimes will be triable by Summary Courts Martial. The composition of these courts is the same as that of field courts martial, but they can sit in any place that is convenient. They are obliged to give their verdict within 19 days from the date of the commission of the crime. There is no appeal against their verdict and sentence, and a death sentence must be carried out within 2 hours.

Note.—The civil authorities can also set up civil summary courts. Such courts are now (autumn, 1926) authorized in the eastern districts of Poland, bordering on the Russian frontier, to deal with brigandage, robbery with violence, arson, murder with a view to robbery, etc.

(e) *Punishments.*—The usual punishments awarded are as follows :—

(a) *Privates.*
Confinement to barracks.
Extra fatigues.
Arrest (light, medium and severe) up to 6 weeks.
Imprisonment, 6 weeks and upwards to 15 years.
Imprisonment for life.
Expulsion from the army (additional to imprisonment of over 3 years).
Death by shooting.

(b) *N.C.Os.*
Confinement to barracks.
Arrest (light or medium).
Imprisonment as above.
Reduction to lower rank.
Degradation to the ranks.
Expulsion from the army (additional to imprisonment of over 3 years).
Death by shooting.

(c) *Officers :*
Reprimand.
Arrest (at home, or in a guard house or a fortress).
Imprisonment.
Expulsion from the service (additional to imprisonment).
Death by shooting.

3. Courts of Honour.

An officer who commits an action which, though not rendering him liable to punishment under the penal code (military or civil), yet is inconsistent with his position as an officer, has to answer for it before a Court of Honour.

Courts of Honour can award :—
(a) Reprimand.
(b) Severe reprimand and caution.
(c) Exclusion from the Corps of Officers.

Courts of Honour for lieutenants and captains are appointed yearly in all regiments and similar formations and in certain staffs, those for field officers are established at the headquarters of each military district, and that for general officers at the Ministry of War. Appeal against decisions of regimental courts may be made to the field officers' court, and against those of the field officers' courts to the general officers' court, but there is no appeal against the decision of the latter.

Courts of Honour consist of seven officers, and are elected each December for the following year, by a general meeting of the officers who come under their jurisdiction.

The procedure is set in motion by order of the commanding officer, or on the motion of a Court of Honour, or by the request of an officer who is implicated in any affair. The Court of Honour then appoints two of its members to make an investigation, and as a result of their report the court decides whether the officer inculpated is to be brought before it or not. The trial then takes place, and a summary of the proceedings is drawn up and signed by the president. The court then gives its verdict.

When there is a question of a dispute or a quarrel between two officers, they are bound to report it to their commanding officer, who will decide whether it is necessary for the case to be put before a civil court, or to be decided by himself, or to be inquired into by a Court of Honour. In the last case the court may order the two parties to be reconciled or it may order a duel in order that honour may be satisfied. But as duels are forbidden by law, no allusion to this is made in the regulations.

There is in addition an Officers' (Voting) Tribunal (Oficerska Trybunal Orzekający) in Warsaw, whose competence is :—

(1) To examine accusations against officers, committed during military service before their entry into the Polish service.
(2) To examine claims of officers of the former Imperial armies to enter the Polish Army.
(3) To deal with affairs coming under the jurisdiction of Courts of Honour, specially submitted to it by the Ministry of War.
(4) Reception into the Polish Army of foreigners.

Under (3) for instance, came the case of a general officer accused of insulting the Związek Strzelecki (Rifle League), which was referred by the Ministry of War to this tribunal, and as a result of which he was obliged to apply to be put on the retired list.

4. Interior Routine of Units.

Officers have powers of summary punishment over their men, including non-commissioned officers, which vary with the rank. For instance, platoon officers can award confinement to barracks up to 3 days (1 day for junior N.C.Os. or extra fatigue duties; regimental commanders can award arrest up to 3 weeks, both to soldiers and officers.

5. Military Prisons.

There is only one military convict prison in Poland at Stanislawow in Eastern Galicia, which has accommodation for 2,000 prisoners, whose sentence is over 3 months' imprisonment.

In each district there is a district military prison (detention barracks) for 600 prisoners (Warsaw for 1,000 prisoners). It's object is to accommodate men awaiting or undergoing trial at the district courts martial, but also holds prisoners undergoing imprisonment not exceeding 3 months.

In each region or garrison where there is a regional (garrison) court martial there is an "areszt," or guardhouse, where prisoners awaiting or undergoing trial by this court are kept, and where men undergoing a sentence of arrest are held.

6. Leave and Furlough.

(a) *Officers.*—Leave is classed in four categories :—
   (a) General leave, for rest and holiday.
   (b) Convalescent leave.
   (c) Leave owing to military duty.
   (d) Casual leave.

Leave for any of these purposes may not exceed 6 months, and may be either with or without pay. Leave with pay, under (a), (b), or (d) may not exceed 8 weeks.

General leave is allowed at the rates of 4 weeks per annum to lieutenants and captains and 6 weeks to senior officers.

Convalescent leave is granted up to 6 months in any year.

Leave owing to military duty is granted up to 2 weeks on change of garrison to settle up private affairs, or up to 8 weeks on return from being a prisoner of war.

Casual leave is leave authorized by the Minister of War on the occasion of public holidays, or leave given for important personal affairs.

(b) *Professional Non-Commissioned Officers.*—Professional N.C.Os. have the same right to leave as officers, with the exception that general leave is limited to 4 weeks per annum.

(c) *Soldiers of the Annual Contingents.*—Leave is only granted to soldiers under instructions specially ordered by the Ministry of War. In general the only circumstances under which they are given leave is to enable them to assist in the agricultural work at the time of the harvest.

7. Moral.

The Polish Army, as a whole, has both good and bad points.

Its clothing and uniform has only been put on a satisfactory basis during the last year or so ; and its barrack accommodation still leaves a lot to be desired, especially in the east.

The wretched conditions under which many officers and N.C.Os. live, who have the greatest difficulty in providing food, housing and clothing for themselves and their families, are obvious to all, and lead to cases of embezzlement and to other questionable means of gaining a little money.

Instruction of the men is carried out in a somewhat unintelligible manner, instructors, both officers and N.C.Os., may know their subject very well from a theoretical point of view, but they are bad at putting it into practice and teaching it to others. They sometimes show great impatience with their men, when slow at understanding or carrying out what is said to them. These are all factors which tend to lower the morale of the private soldier.

On the other hand, in spite of the rough life in barracks, it is very often better than what the recruit is accustomed to at home ; his meals are plentiful and regular, and he is obliged to adopt greater cleanliness. Great efforts are made to teach the ignorant,

THE POLISH ARMY

and to amuse him. Units frequently give amateur theatricals, concerts and cinematograph shows for the benefit of the men, and football and light athletics are encouraged. Every unit has its football team. Also, in spite of occasional roughness of manner, many of the officers take a real interest in the men, and in their comfort and well-being.

Then on top of all, comes the intense patriotism of the true Pole. Every soldier seems to feel all the time that his object in the army is to fight for the defence of his recently won liberty. In many regiments greetings between senior officers and companies, etc., whom they meet contain the words, "For the glory of the Fatherland." This sentiment is a great factor in the moral of the army, especially when the situation is critical, and led to many self-sacrificing episodes during the Bolshevik war.

But the army does not contain only Poles; the recruits include Jews, Germans, Ukrainians and White Russians. In some units these men are given complete liberty to talk their own language and attend their own church, all that is required of them is that they should understand Polish, and be fluent in it if they wish to become N.C.Os. In other units, however, the national feelings are outraged by attempts to bring them into Polish churches and to Polonise them. The Ukrainian and White Russian recruits, who are almost always praised by their officers as being good soldiers and very amenable to discipline, and who seem by all accounts to be quite contented when well treated in the first type of unit mentioned, rapidly react to the stupid treatment in the latter type, and return to their villages with anti-Polish sentiment. The Jewish recruits are never popular, either with officers or men, and seem to have a facility for getting into office jobs and avoiding regimental duty. Some regimental officers refuse to employ them in the office, which sometimes provokes a question in the Diet by some Jewish member who considers that his co-religionists are being unfairly treated.

The general morale of the army depends on the predominance of either its good or its bad points; and though the bad points undoubtedly exist and are difficult to eradicate, yet it seems that on the whole they are being reduced, while the good points grow stronger, and thus the general morale of the army is being steadily raised.

CHAPTER XXV.

ORDNANCE DEPARTMENT.

1. General.

The Ordnance Service is in Poland a branch of the Artillery and is under Department III (Artillery) of the Ministry of War. It used to be called the "Służbauzbrojenia" (Armament Service), but is now called the "Służbaartylerji" (Artillery Service).

The duties of the service are :—

    (a) To supply the army with all weapons, ammunition, explosives and gas warfare stores, and with the necessaries required for their conservation.

    (b) To carry out repairs to the above and to manufacture certain small articles (*e.g.*, fuzes, caps, rifles).

    (c) To carry out research, experiments and trials.

    (d) To inspect weapons in charge of units.

Barrack equipment, field equipment, etc., such as are supplied by the British Ordnance Department, are in Poland furnished by the Intendance or Engineer Services.

The Artillery Service carries out its duties by means of officers and men of the artillery, detached for duties connected with the service. The officers are borne on the strength of the district artillery store (*see* below), which is their permanent unit and in which their records are kept, and the other ranks on the district detachment of artillery service (Oddzial Słuźby Artylerji).

At the Ministry of War the work of the artillery service is directed by the Head of Department III, who receives in the yearly budget a certain sum to be expended according to the programme drawn up by him.

Directly under the Head of Department are the following technical establishments :—

  (*e*) Technical Inspectorate of Artillery. A number of officers whose duty is to inspect all arms and ammunition in possession of the army.
  (*f*) Reception Centre of Artillery Material. An establishment for examining all new arms before being taken on charge.
  (*g*) Institute of Artillery Experiments. This contains a number of workshops for the following duties : (i) scientific research, (ii) small arms, (iii) pyrotechnical, (iv) internal ballistics, (v) external ballistics, (vi) general and analytical.

Under the Head of Department III in the military districts is a chief of the artillery service (who is also, like the B.G.R.A. of a corps, the technical chief of all the artillery in the corps area and the superior commander of non-divisional artillery), assisted by a deputy and a staff in three branches, namely : (i) general, (ii) supply, (iii) accountant. This officer has granted to him by Department III a certain yearly credit for district needs, and has under his orders the district artillery store (*see* para. 3), the district artillery practice camp (if in existence), and a district detachment of artillery service.

The detachment of artillery service provides the personnel for the various ordnance establishments in the district, whether these are under the control of the Ministry of War direct or of the district chief of the artillery service, consequently their establishment varies in each district. It is the unit where the recruits are trained in the duties of the service before they are sent to the ordnance establishments for duty, and is the mobilizing organ for units of the artillery service, such as divisional armament parks, etc. In principle, each arsenal or depot (*vide* para. 3) has a duty company attached to it, to which belong all the personnel employed in the arsenal or depot, and which also contains a guard platoon for guard duties.

In units, duties connected with armament are carried out by the armament officer (oficer broni), who is an officer of the unit specially detailed for this duty, assisted by armament artificers of the artillery service, and assistant armourers, learners supplied by the unit. In each company, squadron, etc., there is also a regimental N.C.O. in charge of arms.

In war time the commander of artillery on the staff of armies and divisions is at the same time director of the artillery service of that formation.

With the army there is an army armament park (Park Uzbrojenia Armji), which is divided into two echelons, with which are reserves of arms, and workshops for repairs. The leading echelon may be about 40–50 kilometres in rear of divisions. Arm and ammunition depots may be formed by this park according to the military situation,

THE POLISH ARMY

employing civilian personnel under military control, or obtaining the services of march units or other line of communication troops. When possible these depots are situated on railways. The war establishment varies according to the number of divisions in the army.

With a division (cavalry or infantry) there is a divisional armament park (Park Uzbrojenia Dywizyjny), which comprises a park platoon and a light repair shop. It keeps a reserve of small arms but not of artillery. The establishment is 5 officers, 138 other ranks, 15 horses, 8 vehicles and 3 motor lorries.

2. Personnel.

The personnel of the artillery service consists of 359 officers (according to the Army List of 1924) ranking from second-lieutenant to colonel, and about 40 reserve officers, with a number of armament artificers, classed as " zbrojmistrz " or master armourers, and " rusznikarz " and " puszkarz " or rifle armourers and gun armourers, who are all skilled tradesmen and professional non-commissioned officers on long service engagements, and of auxiliary unskilled personnel from the annual contingent.

The personnel wear the same uniform as the artillery, that is to say, with collar patches of dark green with black edge.

The officers are now officers of the artillery, possessing special technical qualifications or aptitude, who are appointed for duty in armament establishments. Preference is given to those who have passed through a course at a polytechnic or other higher technical education establishment, or who pass through a course at the Central Armourers' School.

The armourers and artificers are obtained from among the soldiers who are employed in units as assistants to the regimental artificers, or from selected men of the annual contingent serving in ordnance establishments. Those that show skill are allowed to enter the Central Armourers' School at Warsaw for a 6 months' course. If they pass the course satisfactorily they are then allowed to engage for long service as armourers.

The Central Armourers' School also holds periodical refresher courses for officers of the artillery service and for armourers and artificers.

3. Arsenals.

The arsenals and depots of the artillery service are as follows :—

A.—*Arsenals (Zbrojownia).*

No. 1—Brześć-nad-Bugiem. No. 4—Krakow.
No. 2—Warsaw. No. 5—Przemysl.
No. 3—Poznan.

These arsenals have workshops for carrying out repairs to guns and small arms, while that at Warsaw carries out in addition research work, experiments and proofs, and that at Krakow carries out tests of weapons manufactured in the country.

B.—*Ammunition Stores (Zaklad Amunicyjny).*

No. 1—Warsaw. No. 4—Krakow.
No. 2—Dęblin. No. 5—Przemysl.
No. 3—Spala.

C.—*Military Gas Institute.*

Warsaw—for experiments and research.

Anti-Gas Warfare Store.

Zegrze—for holding gas masks and other stores for combating the effects of gas.

Gas School.
Warsaw.

D.—*Armourers' School.*
Warsaw.

The above are directly under the Ministry of War, except for administration for which they are under the chief of the artillery service of the district in which they are situated.

In each military district there is also a depot known as the district artillery store (Okręgowa Składnica Artylerji), whose objects are to keep a reserve of arms and ammunition, to hold mobilization stores for those units supplying the needs of the district (*e.g.*, divisional ammunition parks), and to issue stores as required.

4. Munition Factories.

Munition factories are either State owned or privately owned. The former are controlled by a Central Directorate of State Munition Factories in Department X (Military Industries) in the Ministry of War: with the exception of certain small works directly under Department III.

The larger State factories under Department X are:—

(*a*) *Rifle Factory at Radom (Państwowa Wytwornia Broni).*—It is at present (end 1925) in process of completion, and will not be properly at work till 1926, when its capacity will be 300 rifles per day of 8 hours, or 800 per day working three shifts. For the present rifles are being turned out at the rate of 100 per day at a small factory at Warsaw, from which the machinery will eventually be transferred to Radom. Projects are being considered to add a machine gun branch to it.

(*b*) *Ammunition Factory at Skarzysko, 25 miles S.W. of Radom (Państwowa Zakłady Amunicyjne).*—This is also in process of completion and will hardly be at full work till well on in 1926. It is in two sections, one section for making shell, small arms ammunition, cartridge cases and fuzes, and the other for filling the above with explosives. Its daily capacity will be, working 8 hours a day:—

              1,000—75 mm. shell,
                350—105 mm. shell,
                150—155 mm. shell,
            60,000 rounds S.A.A.,

which figures may be multiplied by 2·7 to obtain the full capacity working three shifts.

(*c*) *Powder Factory at Zagozdzon, between Radom and Dęblin (Wojskowa Wytwornia Prochu).*—This factory is nearly complete. It is in three sections for making smokeless powder (propellant), black powder (for use in sporting cartridges and in mines) and high explosive (ammonite).

The smaller State munition factories are:—

(*d*) *Factory at Warsaw for making fuzes for shell.*
(*e*) *Factory at Toruń for making percussion caps and detonators.*
(*f*) *Factory at Bydgość for making explosives.*

THE POLISH ARMY

Privately-owned munition factories are :—

(a) *Pocisk Ammunition Factory.*—This is in two branches, in Warsaw for making shell, cartridges cases and S.A.A., and in Rembertow, 6 miles outside Warsaw, for making explosives for filling the shell and cartridges. It is capable of turning out 140,000 rounds of S.A.A. and 1,000 shell (75 mm. and 105 mm.) per working day of 8 hours. It has also manufactured a 47 mm. gun, which is being tried.

(b) *Nitrate Explosives Factory at Niewadow, near Tomaszow, S.W. of Warsaw.*—For manufacture of ballistite, guncotton, black powder, trotyl, and a French powder named Poudre B.

(c) *Starakhowice Gun and Ammunition Factory at Wierzbnik, 25 miles south of Radom.*—This is a new branch of the old established firm of Starakhowice, which exploits the mineral and timber resources of the district, and is being erected with the help of Vickers and Schneider Creusot, but the work is lagging and the establishment does not appear to be very efficiently laid out. It is hoped to attain a production of 1,000 shell per 8-hour day, and a quantity of S.A.A. It will also carry out repairs to guns. Fifty per cent. of the shares are in the hands of the State.

It is also projected to build factories for other war material, so that Poland may be independent of import from abroad. An agreement has been made with the Belgian firm of Browning to purchase a number of light Browning machine guns, and for the erection of a factory near Warsaw, but owing to the hesitation of Browning to start work on the factory it is believed that the contract has not yet been definitely signed and it may fall through. Other negotiations are proceeding for the formation of a factory for tanks, and when the type of heavy machine gun to be adopted in the army is finally decided upon, similar negotiations will be started for its manufacture in the country.

CHAPTER XXVI.

AVIATION.

1. General.

Aviation in Poland is of recent growth (since 1918), and up to the present has been practically confined to military aviation. All aeroplanes and pilots who could be collected in 1918 and 1919 were used in the war against the Bolsheviks, and it is only since the conclusion of peace that civil aviation has been thought of: it has developed considerably during the last two years. There are now the following air lines in operation :—

Route	Operator
Warsaw–Prague	Society for Air Traffic in Poland (formerly Franco-Roumanian Air Navigation Co.).
Warsaw–Danzig	
Warsaw–Lwow	Polish Air Line (Aerolot) formerly called Aero-Lloyd.
Warsaw–Krakow–Vienna	
Lwow–Krakow	
Danzig–Copenhagen	
Warsaw–Poznan (direct)	Aero Company.
Warsaw–Lodz–Poznan	

Negotiations are proceeding for the inauguration of a further service, Lwow-Bukarest, to be maintained by the Aerolot Company.

These lines are not all maintained during the winter months.

In October, 1922, a Committee of Civil Aviation was formed under the Railway Ministry. This committee is composed of representatives of the State Departments concerned, of big industries, of aviation companies and of the Polish Aero Club, together with scientific and practical aviators, and its functions are to consider the development, organization and regulations of aviation, to encourage research and to train pilots. So far, little has been done by this committee.

Research work is also encouraged in the military aviation. Officers are engaged on experiments with gliders in the workshops of the Air Force.

The League for Aerial Defence of the State (L.O.P.P.) plays a great part in spreading knowledge of aviation throughout the country and in assisting in the construction of aviation establishments. It was created in 1924 and has now provincial committees and branches all over Poland. It is surprising that even the peasant population are drawn into the League and take an interest in aviation. With the funds it has collected it has bought some half-dozen aeroplanes, which are used in making propaganda flights, has financed a civil aviation school attached to the " Samolot " factory at Poznan, is building an aerodynamic institute attached to the Polytechnic at Warsaw, has built an aerodrome at Lodz, arranges courses of instruction for mechanics and various competitions connected with aviation. Its activity is very great, and it is patronized by all the influential people.

2. Administration.

The Polish aviation troops are part of the regular army, and are subordinated to Department IV (Aviation) of the Ministry of War. This department consists of three sections :—

    (*a*) Organization.
    (*b*) Equipment.
    (*c*) Balloons.

3. Organization.

    (*a*) *In Peace.*—Aviation troops comprise :—

        6 regiments of aviation.
        1 hydroplane division.
        1 balloon battalion.
        1 pilots' school, to move to Dęblin in 1927.
        1 officers' school, to move to Dęblin in 1927.
        1 mechanics' school at Bydgoszcz.
        Central workshops and depot.

The programme for the eventual development of the aviation provides for a total of 12 regiments, 1 hydroplane division, and 1 bombardment division ; but this programme cannot be realized for several years.

An aeroplane regiment consists of :—
>Regimental headquarters (colonel or lieutenant-colonel in command).
>Two or three divisions (either reconnaissance or pursuit) of two squadrons each.
>A training division.
>A mechanics' school.
>A regimental park, with hangar detachment.
>A wireless platoon.
>A photographic platoon.
>A meteorological detachment.
>A reserve cadre.

It is intended to reorganize regiments so that they will be entirely of one type, *i.e.*, reconnaissance, or pursuit, or bombardment.

The regiments only exist in peace, in order to provide better training facilities for all ranks of the aviation service. They are responsible for the training of pilots in their technical duties in war, for the teaching of wireless and other means of signalling, taking and reading of photographs, and training of mechanics, fitters and other tradesmen under the equipment officers.

(*b*) *In War.*—(i) *Provisional Organization.*—In war time the regimental organization is abolished. Divisions of aeroplanes are allotted to formations as required and senior aviation officers appointed to headquarters of formations as technical advisers and as commanders of the divisions allotted. A mobile park is formed and attached to each army. Two or more divisions may be formed into a group under a lieutenant-colonel.

(ii) *Future Organization.*—According to information supplied by the Head of the Aviation Department, it is proposed that the development of the air force shall reach :—
>26 squadrons of reconnaissance and bombardment of 10 machines each,
>22 pursuit squadrons of 10 machines each,
>2 squadrons for night bombing of 6 machines each,

making a total of 580 machines, exclusive of squadron and central reserve.

(*c*) *Workshops.*—The central workshops at Warsaw, to be moved to Dęblin when the new buildings are ready, carry out all sorts of repairs and overhauls to machines and engines and manufacture certain parts, such as propellers, wings, etc. The regimental workshops in general only carry out light repairs, but the Krakow regimental workshops are capable of executing bigger repairs, both to engines and bodies. Propellers are made both at Warsaw and Krakow, as are also wings, fuselages and other non-metal parts. The central depot, in addition to spare parts and instruments, is to hold a reserve of aeroplanes for each squadron, equal to 200 per cent. of the fighting establishment, *i.e.*, 20 machines per squadron, and 400 per cent. of the number of aero-engines. This reserve is being gradually built up. Owing to lack of space at Dęblin, some of these machines are stored with regiments, but they are under the control of the central depot.

4. Command and Staff.

The immediate commander of all the aviation troops is the officer who, at the same time, is the Chief of the IV Department (Aviation) in the Ministry of War. To assist him he has a deputy, and staffs for training, operations, administration and technical questions.

For technical questions and for training, the aviation regiments and balloon battalion are directly subordinate to Department IV. There are no intermediate aviation commands. For general matters, aviation troops come under the command of the military district in which they are situated; and can be ordered by the commander of that district to take part in field exercises with other troops, or to carry out flights for special purposes and even, during times of trouble, in aid of the civil power.

5. Recruiting, Terms of Service and Training.

Recruiting and terms of service for aviation troops are the same as for the rest of the Polish army, but youths who have already some knowledge of a trade are specially selected for service in the technical corps of the army, of which the aviation gets a proportion. Many of the recruits are, however, entirely unskilled.

Recruits receive no technical training during their first year's service, but are employed on non-technical duties in connection with the machines. During that time those that show aptitude for mechanics are noted, and are put in the regimental schools for the second year's service. Here they learn about the aeroplanes and engines, mounting and dismounting them, and carrying out tests and small repairs. At the end of their second year's service those that wish to become permanently employed in the aviation have to pass an examination and are then sent to the Mechanics' School at Bydgoszcz. The course, which now lasts 6 months, will in 1927 be extended to 2 years. If they pass out well they are permitted to take further service in the aviation units as mechanics. They then engage to serve for 12 years. The Mechanics' School also takes those recruits who are by trade metal-workers or wood-workers, or apprentices to these trades, as soon as they join the colours, putting them through the same course as those mentioned above, and under the same conditions.

6. Officers.

(a) Pilots and Observers.

The whole system of training has recently been reorganized and the new scheme, which is described below, is being put into operation as the buildings become available.

Officers of the aviation corps (who have to be qualified pilots and observers and to have a good knowledge of mechanics) are obtained either from cadets or from officers transferring from other arms.

(i) *Cadets.*—Young men wishing to enter the aviation as officers must enter the Podchorązy School at Ostrow (*vide* Chapter VI, para. 2) for 1 year, after which they are sent to the Officers' Aviation School. This school was only opened in November, 1925, and is at present in Grudziądz, but will be moved to Dęblin in 1927. The course will last 2 years and the pupils will be trained to become efficient service pilots and observers and will be taught the beginnings of acrobatic flying. They spend on an average 120 hours in the air. They will be attached to artillery practice camps and divisional training camps during the summer in order to practise co-operation with other arms. After 1 year at this school they become officers, and after the second year are sent to units.

(ii) *Officers of Other Arms.*—Up to the present such officers have been sent to the Pilots' School at Bydgoszcz for an 8 months' course, but in 1926 the course will be lengthened to cover the whole year. The school will go in 1927 to Dęblin. The pupils receive thorough training in piloting, observing, bombing, machine gunnery, photography and wireless, so as to become service pilots or observers. They spend on an average 70 hours in the air, of which 20 are with an instructor, on four or five types of machines with engines up to 400 h.p. As with the pupils of the officers' school, they go into camps with other arms during the summer.

(iii) *Acrobatic Flying.*—This was formerly taught at the Senior Pilots' School at Grudziądz, but is now to be taught in the 11th Regiment (pursuit machines) at Lida. The course will last 4 months, and in the course of time all pilot officers will pass through it.

(iv) *Shooting and Bombing Courses for Aviation Officers.*—Six weeks' courses have hitherto been held in the Pilots' School at Bydgoszcz, but in future 4 months' courses are to be arranged in Dęblin, through which eventually all officers will pass. Here they will fire 10,000 rounds S.A.A. in the air and drop 200 bombs.

(v) *Squadron and Division Commanders' Courses.*—Squadron and division commanders' courses will also be started in 1927 in Dęblin, of 4 months' duration for the former and 2 months for the latter.

(vi) *Special Wireless and Photographic Courses.*—These courses, which are now arranged by Department V (Technical Troops) of the Ministry of War, will in 1927 be taken over by the Aviation Department, for both officers and N.C.Os.

(vii) *Equipment Officers.*—Equipment officers at present are selected from among the older officers of the corps, who are selected to go through a course at the Mechanics' School at Bydgoszcz. In order to maintain sufficient numbers, junior officers may be ordered to do duty as such, and are sent for a similar course before taking up their duties. As in future all officers passing through the aviation instructional schools will receive training as mechanics, the difficulty of getting qualified equipment officers will not be so great.

(b) **Numbers.**

The Army List of 1924 showed a total of 491 officers belonging to the Aviation Corps, which number has been increased by the latest classes trained at the pilots' and observers' schools. There are also some 200 reserve officers. It is stated that there are 700 officer and N.C.O. pilots now in the service. All officers whose duty takes them into the air receive flying pay or flying bonuses, *vide* para. 14 below.

7. Warrant Officers and Other Ranks.

As in all other corps of the Polish army, the senior non-commissioned officers, serjeants and staff-serjeants, are professional soldiers, and a proportion also of the junior ranks, corporal and 2nd corporal.

In the aviation corps these professional N.C.Os. comprise pilots, observers and mechanics who are trained as stated above, and general duty (non-technical) N.C.Os. who are selected from suitable volunteers for promotion from among the annual contingent.

Non-commissioned officers whose duty takes them into the air receive flying pay and flying bonuses at the same rate as officers performing similar duties.

8. Establishments.

War establishments are as follows :—

	Officers.	Other Ranks.	Motor Cars.	Motor Lorries.	Motor Cycles.	Aeroplanes.	Horses.	Wagons.
A.—*Line Division.*								
Headquarters	7	39	2	3	1	—	—	—
W/T section	1	29	—	2	1	—	—	—
Photo section	1	14	—	1	—	—	—	—
2 squadrons, each	14	127	2	10	—	10	4	2
Total Line Division	37	336	6	25	2	20	8	4
B.—*Pursuit Division.*								
Headquarters	6	41	2	1	1	—	—	—
3 squadrons, each—								
(a) single-seater	6	117	2	10	1	10	4	2
(b) two-seater	7	127	2	10	1	10	4	2
Total Pursuit Division								
(a)	24	392	8	31	4	30	12	4
(b)	27	422	8	31	4	30	12	4
C.—*Bombardment Division.*								
Headquarters	7	39	2	1	1	—	—	—
W/T section	1	29	—	2	1	—	—	—
Searchlight section	1	63	1	7	1	—	—	—
Photo section	1	14	—	1	—	—	—	—
3 squadrons, each	8	134	2	11	1	10	4	2
Total Bombardment Division	34	547	9	44	6	30	12	6
D.—*Army Air Park.*								
	7	206	—	20	1	—	—	—

These establishments are provisional only. Line divisions may have 4 squadrons. Pursuit divisions may have only 2 squadrons with 15 machines each. Bombardment squadrons may only have 6 machines.

In each case where the squadron has 10 service machines it holds an additional 5 in reserve.

9. Strength and Distribution of Units.

The location of the air force is at present—

1st Aviation Regiment	Warsaw.
2nd Aviation Regiment	Krakow.
3rd Aviation Regiment	Poznan.
4th Aviation Regiment	Torun.
6th Aviation Regiment	Lwow.
11th Aviation Regiment	Lida (temporarily).
Balloon Battalion and Balloon School	Torun.
Hydroplane Station	Puck.
Central Workshops and Stores	Warsaw.

A big central aerodrome is being constructed at Deblin, where the pilots' school and officers' school will be transferred in the course of 1927. At a later date, when the buildings are completed, the central workshops and stores will also be transferred there.

10. Types of Aeroplanes in Use.

Up to the end of 1926 the standard types in use were—

For reconnaissance	Potez X.V.A.2, with 400 h.p. Dietrich Lorraine engines.
	Potez XXVII.A.2, with 450 h.p. Dietrich Lorraine engines (replacing Potez XV).
	Breguet XIX, with 450 h.p. Dietrich Lorraine engines (also for bombardment).
For pursuit	Spad 61, with 450 h.p. Dietrich Lorraine engine.
For night bombardment	Farman Goliath 60, with two 50 h.p. Jupiter engines.
Hydroplanes for bombardment.	Latham H.B.3, with two 400 h.p. Dietrich Lorraine engines.
Hydroplanes for reconnaissance.	LeO.H.3, Flying boat, with two 300 h.p. Hispano Suiza engines.
	Schreck F.B.A., with 180 h.p. Hispano Suiza engine.
For training	Henriot 19, with 180 h.p. Hispano Suiza engine.
	Henriot 28, with 50 h.p. Rhone engine.

Besides the above machines in regular service, there are a large number of old machines which have gradually been relegated to reserve, of which the following are the principal types :—

Breguet A.14, with 300 h.p. Renault engine.
Ansaldo A.300/4, with 300 h.p. Fiat engine.
Balilla, with 220 h.p. Spa engine.

11. Building and Supply of Aeroplanes.

At the present time Poland can only manufacture the hull of the aeroplane : all engines are bought abroad. The various factories are :—

(a) A private factory, Plage and Laskiewicz, at Lublin, where the non-metal parts of aeroplanes are manufactured and where these parts, together with the engines bought from abroad, are put together. This factory completed in 1924 a first order from the Ministry of War for 300 aeroplanes, namely: Ansaldo A.3 (150), and 150 Balilla. It is now engaged on an order for Potez XXVII aeroplanes. The factory hopes to begin the construction of engines (of a French type) later on.

(b) A factory has been built at Okęcic, just outside Warsaw, on the edge of the future aerodrome. It was supported, both financially and technically, by a consortium of French aeroplane firms and Polish banks, the company having been formed in 1922. Up to the present, however, the factory buildings are barely finished and no machinery has been installed. In 1924 a contract was signed for the building of Spad aeroplanes for the Polish Aviation but was never carried out. The factory has now been acquired by Skoda, and it is stated will carry out the above-mentioned contract and will begin to make aero-engines.

(c) A small factory named Samolot has been set up in the aerodrome of the 3rd Aviation Regiment at Poznan, with capital supplied by the local gentry. It builds Henriot 19 and 28 for engines bought abroad. A school for civilian pilots is attached to this factory.

(d) Another small factory built with Polish capital has been set up at Biala Podlaska, called the Podlaska Wytwornia Samolotow (Podlesian Aeroplane Factory). It has built a series of Potez XV machines and is now building Potez XXVII.

(e) The central aviation workshops at Warsaw (eventually at Dęblin) are also to manufacture Henriot aeroplanes and some seaplanes.

12. Aerodromes, etc.

The following places have permanent aerodromes:—

(*Classified as 1st class.*)
Warsaw.   Dęblin (not opened yet).
Poznan.

(*Classified as 2nd class.*)
Grudziądz.   Krakow.
Bydgość.   Lwow.
Torun.

(*Classified as 3rd class.*)
Lida.   Przemysl.

The following places have aerodromes with temporary hangars, surviving from the war:—

Luck.   Brześć-nad-Bugiem.
Tarnopol.   Lublin.
Wilno.   Bialystok.

There is a seaplane base at Puck.

13. Balloon Units.

There is one balloon battalion, consisting of signal section, photographic section, five balloon companies and a balloon park, and a Central Balloon School, both at Torun.

THE POLISH ARMY

The equipment of the balloon units consists of captive balloons and observation balloons (sausages). There is also a dirigible, which was constructed at Torun, and which made its trial flight there on 11th August, 1922, carrying five passengers.

The war establishments of the balloon units are :—

	Officers.	Other Ranks.	Motor Cars.	Motor Lorries.	Motor Cycles.	Horses.	Wagons.
Battalion headquarters	5	23	1	2	1	—	—
Balloon company (motor transport)	7	146	1	9	1	—	—
Balloon company (horse transport)	7	162	1	—	1	70	29
Balloon park	3	90	—	4	1	35	13

Each company has one balloon.

14. Aviation Corps Pay.

Additional flying pay and bonuses are given to officers and men of the Aviation Corps and to certain qualified personnel of other arms, at the following scales :—

Additional Flying Pay.

Category I .. .. For officers—100 per cent. of the pay of rank according to rate (*a*) (*see* Chapter XXIII (1)).
 For N.C.Os.—100 per cent. of the pay of category 10 according to rate (*a*).
Category II .. .. 75 per cent. of the above rates of pay.
Category III .. .. 50 per cent. of the above rates of pay.
Category IV .. .. 30 per cent. of the above rates of pay.
Category V .. .. 25 per cent. of the above rates of pay.

The personnel to whom the additional flying pay is given is as follows :—

Category I.
 (*a*) Pilots and machine gunners of aeroplane units.
 (*b*) Pilots of dirigibles.

Category II.
 (*c*) Observers of aeroplane units.

Category III.
 (*d*) Technical controllers in factories and workshops if their control necessitates flight.
 (*e*) Pupils of flying schools (pilots, observers).
 (*f*) Technical officers, wireless operators, photographers and other officer specialists who go up in aeroplanes or dirigibles to carry out their duty.
 (*g*) Mechanics, wireless operators, armourers, and other non-officer specialists who go up in aeroplanes to carry out their duty.

Category IV.
  (*h*) Observers of captive balloons, pilots and observers of free balloons, observers of dirigibles.
  (*i*) Balloon mechanics, wireless operators, armourers, photographers, and other specialists who go up in dirigibles, captive or free balloons to carry out their duties.

Category V.
  (*k*) Pupils of balloon schools.

The personnel under (*a*), (*b*), (*c*), (*d*) and (*h*) draw this additional flying pay monthly in advance during each half-yearly period provided they carry out the necessary qualifying flights. (Pupils of flying schools begin to draw it from the first day of the month after they have satisfactorily finished the school course.)

The personnel under (*f*), (*g*) and (*i*) receive at the end of the month the additional flying pay at the rate of one-thirtieth the monthly amount for each day on which they went up in the air and carried out their work satisfactorily, irrespective of number of flights and duration during any one day.

Pupils of schools and courses, included under (*e*) and (*k*), receive the additional flying pay for the whole normal duration of the course at the school, but at the end of the course, provided they finish it satisfactorily.

The qualifying flights and periods required for the above rates of additional flying pay are as follows :—

(1) *Aeroplane Units.*
  (*a*) Pilots. Six hours in the air, including 30 landings, one long distance flight over 300 kilometres, and two flights at a height of 3,000 metres.
  (*b*) Observers. Six hours in the air, at least 10 separate flights, with 2 photographic tasks and 2 wireless tasks, satisfactorily carried out.

(2) *Balloon Units.*
  (*a*) Pilots, observers, or machine gunners in dirigibles—one 2-hour flight.
  (*b*) Pilots in free balloons—two 2-hour flights.
  (*c*) Observers in captive balloons—8 ascents, totalling at least 10 hours.

(3) *Schools and Courses.*—The normal duration of courses, which is—
  (*a*) Pilots' school—8 months.
  (*b*) Observers' course in aeroplane regiments—$1\frac{1}{2}$ to 3 months.
  (*c*) Balloon observers' course in the balloon battalion—2 months.

Flying Bonuses.—The following bonuses are granted :—
  (*a*) For officer instructor pilots of aeroplanes, for each time they go up with a pupil .. .. 0·4 points.
  For N.C.O. instructor pilots of aeroplanes, for each time they go up with a pupil .. .. 0·3 ,,
  (*b*) For officer instructor pilots of balloons, for each time they go up with a pupil .. .. 0·3 ,,
  (*c*) For special flights, per hour .. .. 25 ,,

(d) For pilots of factories and workshops—
  (i) For taking up a new type of machine for the first time   256 points.
  (ii) For taking up a new machine of old type for the first time .. ..   64 ,,
  (iii) For taking up a repaired machine for first time after repairs .. ..   39 ,,
(e) For aeroplane or balloon foreman mechanics, working at assembling machines, if they go up in the machine they have assembled .. ..   48 points monthly.

These " points " are multiplied by the multiplier, *vide* Chapter XXIII, para. 1, to obtain the sum due to the individual. These payments are made monthly in arrear.

15. Methods of Communicating with Aeroplanes.

For communication from the ground to an aeroplane strips of white cloth are used, while the position of units (divisions, regiments, battalions, artillery regiments, etc.) is indicated by sheets of cloth of various shapes and carrying various markings. Stars denote army headquarters; circles, divisions (and brigades); half circles, regiments; and triangles, battalions. Cavalry are distinguished by similar figures with the addition of a square cloth with a red circle in the middle. Artillery units are distinguished by squares or rhomboi.

Aeroplanes communicate with the ground by various forms of lights or clouds of smoke, and also by wireless. There are several sets of wireless in use, left over from the war, but it is intended to introduce a new type for general use, and trials have been held with both French and English types.

Ground signals and wireless signals are shown at Plate II, A, B and C.

A few R.K.G. wireless telephones have been bought and were tried in aeroplanes during the manœuvres of 1925, and good results, it was stated, were obtained.

CHAPTER XXVII.

MILITARY EDUCATION.

1. General.

Poland, from an educational standpoint, is in a very backward condition, due to the suppression of the Polish language in the past, and to the mixed character of the population in certain districts. In introducing the Military Service Bill for 1922 the Minister of War admitted that 70 per cent. of the recruits were illiterate. Hence the military education of the private soldier has to begin with the Polish language and the three " R's "; and the recruit spends part of his first winter's training in elementary education.

Officers, on the other hand, are almost entirely drawn from the middle classes who, provided they were willing to learn in a foreign tongue, had good opportunities of State education in the middle and higher schools, polytechnics and universities set up by the former occupying Powers, which are now, under the Poles, being rapidly extended and are always over full. Consequently, it was easy to fix a standard of education for officer candidates.

The general system of education in the army is that of elementary education of the recruit in his own unit by his own officers and N.C.Os.; special schools for N.C.Os. and officers where the training is partly military and partly educational; and in larger towns evening classes available for N.C.Os. and privates in the State schools.

Games and light athletics are encouraged in units, and physical training forms part of the daily routine.

2. Military Orphanages.

The only organization of this nature is an orphanage for the orphans of fallen officers, in Warsaw. It is mainly supported by charity, getting but a small grant from the government, and contains not more than 100 small children.

3. Cadet Schools.

Three " cadet " schools (Korpus Kadetow) exist at Lwow, Ostrow and Rawicz, and give a training equivalent to the five upper classes of a middle school. They are organized on military lines; the cadets wear a special uniform and do a certain amount of military training. There is, however, no obligation on a cadet to become an officer and they may, on completion of their course, return to civil life. Those who desire to become officers pass into the Podchorąży School (*vide* Chapter VI). The two first-mentioned schools have about 800 cadets each. The third, at Rawicz, was formed only in September, 1925, with one (the lowest) class, and each successive year a new lowest class will be formed until the full establishment is reached.

4. Regimental Officers' Schools.

These schools are of two kinds, namely, officers' training schools and technical schools (*see* para. 5). The pupil receives his commission as an officer at the end of the second year at the former; at the latter specialist training in technical arms is given.

The regimental officers' schools exist for infantry, cavalry, artillery and engineers, to which the future officer passes after he has done the 1-year general course at the Podchorąży School at Ostrow* (*vide* Chapter VI). These so-called officers' schools are :—

Officers' Infantry School.—Located in the same building and under the same command as the Podchorąży School at Ostrow. The course lasts 2 years in all. When full it will hold 250 pupils in each year.

Officers' Cavalry School.—Part of the Central Cavalry School at Grudziądz. (Also for horse transport officers). Two years' course for 250 pupils in all.

Officers' Artillery School, Torun.—The course lasts 3 years, the pupil becoming an officer at the end of the second year. 300 pupils in all are on the establishment.

Officers' Engineer School, Warsaw.—For future officers of engineers, signals, railway troops and motor transport. The establishment will eventually be 100 pupils in each course, but at present there are only about 40–50 per course. After 2 years the pupils

---

* This school was at Warsaw, but after having taken an important part in the fighting against Marshal Pilsudski during the coup-d'etat of May, 1926, was removed to Ostrow.

are made second-lieutenants; those of the engineers are kept for a third year's application course; those of the other branches being sent for the third year to the training school or camp of their branch.

Officers' Aviation School.—*Vide* Chapter XXVII.

Officers' Medical School.—*Vide* Chapter XIX.

Officers' Naval School, Torun.—The course lasts 3 years, which includes courses at sea during the summer in the training ship " Lwow," a sailing ship with auxiliary petrol engines.

The further training of officers, after they have already served as such, is carried out as follows :—

Infantry Officers.—At present 5 to 6-months' courses are arranged at the former N.C.O.s' School at Chelmno for those officers (captains and lieutenants), who obtained commissions during war time and have not been to a proper officers' school. Three months' courses for majors and lieutenant-colonels are held in the training camp at Grupa (near Grudziądz) during the summer.

Cavalry.—Eight-months' courses for senior officers, captains and majors are held at the cavalry school at Grudziądz. Occasionally short courses of 3 months are held for lieutenant-colonels and colonels.

Artillery.—Courses at the Central Artillery Training Camp at Torun for lieutenants (battery commanders' course, lasting 4 months), for captains (group commanders' course, lasting 4 months), and for senior officers (regimental commanders' course, lasting 3 months).

Engineers.—Eight-months' courses are held in the Officers' Engineer School at Warsaw for those officers who have not been through a proper school before appointment. One-year's course in fortification for majors and colonels was started in 1925, at the same school, and other refresher courses for engineer officers are also held.

Musketry, etc.—At the Central Musketry School at Torun courses in small arms training, lasting 3 months, are periodically held for captains and lieutenants of infantry and cavalry and a few from other arms.

Physical Training.—The Central School of Gymnastics and Sport at Poznan holds 3½-months' courses for junior regimental officers, and 9-months' longer courses; also 1-year courses in swordsmanship for a few specially selected officers.

Medical Officers.—Refresher courses in the duty of medical officers, lasting 3 months, are periodically held at the Central School of N.C.Os. of the Medical Service at Przemysl.

Veterinary Officers.—Courses are held at the Cavalry School, Grudziądz.

In addition to the above, special courses are arranged :—

(a) For general officers and colonels of all arms. A course of higher military studies, lasting 10 months, for about 20 officers, at Warsaw.

(b) For colonels of artillery. A course of higher artillery work for about 12 officers, lasting 3 months, at Warsaw.

(c) Short 2-months' courses are also held at the Staff College for officers appointed or likely to be appointed quartermasters of regiments (*i.e.*, officer in charge o mobilization arrangements).

5. Technical Schools and Courses.

The Politeknikum, Lwow.—This is a State establishment for giving higher technical instruction (mathematics, engineering, chemistry, etc.). Officers of the Technical Corps may be specially seconded to it from their units for a course of study.

Sound Ranging, etc.—Three-months' courses are held at the School of Artillery Ranging at Torun for specially selected lieutenants of artillery.

The Signal Training Centre, Zegrze.—Recently appointed second-lieutenants of signal troops are given their final 8 months' specialist training after leaving the Officers' Engineer School. Refresher courses of 4 months' duration are held for senior officers of signal troops, and 6 months' courses for regimental signal officers of other arms are held yearly.

The Motor Transport Training Camp, Warsaw.—Second-lieutenants on appointment from the Officers' Engineer School do an 8 months' course, and refresher courses are held from time to time for senior officers.

The Railway Troops Training Camp, Jablonna.—Second-lieutenants on appointment from the Officers' Engineer School do an 8 months' course, and refresher courses are held from time to time for senior officers, also 3 months' courses for officers of armoured trains.

The Tank Training Camp, Przemysl.—Courses are held when required.

6. The Staff College at Warsaw.

The course at this college lasts 2 years, and comprises 60 students at each yearly course. Candidates for entry have to pass a qualifying and competitive examination. The first year is devoted to the study of a division, and of a cavalry brigade, and of the use of the different arms. The second year is devoted to the study of higher formations, strategy and politics, preparation for war and its conduct, and the effect of war on economic life.

Owing to the climate of Poland the winter months are devoted entirely to indoor study. Between November and June of each year the pupils remain in Warsaw, from July to September they travel throughout Poland, carrying out staff rides, visiting military and industrial establishments, etc., and during October they have 1 month's leave. At some period during the course students are attached to an arm other than their own, or to the staff of a small formation during field training. All students are taught French.

To the Staff College is affiliated the Higher Intendance School, whose pupils participate in certain of the work and exercises of the Staff College, *e.g.*, general tactics, staff work, organization, military history and the French language.

7. Schools for Non-commissioned Officers.

N.C.Os. get their early training in their units, but in order to render the system more uniform throughout the army and to provide better instruction than can be given in the regiments, certain schools for the training of N.C.Os. have been formed.

These are :—

(a) In each military district there is an instructional battalion for N.C.Os. of infantry, where the training lasts 6 months.

There is also a Central Infantry N.C.Os.' School at Grudziądz, where the course is eventually to last 1 year, but at present a shortened course of 5 months is being held. This school contains 600 pupils.

(b) Artillery N.C.Os.' School at Torun. The course here will also eventually be 1 year, but is for the present being reduced to 5 months. There are 250 pupils.

(c) Central Musketry School at Torun. For N.C.Os. of Cavalry and Infantry. The training consists of machine gunnery.

(d) Central School for N.C.Os. of the Medical Service at Przemysl. A 6 months' course.

N.C.Os. of other arms have no special schools for their instruction, but courses for 150 N.C.Os. are being held at the Cavalry School at Grudziądz and similar courses are organized for engineer N.C.Os. at the Engineer Training Camp at Warsaw, and for others at the training centres for the technical arms, signals, motor transport and railway troops.

8. Military Education in Civil Schools.

As was stated in Chapter XXI, paragraph 4, great attention is being paid to the development of the military spirit in the nation, and a law has been drafted to enforce it. Pending the passage of this law the Ministry of Education, in collaboration with the Ministry of War, has ordered physical and military training to be given in all schools, whether State or private.

Physical training, including games, is to be carried out in all elementary schools by both boys and girls for 2 hours weekly, and also in middle schools. In addition, in middle schools, boys in the last three classes are to carry out military training, including field service duties, musketry and bombing. This is generally done by the organization known as the Hufiec Szkolny, or School Corps, membership of which used to be voluntary, but will now be obligatory. In the 6th class of his school, the youth goes through the training of the individual soldier; in the 7th class, that of the section; and in the 8th class, the final class of a middle school, that of the *groupe de combat*. The training periods consist of 3 periods of 50 minutes each per week, two lectures and one field exercise or musketry exercise per month.

In the higher training establishments, universities and so on, military training is equally obligatory on all those who have not done military training as prescribed by the law of universal military service, but actually the organization of this training is in its infancy.

In girls' schools, physical training is also obligatory, and in addition, for the higher classes, instruction is given in medical duties, first aid, and so on, to those who wish it.

Medical examinations and physical tests are made obligatory for both sexes.

The physical training is given by one of the school teaching staff, who must have been through a course of physical training, and be approved by the Ministry of Education. Military training may be given also by a member of the teaching staff with the necessary qualifications, approved by both the Ministries of Education and War, or may be given by an officer of the p.w. cadre of the regiment in whose territorial district the school is situated.

Camps are arranged in summer by the various military districts, attendance at which is voluntary on the part of the boys; the camp and instructional staff being again the p.w. officers. The boys receive free rations, and all camp and training appliances are provided by the military authorities. Attendance at these camps is very popular, and there are always more applicants than vacancies. The training includes—

(*a*) Physical training, grenade throwing, bayonet fighting, hygiene.

(*b*) Musketry, and care of arms.

(*c*) Field training, including appreciation of terrain, signalling and field engineering.

(*d*) Army organization and interior economy.

(*e*) History of Poland and general subjects.

To define the programme of instruction and to provide instructors (not for schools only but for the societies mentioned in Chapter XXI, paragraph 4) the Ministries of Education and War have made the following arrangements: A Council of Physical Training and Military Preparation has been set up, composed of representatives of the Ministries of War, Education and Public Works, of the various authorised societies, and others, who will draw up the general organization throughout the country and supervise its execution.

A Central Institute of Physical Training is to be created, at which qualified instructors of physical training will be prepared. At the present time these instructors are trained at the military School of Gymnastics and Sport at Poznan, or in special courses arranged when and where convenient; but the supply is not sufficient to meet requirements.

Advanced courses of training or summer camps are arranged, where school teachers and other suitable persons are given training sufficient to enable them to act as instructors in schools or approved societies.

To encourage the development of the military spirit, various competitions, musketry meetings, sports, and so on, are arranged frequently, at which both school detachments and approved societies compete, and at which prizes are given. The senior military officers make a point of encouraging these by their presence and assistance.

Reduction of the period of military service and other privileges, such as choice of arm or regiment, are given to those youths who pass the qualifying tests of physical development and military training before being called up for military service (*see* Chapter XXI, paragraph 4).

9. Study of Foreign Languages.

All Polish officers, and a large proportion of the men, can speak one other language besides Polish, even though they may be unable to read and write it ; but in the course of time the German and Russian languages will tend to decrease among the Polish peasantry, as facilities now exist which enable him to be taught in his own language. There will, however, continue to be a large number of citizens to whom German or Russian is the mother tongue. French or German is an obligatory subject in all middle schools, and French is taught during the first year at the Staff College. Officers are encouraged to study foreign languages by the holding of interpretership examinations, success at which gives the officers preference in certain Staff appointments, and, in the case of certain languages, the right to 3 months' leave in the country with special allowances.

10. Welfare.

The position of a Polish officer, unless he has money of his own, is difficult. Even with the increase of pay granted in the summer of 1926 his income is very small, and officers find it difficult to make both ends meet. Consequently many of them try to increase their income by other means, sometimes dishonest, and to make economies at the cost of their health. Many of them only have one square meal a day.

The question of quarters is unsatisfactory also. In most garrison towns lodgings are hard to get, and officers and their families are overcrowded, or live in badly built or dilapidated houses. Very few barracks have sufficient quarters for the officers, and in fact, a proposal to compel unmarried officers to live in barracks was rejected on the grounds that it was an interference with the liberty of the individual.

The soldier, on the other hand, is in a much better position, as his lodging, clothing and feeding is provided for. The barracks vary very greatly, in some places they are cold and draughty huts, while in others, especially in Poznan, they are up-to-date barracks equal to the latest construction in England.

In most garrison towns there is a club for officers, and often a small library.

In all barracks there is a reading room and canteen for the soldiers, the latter often run by a soldiers' co-operative.

Serious endeavours are being made to arrange classes of instruction for the soldiers, so as to teach them some useful subject that will help them on their return to civil life, and to teach the illiterate soldiers the three " R's." Soldiers are also encouraged to cultivate plots of land in the barracks and produce vegetables, etc., and in a few places, especially in the Poznan district, there is a large farm entirely cultivated by the soldiers under the direction of the higher authorities.

CHAPTER XXVIII.

UNIFORM.

1. General Notes on Uniform.

When the Polish Army was formed in 1918 and 1919 the troops were clothed in whatever uniform was available. Stocks of German and Austrian uniforms were issued, with the decorations taken off, while others were clothed in bought American uniforms or French horizon blue uniforms issued to the troops organized in France.

These are, however, now replaced by a universal pattern uniform of khaki. The same uniform is in use both for home service and in the field.

2. Details of Uniforms.

Tunic.—Of khaki serge, with upright collar, 6 metal buttons, and 2 side pockets with the opening sloping downwards from the front to the side. On each side of the collar opening is a patch of coloured cloth, about 4 inches long, with rear edging of different colours, varying with the arm, except in the cavalry and horse artillery, who wear in the same place a miniature pennon of identical colours with those of the lance pennon. The collar patch for all ranks bears along the edge in front and along the bottom for about 4 inches from the hooks a zig-zag line of silver braid. This is narrow for other ranks, medium for officers, and broad for general officers. On the shoulder straps are worn the badges of rank and the number of the regiment.

The collar patches of the different arms are :—

Arm.	Collar Patch.	Edging.
General officers	Dark blue velvet	Crimson.
Infantry	Blue	Yellow.
Artillery (except Horse)	Green	Black.
Engineers	Black	Red.
Signals	Black	Blue.
Aviation	Yellow	None.
Railway troops	Black	None.
Motor transport	Black	Yellow.
Horse transport	Brown	Light blue.
Gendarmerie	Red	Yellow.
Medical	Cherry	Blue.
Administration	None	White.
Intendance	None	Crimson.
Corps of Controllers	Black	Crimson.
Corps of Administrative Control	Brown	Black.
Topographical	Black	White.
Veterinary	None	Dark green.
Justice	None	Black.

THE POLISH ARMY

Trousers, or Breeches.—Of plain khaki serge or cord. General officers wear a double dark-blue stripe down both breeches and trousers.

Head-dress.—The national headgear of the Polish squirearchy in the old days was a cap with a four-sided top, from which was developed the lancer helmet formerly adopted in most armies.

This same cap, or czapka, has been modified and made into the headgear for all ranks of the Polish Army, which therefore consists of a stiff round cloth cap, a brown leather peak and a soft square top, of which one point is in the centre of the front. A band of coloured cloth, varying with the regiment (black for horse artillery), is worn round the cap in cavalry. On the front of the cap are worn badges of rank. Officers have two lines of silver braid across the top of the cap, joining opposite corners. Round the circular portion of the cap junior officers have one row, and field officers have two rows of silver braid; general officers have a broad zig-zag stripe of silver lace. A silver eagle is worn on the front of the cap between the badges of rank and the front corner of the square top.

Steel Helmet.—A steel helmet of French pattern is worn when ordered, on manoeuvres, and in war. A silver eagle is attached to the front.

Greatcoat.—The soldier's greatcoat is of khaki cloth, single-breasted, with broad collar, belt and shoulder straps.

The officer's was of similar pattern and stocks are still being worn, but the new pattern is similar to the English pattern double-breasted greatcoat, with cloth straps behind and double cuffs, only with 6 buttons down each row in front instead of 4.

Across the front points of the collar, when turned down, is a stripe of the colour (or colours) forming the patch on the collar of the tunic.

During the winter fur coats of no standard pattern, with fur collars, are allowed to be worn. Khaki mackintoshes are also permitted. These are supposed to carry badges of rank on the shoulders.

Boots.—All mounted men wear black leather jack boots with spurs. Dismounted men wear as a rule ankle boots with puttees, though sometimes loose leather high boots may be worn, in accordance with the custom of the peasantry, who normally wear long loose boots. Some regiments have American canvas gaiters instead of puttees. Officers may wear brown leather field boots and spurs instead of black.

Belt.—Other ranks wear a plain leather belt. Officers wear a Sam Browne belt, to which a sword is attached by means of leather slings, and not in a frog.

The officer's scabbard is of steel with two rings, to which are attached the two slings depending from the Sam Browne belt. A sword knot of silver and crimson is attached to the belt. The scabbard of the soldier is also of steel, but with one ring, to which is attached the strap attached to the plain leather belt. His sword knot is also of leather.

THE POLISH ARMY

The colours of the cavalry and horse artillery are :—

Regiment.	Colours of Pennon on Lance and on Collar.	Cap Band.
Horse Artillery	Black and crimson	Black.
1st Chevauxlegers	White with crimson line in centre	Crimson.
2nd ,,	White with crimson line in centre	White.
3rd ,,	White with crimson line in centre	Crimson.
1st Lancers	Crimson and white	Crimson.
2nd ,,	White and dark blue	White.
3rd ,,	Yellow and white	Yellow.
4th ,,	Light blue and white	Light blue.
5th ,,	Divided in 3 triangles : white, crimson, blue	Crimson.
6th ,,	Light blue with white line	Light blue.
7th ,,	Divided in 3 triangles : 2 red, 1 white	Crimson.
8th ,,	Orange	Orange.
9th ,,	Crimson and white with white and crimson centre line.	Crimson.
10th ,,	Crimson and white with white and blue centre line.	Crimson.
11th ,,	Crimson with white line	White.
12th ,,	Crimson and dark blue with white line	Crimson.
13th ,,	Pink with blue line	Pink.
14th ,,	Yellow with white line	Yellow.
15th ,,	White and red	Red.
16th ,,	Blue and white with red line	White.
17th ,,	White and yellow with red line	Yellow.
18th ,,	White and light blue with red line	Light blue.
19th ,,	Divided in 3 triangles : 2 blue, 1 white	Dark blue.
20th ,,	Crimson with blue and white line	Crimson.
21st ,,	Blue with yellow and white line	Blue.
22nd ,,	Divided in 3 triangles : 2 white, 1 red	White.
23rd ,,	White and brick red	Brick red.
24th ,,	White with yellow line	White.
25th ,,	White and red with blue line	Red.
26th ,,	Pink and white with blue line	Pink.
27th ,,	Yellow and white with white and blue line	Yellow.
1st Mounted Rifles	Olive green and crimson	Olive.
2nd ,, ,,	Olive green and crimson, blue line	Olive.
3rd ,, ,,	Olive green and crimson, yellow line	Olive.
4th ,, ,,	Olive green and crimson, white line	Olive.
5th ,, ,,	Olive green and white with red line	Olive.
6th ,, ,,	Olive green and white	Olive.
7th ,, ,,	Olive green and white with yellow line	Olive.
8th ,, ,,	Green and white with blue line	Olive.
9th ,, ,,	Green and yellow with crimson line	Olive.
10th ,, ,,	Green and yellow with white line	Olive.
Pioneer Squadrons	Crimson and black	Black.

THE POLISH ARMY

Special Distinctions.

Unit.	Badge (embroidered except where otherwise stated).	How Worn.
Mountain Divisions (All arms).	Silver swastika and oak twig (a)	On collar.
	White metal swastika, oak twig, and feather	Right side of cap.
16th Division and 63rd Infantry Regiment which originally belonged to this division.	Metal shield bearing an eagle (66th Regiment a griffin).	On collar patch.
77th Regiment	White metal bear	On shoulder strap.
1st Chevauxlegers	Monogram J.P. (Josef Pilsudski)	On shoulder strap.
8th Uhlans	Monogram J.P. (Josef Poniatowski)	On shoulder strap.
Machine gun companies	Clip of five cartridges	Left sleeve.
Pioneer platoons (infantry)	Crossed axes	Left sleeve.
Telephonists	T with single-forked lightning	Left sleeve.
Telegraphists	T with double-forked lightning	Left sleeve.
Wireless operators	T.R. with triple-forked lightning	Left sleeve.
Tanks	Dragon	Left sleeve.
Bridging battalion	Crossed axes and anchor	Left sleeve.
Motor transport troop	Winged motor within circle	Left sleeve.
Railway troops	Winged wheel	Left sleeve.
Armoured cars and trains	Plumed helmet	Left sleeve.
Aviation	Eagle in flight	Left sleeve.
Pilots	White metal eagle in flight holding in beak a laurel wreath.	Hanging from collar on left side of tunic.
Observers	White metal eagle in flight holding in beak a laurel wreath with arrows.	Hanging from collar on left side of tunic.
Officers' Schools	Star between two laurel branches (a)	On collar.
	Letters S.O. in metal	On shoulder strap.
Podchorazy School	Sword and oak twig (a)	On collar.
	Monogram S.P. in metal	On shoulder strap.
N.C.Os.' schools	Crossed rifles with wreath (a)	On collar.
Intendants	Leaf	On collar.
Corps of Controllers	Winged staff with arrows	On collar.
Chaplains	Cross (shape varies with denomination)	On collar.
Rabbis		
Medical officers	Rod and serpent between two twigs	On collar.
Veterinary officers	Rod and serpent	On collar.
Topographers	Orb and twigs	On collar.
Shoeing smiths	Horseshoe	Left sleeve.

N.B.—Badges marked (*a*) may be alternatively of metal.

3. Badges of Rank.

Badges of rank are worn on the cap and shoulder strap and are as follows:—

General Officers.	Cap.	Shoulder Strap.
Marshal	Broad zig-zag line of silver lace and crossed batons.	Bar of zig-zag silver lace and crossed batons.
General	Similar lace and 3 stars	Similar lace and 3 stars.
General of division	Similar lace and 2 stars	Similar lace and 2 stars.
General of brigade	Similar lace and 1 star	Similar lace and 1 star.
Field Officers.		
Colonel	Two lines of silver braid and 3 stars.	Two bars of silver braid and 3 stars.
Lieutenant-Colonel	Two lines of silver braid and 2 stars.	Two bars of silver braid and 2 stars.
Major	Two lines of silver braid and 1 star.	Two bars of silver braid and 1 star.
Junior Officers.		
Captain	One line of silver braid and 3 stars.	No bars. 3 stars.
Lieutenant	One line of silver braid and 2 stars.	Two stars.
Second-Lieutenant	One line of silver braid and 1 star	One star.

N.C.Os.	Cap.	Shoulder Straps of Tunic and Greatcoat.
Starszy Sierżant and corresponding ranks (warrant officers).	Two chevrons	Stripe round edge of shoulder strap and one central lengthwise bar.
Sierżant (staff-serjeant)	One chevron	Stripe round edge of shoulder strap.
Plutonowy (serjeant)	Three bars	Three bars across shoulder strap.
Kapral (corporal)	Two bars	Two bars across shoulder strap.
Starszy szeregowiec. Senior private (lance-corporal).	One bar	One bar across shoulder strap.

These chevrons, bars and stripes, which used to be of crimson cloth, are in future to be of silver braid with crimson edging, total width 10 mm. on the shoulder strap, 5 mm. on the cap.

Professional N.C.Os. wear a distinguishing mark of chevrons on the left sleeve of tunic and greatcoat, with the point downwards at the bend of the elbow. One narrow chevron ($1\frac{1}{2}$ cm. wide) is granted after 3 years' professional service, and after each successive 3 years another is added, at a distance of $\frac{1}{2}$ cm. above the first. When three have been earned they are replaced by a broad chevron of 3 cm. width.

4. Staff Distinctions.

Staff officers wear the uniform of their arm, but with a silver eagle on the collar patch. General officers wear the same silver eagle.

THE POLISH ARMY

Staff officers, adjutants of regiments, A.D.Cs. to generals, and gendarmerie officers wear aiguillettes of colour varying from silver to grey-green. Gendarmerie privates wear similar aiguillettes of yellow braid.

5. Uniform Worn by Semi-Military Bodies.

The Sokol Society has a special semi-uniform which consists of a coat, buttoned up to the neck, but with the upper button and collar left open to show the shirt, which is crimson and braided across the front. Breeches, trousers and boots of no special pattern. The hat is of the same shape as the military czapka and carries a falcon's feather on the right side.

The Cadet Schools of Lwow, Modlin and Rawicz wear a blue serge uniform with yellow piping at the seam of the trousers, and similar piping, together with silver lace, on the collar of the coat. They wear an exaggerated high form of the czapka, also of blue cloth, with a large white metal plaque and the Polish eagle on the front.

Veterans of the rebellion of 1863 wear a blue uniform, with crimson facings and crimson collar patch with the silver zig-zag line on it. Their czapka is also of blue with a silver eagle, which bears the date 1863 and the letter W. As all veterans are granted the rank of at least second-lieutenant, they wear these badges of rank also, and are entitled to salutes from the troops.

6. Identity Discs.

Identity discs are issued on mobilization. They are flat, square metal tablets, worn on a cord round the neck and marked with the owner's name and Christian name, the commune in which he is domiciled, with its district and province. Discs taken off casualties are sent to the recruiting district corresponding to the place of birth, where the man is identified from the registers.

7. System of Supply of Uniforms.

Department VII at the War Ministry is responsible in general for the supply of uniform to the army. Some military districts have their own uniform factories, run by them as a business concern, and supply themselves therefrom and accept orders from other D.O.Ks., and only demand on Department VII for those articles which they do not manufacture.

Issue is made from district stores to divisional stores and thence to regimental stores. The latter are supposed to keep an extra good suit of uniform for every man, issuable only for ceremonial occasions and returned to store afterwards.

8. Personal Kit.

Each soldier, professional or conscript, is entitled to :—

2 sets of cloth uniform.
1 set of summer uniform (canvas or drill) (2 sets in technical units).
2 sets of underlinen.
2 pairs of thick drawers.
2 pairs of boots.
1 greatcoat.
1 jersey or waistcoat.

For their recruits' training on the barrack square, recruits are issued with an additional set of old uniform.

178   THE POLISH ARMY

9. **Medals and Decorations.**

No war medals exist.

Two military decorations are given for distinguished service in war. These are the Order " Virtuti Militari " and the decoration " Cross of Valour " (Krzyz Walecznych).

The Order " Virtuti Militari " is divided into five classes. The highest class, Grand Cross, is only given to Supreme Commanders as the reward for a successful operation which has given a decisive result and saved the country. The only holders of it are therefore Marshal Piłsudski, Marshal Foch, and the Kings of Italy, Belgium, Jugo-Slavia and Roumania. The 2nd, or Commander's, Class is given to generals for a successful tactical operation or heroic defence of a position. The 3rd, or Chevalier's, Class is given to an officer or other rank, already holding the 4th Class, for exceptionally brave conduct. The 4th, Gold Cross, Class is given to an officer or other rank already in possession of the 5th Class, and the 5th, Silver Cross, Class is given to officers or other ranks for brave conduct in the field. Each award carries with it a yearly pension of 300 zloty (about £13). The ribbon is of blue with black edges. According to the rules of the Order the cross is never to be taken off, but is to be worn for ever.

The Cross of Valour is given for distinguished conduct in battle. It is a bronze cross attached to a crimson ribbon with white edges. Up to four bars may be given for subsequent occasions.

Other orders and decorations are :—

The White Eagle.—Granted to civilians as well as soldiers. Consists of : (a) The Cross. Of red enamel, with silver edges and rays, carrying a white eagle. Worn on sash of light blue. (b) The Star. Worn on left breast. (c) The Chain.

Polonia Restituta.—Divided into five classes. A white enamel cross, with a Polish eagle in the centre. The star has in the centre the monogram R.P. It is worn with a red ribbon with white edges.

Cross of Merit.—In three classes, gold, silver and bronze cross. Carried on a crimson ribbon with blue edges, on the left breast.

Besides these orders there is a large number of badges commemorating the fact that the wearer has passed through certain military schools, or that he has been in a certain military formation before the restoration of Poland (*e.g.*, 1st Brigade of the Legions, Haller's Army, Bayonne Regiment), or that he took part in a certain operation (Defence of Lwow, Defence of Silesia, Battle of Rokitno), or that he was in a certain regiment or division that specially distinguished itself on one occasion (34th Infantry Regiment, 1st Horse Artillery Division), or that he was a victim of the political trials of the former partitioning Powers (*e.g.*, Marmoros Sziget trial), and so on. At least 100 of these are authorized to be worn.

CHAPTER XXIX.
NAVY.

1. **Historical Sketch.**

When Poland recovered her independence in 1918, great hopes were placed on the utterances of certain statesmen, that she would be given full access to the sea. Preparations were at once made for the formation of a navy, and a British Naval Mission

THE POLISH ARMY

came to assist in its organization. The hopes were, however, disappointed, as the Treaty of Versailles only gave Poland a small, sandy, useless sea coast, with no port, and shallow water close to the shore. Danzig, which Poland had hoped to obtain, was made into a Free City in which Poland was given a privileged position, the control of her foreign relations and the free use of the port.

During the Bolshevik war a political strike among the Danzig dock labourers prevented the unloading of ships with war material destined for the armies in the field, and Poland determined to see if something could be done to render her independent of Danzig. She decided to develop the fishing village of Gdynia into a naval and commercial port, and work in this direction has already been started.

To give protection to the commercial ships bringing war stores to Poland, she has determined to have a small sea-going fleet, based on Gdynia.

She has also organized a river fleet for use on the waterways, especially in Eastern Poland; and this river fleet together with the sea-going fleet represents the Polish Navy.

2. Administration.

The administration is entirely in the hands of the Army. The Navy Department is a special department directly under the Minister of War, in touch with the General Staff, the Administrative Staff, and the Chief of the Corps of Controllers in their respective provinces. The department is under an Admiral, has a staff of some 30 officers, and is located in Warsaw. The headquarters of the sea-going fleet is at Gdynia, and of the river flotillas at Torun and Pinsk.

The commercial fleet is also administered by the Department of the Navy.

3. Personnel.

(*a*) The professional personnel, both officers and petty officers, is largely drawn from Poles who had previously served in the Russian, Austrian and German navies. As they retain the rank they then held there is an unnecessarily large number of Admirals. Besides these there are a few young men who have joined since the formation of the navy.

The rank and file are drawn from a quota of the annual contingent called up for military service.

The total establishment is about 250 officers and 2,100 other ranks, of which 570 are on a long service engagement.

(*b*) Officers are obtained from among young men who enter the Podchorąży (Cadet) School at Ostrow, where in company with cadets wishing to enter the army, they do one year's general military training. Having completed this they are sent to the Naval School at Torun for a further three years' course, which includes voyages during the summer in the training ship " Lwow." The " Lwow " is a sailing ship with auxiliary petrol engine.

Several officers have been to France to study in the naval schools in that country.

(*c*) Warrant officers and specialists. Apart from those who had already served in the old navies, the complement of warrant officers and specialists is drawn from the lower ranks, after passing through a course at the School of Naval Specialists at Torun. This school trains signalmen, telegraphists, navigators, torpedo gunners, gunners, engine room hands, stokers, electricians and petty officers.

(*d*) **Seamen.** The rank and file are obtained partly from the yearly contingent and partly from volunteers. The medical qualifications required for sailors are stricter than those of the ordinary soldier. They serve for two years, as in the army.

(*e*) **Reserve.** The reserve comprises all officers and men who have done their period of military service in the navy.

4. Fleet Organization.

The navy is divided into two fleets :—
- (*a*) The sea-going fleet.
- (*b*) The river fleet.

The sea-going fleet comprises :—
A division of torpedo boats (6 ex-German T.B.s).
A training division (2 gunboats and 4 minelaying trawlers).
A hydroplane division.
The naval port of Gdynia, including the land defences.

The river fleet consists of the Vistula flotilla, based on Torun and Modlin, and the Pinsk flotilla, based on Pinsk. The river fleet contains 4 monitors, 6 river gunboats, 25 various motor boats, and a few others.

The list of vessels is given in the Appendix to this chapter.

5. Programme.

The naval programme has not yet been decided upon. A programme has been drawn up for 3 light cruisers, 6 destroyers, 12 torpedo boats, 12 submarines and 36 smaller craft in the sea-going fleet, but it has not yet been approved and financial difficulties will prevent its realization for some time. Meanwhile only 2 new destroyers of 1,545 tons have been bought in France, and the old cruiser "Desaix," for use as a training ship.

As regards the river fleet, a firm at Krakow has recently delivered two river monitors of 70 tons.

6. Ports.

The only port is Gdynia, which in 1920 was merely a fishing village, on a sandy shore, protected from the open Baltic by the Hela sand spit.

The full scheme of construction provides for an outer port of over a million square metres surface, to be protected by breakwaters, with wharves and other unloading facilities, and divided into a commercial port and a naval port, and a large inner basin to be excavated out of the marshy ground for about a mile inland. This inner basin is to have a surface of nearly half a million square metres, and is to be provided with docks, wharves, stores—in fact, is to become a large, important commercial port rivalling Danzig.

The outer port is now under construction, and should be completed by the end of 1928, but work has only recently been begun on the inner port, which, according to the programme, will not be finished until 1930.

THE POLISH ARMY

In addition to the wharfage, railway lines, water pumps, naval barracks (now ready), a lighthouse, and minor works are being carried out.

7. Naval Expenditure.

The budget for 1927-28 contains a provision of zloty 10,994,928, or about £250,000, for the current expenses of the Navy, which does not include purchase of new ships, or expenditure on Gdynia.

APPENDIX TO CHAPTER XXIX.
LIST OF SHIPS OF THE POLISH NAVY.

Name.	Type.	Tonnage.	Draught. ft.	in.
"Desaix"	Cruiser (old)	—	—	—
"Wichr"	Destroyer	1,545	—	—
"Burza"	Destroyer	1,545	—	—
"Komendant Piłsudski"	Gunboat	342	9	6
"General Haller"	Gunboat	342	9	6
"Mazur"	T.B.	415	8	4
"Kujawiak"	T.B.	335	7	8
"Krakowiak"	T.B.	365	7	4
"Ślązak"	T.B.	365	7	4
"Podhalanin"	T.B.	365	7	4
"Jaskolka"	Trawlers	196	4	8
"Mewa"	Trawlers	196	4	8
"Czajka"	Trawlers	196	4	8
"Rybitwa"	Trawlers	196	4	8
"Krakus"	Auxiliaries	55	5	8
"Wanda"	Auxiliaries	55	5	8
"Warszawa"	Monitors	125	2	6
"Horodyszcze"	Monitors	125	2	6
"Pinsk"	Monitors	125	2	6
"Mozyrz"	Monitors	125	2	6
"General Sosnkowski"	River gunboats	200	2	8
"Hetman Chodkiewicz"	River gunboats	110	2	4
"Admiral Dickman"	River gunboats	100	2	0
"General Szeptycki"	River gunboats	100	2	0
"Admiral Sierpinek"	River gunboats	65	1	8
"General Sikorski"	River gunboats	35	1	4
"Wilno"	River motor gunboats	70	1	4
"Krakow"	River motor gunboats	70	1	4
"Stefan Batory"	Auxiliaries	—	—	—
"Hetman Zolkiewski"	Auxiliaries	—	—	—
"Neptun"	Auxiliaries	13	2	0
"Linc" type—5 motor boats	—	7	1	4
"Pra Ga" type—10 motor boats	—	5-12	—	—
Various—10 motor boats	—	—	—	—

APPENDIX I.
TACTICS AND DRILL.

General Remarks.

The fundamental principles on which the instruction of the Polish Army are based are those in force in the French Army. Thus, though Polish field service manuals deal mainly with a war of movement, position warfare being referred to as a secondary possibility, the principles enunciated in the manuals are generally applied, in tactical schemes and war games, to troops engaged in the latter. With this teaching, which is enforced by the French Military Mission, many senior officers of the Polish Army are dissatisfied, though at present they are unable to change it. It does not take into account the peculiar conditions of Poland's geographical characteristics, namely, a vast country consisting of a broad, flat plain, with no natural boundaries, covered with patches of forest varying from small copses to extensive woods, between which the ground is quite open, offering no obstacles to movement and very few to view. Only in the south mountains and, in the east marshes, alter the general character of the country.

In drill, the same French influence appears to misunderstand the Polish character. While with the French soldier, it may be desirable to relax the outer aspects of discipline, allow him to dress as he pleases, criticise his orders, and carry out his movements in what seems to be a somewhat disorderly manner, yet the Polish character needs stricter outward signs. Consequently, the modified parade-schritt which is used on ceremonial parades everywhere in Poland, and becomes almost Prussian in Poznania, is looked upon with disfavour by the French, who also decry the time spent in manual exercises with the rifle, though these undoubtedly result in smartening up the rather lumpish Polish recruit.

Infantry Training.

The training of the infantryman is based on the "drużyna," or *groupe de combat*, consisting of 13 men, namely, a commander, a rifle section and a light machine gun section.

As yet the necessary training manuals have not been fully issued, those that are in circulation deal only with the individual training of the soldier in musketry, bayonet fighting, bombing and machine gunnery. No manuals dealing with the employment of infantry in war have been published yet, with the exception of Field Service Regulations, dealing with combined action of all arms.

Cavalry Training.

Cavalry tactics are based on the platoon (troop), which consists of three sabre sections and one light machine gun section.

Here again, cavalry training which has been issued deals almost entirely with the training of the unit, only a few pages being devoted to the use of cavalry in action.

Artillery Training.

Training manuals for artillery are inadequate. So far, handbooks describing the gun drill for the different natures of guns have been issued, and instructions for opening fire and ranging. A provisional handbook on the general employment of artillery in war has also been issued, but instructions for selection of positions, getting into action, observation and control of fire, and the technical employment of the various natures of shell and of fire are not, as yet, issued.

Other Arms.

In general, handbooks dealing with technical subjects have been published, such as various signalling instruments, engineer equipment, gas masks, the construction of aeroplanes and so forth, but instructions dealing with the use of them in war are absent. Consequently, there are no Signal Training, Tank Training, Aviation Field Service Regulations and so forth, except one or two very short provisional pamphlets.

Tactical Doctrine—Preliminary considerations.

Battle is the getting of the mastery over the enemy's freedom, and to obtain victory there must be a firm determination to conquer. The final victor is not he who has less casualties or greater booty, but he whose will is strongest, whose moral strength is greatest.

THE POLISH ARMY

The object of all fighting, offensive or defensive, is to destroy the enemy, therefore the object of each unit must be to cause the enemy the greatest losses. Careful preparation gives the best chances of success, and operations must be carried out according to the plan prepared by the commander, which must state the task to be accomplished, the plan of the commander, the arrangements to carry it out, and explanations facilitating its execution.

Units should be grouped in depth, thus giving the possibility of retaining fresh reserves to the very end, though this must not be a reason for failing to use them at the decisive moment. Every effort should be made to attain surprise.

Proper communications must be assured on all occasions, it being the duty of superiors to maintain contact with inferiors; while the responsibility of keeping contact with the neighbouring unit or formation is laid on both of them. Personal contact should be frequent. While the responsibility and the general supervision of communications is laid on the commanders and the chief staff officers, the technical execution of the plan is the duty of the chiefs of communication, and, in smaller units, the signalling officer.

Every commander conducting an operation must be supplied with, and obtain the necessary information on which to base his plan of operations; he is also responsible for the immediate security of the troops under his orders at all times, whether at rest or on the move, and for taking measures to ensure their freedom of action.

Advanced, Flank or Rear Guards.

The occasions when cavalry alone are necessary as advanced guard are rare; normally the advanced (flank or rear) guards should be composed of all arms, but the principal component should be infantry. In all cases a detachment of cavalry should be added for patrol work. Artillery, sappers, and other arms should be added when they are required, and if they are sufficiently protected. No more troops should be used than are absolutely necessary to ensure efficient protection.

In the approach march, each column sends out an advanced guard of all arms. The infantry should be from one-sixth to one-third of the total in the column. If cavalry are available they may be sent out as an independent covering and reconnoitring force. Machine guns, guns, armoured cars and cyclists may be included; if guns are kept with the main body, artillery reconnaissance detachments should accompany the advanced guard, and the guns should be close to the head of the main body.

The advanced guard divides itself into main guard (oddział główny), vanguard (oddział przedni) and point (szpica). The first-named includes the mass of the infantry and the guns; the vanguard, the cavalry, a detachment of infantry and sappers, if required; the vanguard puts out its cavalry, with a small supporting infantry detachment as point. The advanced guard commander should accompany the point or vanguard, the commander of the whole column the main guard. The advanced guard should be at such a distance in front as to protect the main body from being delayed, from being surprised by artillery fire, but not so far that the main body cannot support it in action; the distance should always be laid down by the column commander.

When the situation on the flank is such that the column cannot be protected by flank patrols, flank guards must be sent out, which vary in composition and size according to the possibility of attack from a flank. If possible, they march on a parallel road on the flank, but if such roads are absent, or if danger only exists at certain points, stationary flank guards may be used which remain in position till the danger is past and then rejoin the column.

In a retirement, the duty of a rearguard is to separate the main body from the enemy and to safeguard it from attack. Its formation is like that of an advanced guard, but it must have strong artillery support and be in constant touch with the commander of the main body. It moves, if possible, in line of march, unless the action of the enemy obliges it to move in battle order. It moves by bounds from position to position and attempts to delay the enemy by holding defiles, destroying bridges, making obstacles and forcing him to deploy.

Advanced Guard to Independent Cavalry.

Independent cavalry protects itself in a similar manner by sending out an advanced guard. But in front of the point of this, it is laid down that three reconnaissances should be sent out, one along the line of march some 6-8 kilometres in front of the point of the advanced guard, and the others to the right and left. The point, in open country, may be reduced to some six cavalrymen under an officer, in closer country it must be stronger so that the officer in command can send out patrols, of two men each, to search the country. These patrols are called "szperaczy" (searchers). The point moves by bounds, when the searchers report the ground in front to be clear. The commander of the point should never lose sight of the searchers and should have a series of arranged signals with them.

Outposts (Czaty).

Depending on the situation, outposts may be put out independently by each body of troops, or the protection of the whole may be secured by outpost troops under one command, or by sending out protective detachments.

The object of outposts is to prevent the enemy from discovering the dispositions of the main body, either from the ground or from the air, to protect it from disturbance, and, in case of attack, to resist sufficiently to give it freedom to deploy and manœuvre.

Cavalry cover the operation of putting out outposts and by day reconnoitre in front of them. Infantry form the principal body of outposts, using their fire, including machine guns, mortars and infantry guns, to hold points whose possession is necessary for the protection of the main body. Artillery can be used, not only to assist in the defence of these points, but to fire on bridges, defiles, etc., and to co-operate in beating off aeroplanes, tanks, armoured cars and armoured trains. Technical troops are added to outposts for strengthening and constructing positions. No more troops should be used than are necessary to ensure efficient protection.

Outposts should be put on roads leading towards the enemy and on points from which the enemy could observe the outpost disposition. They should be concealed from the enemy and always ready to resist attack. The commander decides the degree of readiness. As a rule pickets, outposts and outpost reserves should not pitch tents, take off equipment (except packs), but they may cover themselves with tent sections, except the head. The two former may not light fires or smoke. Pickets never let their rifles out of their hands. Outpost troops do not pay salutes, nor sound trumpets or drums.

The position of main outposts is selected with a view to defence, that of pickets for observation. The outpost line is divided into sections. In close country it is best to put outposts at road junctions. In mountainous country a light chain of outposts is the best and as the terrain imposes on the troops the necessity of operating in small columns, each must assure its own protection.

When night comes during a battle, troops in the front lines are responsible for putting out battle outposts, without waiting for orders, bivouacing on the ground they hold, putting out pickets in the foreground and patrolling constantly.

As a rule a company of infantry forms the main outpost (czaty główne) and occupies a position on the main line of resistance. Its machine guns are so situated as to cover approaches, if possible with enfilading fire. One platoon is always kept on the alert on the defensive position. This company puts out pickets (placówka), whose main duty is observation and warning, in positions which constitute a first line of resistance. Such pickets may be one or more *groupes de combat*, rarely a whole platoon. Important ones are under an officer. They should be given light machine gun, rifle grenades and signalling equipment. These pickets put out sentry groups (czujki), normally of two men, relieved every one or two hours.

Long distance patrols, cavalry, supported by infantry (the latter up to 1-3 kilometres) are sent out by the outpost commander. Patrols from pickets are sent out by the picket commander under the direction of the outpost company commander.

At night, the greater part of the cavalry (divisional cavalry that has covered the outposts during the day) is withdrawn to reserve, except for a small number reduced to a minimum, of outpost cavalry. The duties of protection devolve on the infantry, who must exercise greater alertness, and, by listening posts and greater frequency of patrolling, ensure security.

The Battle.

The division is the basic unit of tactical operations and is able to act alone and to carry all military operations to a finish. It generally acts as part of an army, in its defined sector of operations. This sector may be broad with a feeble enemy. It must not be confounded with the battle front on which it fights, which, against a well organized enemy is not to be greater than 4 kilometres in the offence and 5-7 kilometres in defence, but in position warfare this may be reduced to 2 kilometres in attack, or in defence extended to 10-12 kilometres.

THE POLISH ARMY

The sector of operations is much less clearly defined; when armies are in contact, the sector of a formation may be reduced almost to the width of its battle front. On the other hand, if a division is engaged on a flanking operation, both the sector of operations and the battle front may be greatly increased, the former in specially favourable circumstances even to 40–50 kilometres.

In its sector, a division engages in one or more actions, that is to say, detachments allotted to a fight take up a battle front corresponding to their strength, the intervening spaces being merely lightly covered; but the commander remains responsible for the whole of his sector.

Infantry acts by fire and movement, but movement, inspired by the will to come to close quarters, can alone obtain success. It is an indispensible condition to co-operate closely with tanks and artillery. Except in cases where the enemy is not in a prepared position and his artillery is not yet in action, the attack should be carried out steadily and methodically without impatience. Infantry gets exhausted, physically and morally, quicker than other arms, therefore it must be spared useless fatigue and losses. In a stubborn battle losses are heavy and the conditions hard, therefore efforts must be made to relieve exhausted troops in good time, by disposing troops in depth, ready to relieve one another.

Artillery must act in close co-operation with other arms, especially with infantry, and must rely on them for protection.

Cavalry acts by its swiftness of movement, but must be able to fight on foot. It acts mounted against hostile cavalry who accept such fighting, against demoralized, or exhausted, or surprised infantry and against artillery in action from the flank or rear, or on the march. Cavalry is easily annihilated, and takes a long time to create, therefore it must not be wasted. Its chief task is to obtain information and to maintain touch.

Aviation's principal task is observation and liaison between neighbouring formations, between different arms, especially between infantry and artillery, and between commanders and their subordinates, but if the army is richly endowed with aeroplanes, they may be used for destroying the enemy, principally by firing on important points, and those lying out of range of artillery fire, or against infantry and guns in action. If the number of aeroplanes is very great, pursuit and bombardment units may be used to seek out and destroy the enemy's air forces.

The task of tanks is to destroy the enemy's technical installations and troops by sudden attack at short range, always in closest touch with advancing infantry. In order to ensure this, tank units are always to be under the command of the infantry commander. They are particularly susceptible to artillery fire, therefore their own artillery must be able to protect them by keeping down the enemy's gunfire. Where the enemy is situated in a terrain with a number of good observation points, tanks should not be used.

To counter the effect of enemy tanks, special defensive arrangements are necessary, such as machine guns firing armour-piercing bullets, single guns carefully located, or massed artillery fire. Anti-tank defensive measures must be carefully concealed from observation, especially from the air. Infantry must be trained not to panic when hostile tanks arrive, remembering that the field of view of a tank crew is very limited and therefore that they can easily escape their notice while the tanks pass, and be ready to attack the following infantry. To flee from tanks is fatal.

The commanders of tank platoons lead their platoons into action and are directly under the orders of the unit (battalion) with which they are co-operating. Commanders of tank companies are directly under the regiment or brigade to which they are allotted, remain with their commanders as technical advisers, and are responsible for the supply of petrol and ammunition, and for relief by fresh tanks, for which purpose they should keep a few in reserve. Their tactical duties end when they have allotted platoons to battalions. Tank regimental commanders' duties are analogous.

The Attack, or Encounter Battle.

Every unit, detailed for attack, must act as though it was making the decisive attack.

The attack is envisaged in three phases. The first phase consists in bringing the division to close touch with the enemy and to a position from which the main attack is delivered (approach march), during which further information is supplied to the commander on which to base his plan of attack, and in which enemy covering troops are driven in. Aviation is useful, not only to obtain information about the enemy but to keep the commander informed of the situation of his own advanced troops, and to observe artillery fire. The leading infantry occupies ground to permit of the coming into action of its own artillery and of the development of the main attacking troops. The commander of the division is well to the front, with his staff, controlling the situation, as it is the last occasion on which he will be able to control his whole force.

The second phase is the development of the attack by the whole force. A frontal attack is simplest and may give decisive results, but requires superiority of modern technical weapons. Flank attacks, combined or not with a frontal attack, give excellent results, but often the enemy retires without waiting for the fight. The commander must not expect to have complete information during the approach march and must make his dispositions based on such information as he has been able to get, or he will lose the initiative. He divides his forces into attacking troops and reserve (if necessary also troops on a defensive sector) and regulates the progress of the attack by defining a number of successive objectives to be reached. The final main objective is the line of the hostile field artillery.

A battalion in attack deploys on a front of from 500 to 1,000 metres, with a continuous front swept by the fire of infantry guns and machine guns. If the advance is over 2,000 metres a second battalion must be used to form a fresh wave, and over 4,000 metres a third (from the reserve) each fresh wave passing beyond the first further forward. In the attack on a prepared defensive system the battle front of a battalion must be reduced to 300–400 metres, and its limit of advance to 1,500.

Artillery is used for immediate infantry support, counter battery work, and on occasions for preparatory bombardment or firing on enemy communications. The allotment of guns to infantry is either reinforced, *i.e.*, one group (three batteries) to each battalion attacking in front line, or medium, *i.e.*, one group to two battalions, or weak, *i.e.*, one group to three or more battalions. These groups remain, in principle, under the control of the divisional artillery commander. Exceptionally, when an attacking detachment is operating outside the area in which the divisional artillery is situated, then a group may be placed under the direct orders of the infantry commander. For calculating guns required for counter battery work, it is reckoned that half a battery can silence one hostile battery provided the preliminary operations have shown superiority in artillery.

If tanks are used, the normal proportion is one platoon of tanks to one battalion of infantry, and each successive battalion must be accompanied by a fresh platoon. A division should therefore have one tank battalion allotted to it.

Aviation is allotted to armies, or if there is an intermediate formation between armies and divisions, then to that formation. The number of co-operation squadrons in an army corresponds to the number of divisions. The commander of the aviation must ensure continuity in carrying out his task, namely, making reconnaissances, control of fire, and co-operation with infantry. If his machines are too few, he must allot their tasks so that during the artillery preparation they are at the disposal of the guns, and during the infantry attack they are used with the infantry.

The foundation of the attack is the forward movement of the infantry and all other arms must contribute to facilitate this. The infantry moves forward as far as possible before opening fire itself, and when further movement is impossible, the *groupes de combat* commence the combined action of fire and movement.

The final phase is the assault, and the manner in which this is carried out depends on circumstances, and on the difficulties encountered in arriving at assault distance. This distance may be reckoned at about 300 metres, being the distance which compels supporting artillery to lengthen their range in order to avoid causing losses to their own infantry. If it is possible the assault should be made by whole battalions, which necessitates holding up the general forward movement until a given signal; or till a given moment, when the artillery lengthens its range and the infantry assaults. Often, however, the signal for the assault is given by the leading *groupes de combat*, energetically led, who find and exploit a weak spot, and carry their neighbouring *groupes* with them. This moment should be used by the aviation for bombing or machine gunning enemy infantry and reinforcing troops. The captured position should be at once strengthened, fire directed on the retreating enemy, and pursuit arranged.

The Pursuit.

The pursuit must be constant and energetic, if the enemy has lost a rallying point, it can afford to neglect tactical liaison, and in this case cavalry, supported by armoured cars and trains, will reap great success. In modern battles it is, however, difficult to say when the enemy is completely exhausted, and modern weapons give him such fire power from small detachments that the pursuit must be generally carried out by all arms, preferably by fresh troops, in close tactical liaison and ready to fight at any moment. As the enemy will try and fall back by night, the pursuit must keep close contact even by night to prevent him falling back unmolested.

Pursuing troops must be given lines of pursuit, not tactical objectives. They must press on, leaving rallying points to be dealt with by troops following after.

THE POLISH ARMY

The Defence.

Passive defence is fatal. Every defence must try to destroy the enemy's forces, either by an eventual counter-offensive with reserves, or by exhausting him in repeated attacks. No commander must be content to beat off an attack, but must make the attacker pay for it by counter-attack at favourable moments.

The defence can either be to gain time or a suitable opportunity for counter-attack, or it may be the determined defence of a position which it is required to prevent falling into the enemy's hands.

In principle the defence is organized along a single line, the main line of resistance, but in order to hold this line troops are disposed in depth so as to cover it in front, and to find suitable positions for reserves. This covering position should prevent observation by the enemy of the main line, and should compel him to adopt fresh grouping of his artillery before proceeding to attack the latter. But troops in the covering position should never be drawn into decisive action, therefore they should never be reinforced from the main line, but gradually fall back on it. To enable reserves to deploy for counter attack under favourable conditions, a line of reserves should be formed, behind which they are placed either in one mass or in groups.

A divisional defence area forms a sector, divided into sub-sectors for regiments. Each defensive line consists of a number of centres of resistance, organized in depth, and which cover by their fire the intervening ground. These are the framework of the defensive position and each is generally garrisoned by a battalion, working in close touch with a named artillery detachment. Each centre of resistance is composed of a number of points of resistance, the garrison of each of which is normally a company. It must be organized so that the various *groupes de combat* can bring flanking fire on to the ground in front and mutually support each other, and should have its own reserve.

A centre of resistance of a battalion can hold a front of 1,000 to 1,500 metres, and the same depth, and should be about the same interval from the next one to the flank. If the interval between them is not properly covered by fire, stronger reserves are necessary.

Artillery should also be stationed in depth and should not be in front of the line of reserves. This involves long range fire to support the covering position.

A defensive position should be selected by means of the map and by personal reconnaissance. First of all the centres of resistance are chosen, taking into consideration the object to be defended and the ground in front over which the enemy will come. The organization of the centre rests with the troops who will occupy it. Anti-tank defence needs special consideration, involving the selection of natural and artificial obstacles, machine guns firing armour-piercing bullets, single guns firing at close range (1,500 metres) and the mass of artillery.

If the enemy succeed in getting a footing in the defensive line, the divisional commander will deliver an immediate counter-attack with his reserves and artillery, assisted by tanks.

The Retreat.

To withdraw troops from contact with the enemy by day will cause heavy losses and perhaps complete disorganization, therefore such a withdrawal must be carried out at dusk or at night. Covering troops must intensify their fire in order to deceive and delay the enemy, and must be ready to sacrifice themselves to ensure the safety of the main body.

If the retirement is over a considerable distance, it should be covered by properly constituted rearguards under energetic officers.

No troops should withdraw from one position to another without orders from higher authority.

Wood Fighting.

Troops approaching the enemy through a forest should move in small compact bodies, at such intervals as to be able to deploy quickly and open fire. All units are responsible for their own local protection. Rifles should be carried loaded and bayonets fixed. Reserves should follow in echelon, protecting flanks and rear.

Communication must be maintained without interruption and direction should be kept by means of the compass or by the help of reliable guides. Clearings parallel to the front should be used to regulate the forward movement.

The characteristic of wood fighting is short, sharp bursts of fire and energetic attack with the bayonet.

A defensive line should not be selected at the edge of a wood.

Fighting in Villages.

This type of action resolves itself into a series of combats for individual buildings. As the unexpected appearance of armoured cars may cause heavy losses, good observation and communication should help to beat off enemy armoured cars.

The irregular nature of the front after a village is captured renders it very liable to counter-attack, for this reason intercommunication should be re-established at the earliest moment.

Night Fighting.

Night fighting gives the advantages of surprise and tends to reduce casualties, but its disadvantage is the difficulty of intercommunication. Night operations, therefore, should be carefully prepared and be simple to carry out.

Night attacks should be made early in the night if they are merely the continuation of the previous day's fighting, or if it is required to prepare the ground captured for defence before daybreak, or if the enemy is in retreat. They should be made just before the daylight if it is desired to exploit the success.

The success of night operations depends essentially on surprise, therefore all preliminaries which would warn the enemy of its preparation must be avoided. Troops must get all available information about the ground, each unit should have its objective carefully defined, and communication between infantry and artillery should be carefully regulated.

Night operations begin with the march out of troops to a position of " departure " (forming up place) from where, at a given signal, at a given time, the attack is launched.

A high degree of readiness and good methods of taking up positions in the event of a night alarm, are the best guarantee of a successful defence against night attacks. If the enemy succeeds in getting a footing in the line, a counter-attack must be made at once, the arrangements for which must have been thought out before and carefully prepared.

APPENDIX II.

GLOSSARY OF MILITARY TERMS.

1. The Polish Orthography.

The Polish alphabet contains all the letters in use in the English alphabet except q, v, x and y; (x and y are used in one or two special words).

On the other hand it has two additional nasalised vowels, ą and ę, pronounced like the French " on " and " in " respectively ; and places diacritical marks on several consonants, altering their pronunciation. J is a semi-vowel pronounced like our y. The vowels are pronounced as in German, that is to say, u is pronounced " oo " and not like the French u, the accentuated ó is pronounced like a short u, as in the English word " bull."

The consonants have two forms, hard and soft. In all cases except l, the simple consonant is the hard form, and the soft form is made from the hard form in various ways. The vowel i can only follow a soft consonant, others can follow either. The consonants, with their hard and soft variations, are :—

Hard.	Soft.	Hard.	Soft.
b*	bi	m*	mi
c	ć, cz	n*	ni (ń)
d*	dz	p*	pi
f*	fi	r*	rz
g*	gi	s*	ś, sz
h*	hi	t*	ć
k*	ki	w	wi
ł	l	z	ż, ź

Those marked * are pronounced as in English, the g being always hard as in " go."

The pronunciation of the soft consonants whose soft form is formed by i is the same as of the corresponding hard consonant, except that the sound like an English y follows the consonant sound, e.g., " pies " (a dog) is a monosyllable pronounced " pyess."

When an i follows a soft letter that would obviously carry an accent to mark its softness, the accent is left out, as the fact that the i follows is sufficient to show that the preceding letter is soft, e.g., siła, strength.

The softening of the other consonants alters their pronunciation as follows :—

Hard.	Soft.
c—ts	cz—tsh (ch as in " church ").
	ć is between c and cz.
d—d	dz—dj.

Soft l is pronounced close to the teeth and is like the French l, or the l in the English word "leave." Hard ł is pronounced in the throat and resembles the l in the English words " kill " or " lion." It is often said that it is pronounced like an English w, but this is not quite correct ; it has a sound rather between w and the consonantal y. The difference between the two, ł and l, is clear if we take the case of an English word with a hard l, such as " kill " or " Lyallpur," which phonetically are pronounced as near as can be expressed like " kiy " and " Yayypur," but the Eurasian, speaking Chee-chee, cannot pronounce these hard l's, and says " kill'i " and " L'iyall'ipur." The Polish names Piłsudski, Łos, and Łódz, are pronounced more like " Piyusudski," " Wash," " and " Woodj."

Hard.	Soft.
n—n	ni (ń)—French gn in " Boulogne."
r—r	rz—zh, or j as in French " jour,"

the r ceasing to be sounded, *e.g.*, przemysł (trade)—" pzhemys'w," while the town Przemysl (with soft l) is pronounced " Pzhemysl'i."

s—s	sz—sh.
	ś is halfway between s and sz.
t—t	ć is halfway between c and cz, q.v.
w—v	wi—vy.
z—z as in zebra. }	ż—j as in French " jour."
	ź is halfway between z and ż.
	Note.—ż is often written ʒ.

These soft and hard forms exist in Russian just as much as in Polish, the only difference being that they are not marked in writing, and this makes the difficulty in transliteration; *e.g.*, the Commander-in-Chief of the Red Army is Kameneff, so spelt in Russia, but as the m and the n are soft, in Polish it becomes " Kamieniew." So the fortress of Brest becomes in Polish " Brześć," as in Russian the r is followed by a soft vowel and the t by a soft sign.

2. Glossary of Military Terms.

In the following glossary substantives are given in the nominative singular except that when the singular is not used the nominative plural is given. Adjectives standing alone are given in the nominative masculine singular and, when with substantives, are in agreement with them. Verbs are given in the infinitive.

In the second column, which represents attempts to give the true pronunciation by means of English values for letters, the letters should be pronounced exactly as in English, with the following remarks :—

    ai is as the long i in " time."
    g is always hard as in " gun."
    i is as the short i in " tin."
    kh represents the sound of ch as in " loch."
    l is always liquid.
    y is always consonantal as in " yacht," even when it follows a consonant, so that the Polish word " koń " transliterated as " kony " is a monosyllable rhyming with the French town Boulogne.
    zh represents the sound of j in the French " jour."
    z is as in " zebra."

The accent is, without exception, on the penultimate syllable.

Amunicja	Amooneetsya	Ammunition.
Areszt	Aresht	Detention.
Armata	Armata	Gun.
Armja	Armya	Army.
Artylerja	Artilerya	Artillery.
Artylerja ciężka	Artilerya tchyenzhka	Heavy artillery.

Artylerja konna	Artilerya konna	Horse artillery.
Artylerja polowa	Artilerya polova	Field artillery.
Artylerja zenitowa	Artilerya zenitova	A.A. artillery.
Atak	Atak	Attack.
Atakować	Atakovatch	To attack.
Azot	Azot	Nitrogen.
Bagnet	Bagnet	Bayonet.
Baon	Baon	Battalion.
Balon	Balon	Balloon
Balon uwięźny	Balon oovyenzhni	Captive balloon.
Bataljon	Batalyon	Battalion.
Baterja	Baterya	Battery.
Bęben	Bemben	Drum.
Bezdymny	Bezdimni	Smokeless.
Bezpieczeństwo	Bezpyechenstvo	Safety.
Bezpośredni	Bezposhredni	Immediate, direct.
Biedka	Byedka	Cart.
Biskup polowy	Biscoop polovi	Chaplain General.
Bitwa	Beetva	Battle.
Biwak	Beevak	Bivouac.
Błoto	Bwoto	Marsh.
Boczny	Botchni	Flank, side (adj.).
Bok	Bok	Flank, side.
Bomba	Bomba	Bomb.
Broń (palna)	Brony (palna)	Arm of the service, armament, weapon (firearm).
Bronić	Bronitch	Defend.
Brzeg	Bzheg	Bank (of a river).
Budynek	Boodeenek	Building.
Cel	Tsel	Target.
Celować	Tselovatch	To aim.
Celowniczy	Tselovneetchi	Layer.
Celownik	Tselovnik	Range, back sight.
Chorągiew	Khorongyev	Flag.
Chorąży	Khoronzhi	Ensign.
Ciężki	Tchyenzhki	Heavy.
Cofnąć (się)	Tsofnontch (she'n)	To retreat.
Ćwiczebny	Tchveetchebni	For drill, training (adj.).
Ćwiczenie	Tchveetchenie	Exercise, drill, training.
Czaty	Tchati	Outposts.
Czołg	Tcho-w-g	Tank.
Czołowy	Tchowovi	Leading, in front.
Daleki	Daleki	Distant.
Dalekonośny	Dalekonoshni	Long range.
Defilada	Defilada	March past.
Dobosz	Dobosh	Drummer.
Dowódca	Dovudtsa	Commander (the usual word).
Dowództwo	Dovudstvo	Headquarters.
Droga	Droga	Road.
Drut (kołczasty)	Droot (ko-w-tchasti)	Wire (barbed).
Dwukolka	Dvookolka	Cart (two-wheeled).
Dym	Dim	Smoke.
Dyszel	Dishel	Pole.
Dywizja	Divizya	Division (of all arms).
Dywizjon	Divizyon	Division = 2 squadrons.
Działo	Dzhyawo	Gun.

THE POLISH ARMY

Emeryt	Emerit	Pensioner.
Etat, etatowy	Etat, etatovi	Establishment (subs. and adj.).
Ewidencja	Evidentsya	List, register.

F.

Garłacz	Garwatch	Rifle grenade attachment.
Gaz	Gaz	Gas.
Generał	Generaw	General.
Gołąb pocztowy	Gowomb potchtovi	Carrier pigeon.
Goniec	Gonyetz	Messenger, orderly.
Górski	Gurski	Mountain (adj.).
Grajek	Graiyek	Bandsman.
Granat	Granat	Explosive shell (contrasted with shrapnel).
Granat karabinowy	Granat karabinovi	Rifle grenade.
Granat ręczny	Granat rentchni	Hand grenade.
Granica	Graneetsa	Frontier.
Grenadjer	Grenadyer	Bomber.
Hamulec	Hamoolets	Brake.
Haubica	Howbeetsa	Howitzer.
Intendantura	Intendantoora	Intendance service.
Inżynier	Inzhinyer	Engineer.
Inżynierja	Inzhinyerya	Engineers.
Jaszcz	Yashtch	Ammunition wagon body.
Jazda	Yazda	(1) Cavalry. (2) Riding, journey (on horseback).
Jenerał	Yeneraw	General.
Jeniec	Yeniets	Prisoner.
Jezdny	Yezdni	Driver (of horses).
Kadra	Kadra	Cadre.
Kapela	Kapela	Band.
Kapelmistrz	Kapelmistsh	Bandmaster.
Kapral	Kapral	Corporal.
Karabin	Karabin	Rifle.
Karabin maszynowy	Karabin mashinovi	Machine gun.
Karabinek	Karabeenek	Carbine.
Kara	Kara	Punishment.
Kąt	Kont	Angle.
Kątomierz	Kontomyezh	Goniometer.
Kawalerja	Kavalerya	Cavalry.
Kierownik	Kyerovnik	Director (personal).
Kierunek	Kyeroonek	Direction.
Koło	Kowo	Wheel.
Kołyszka	Kowishka	Cradle (of gun).
Komenda	Komenda	(1) Order. (2) Commandantur.
Koń	Kony	Horse.
Koń dyszlowy	Kony dishlovi	Wheel horse.
Koń juczny	Kony jootchni	Pack horse.
Koń wierzchowy	Kony vyezhkhovi	Riding horse.

Koń zaprzęgowy or pociągowy	Kony zapzhengovi or potsiongovi.	Draught horse.
Konwoj	Konvoy	Convoy.
Krok	Krok	Step, pace.
Kucharz	Kookhazh	Cook.
Kuchnia polowa	Kookhnya polova	Field kitchen.
Kula	Koola	Bullet.
Kuźnia	Koozhnya	Forge.
Kwatery	Kvateri	Billets.
Kwatermistrz	Kvatermistsh	Quartermaster (officer in charge of administration in regiment).
Krawiec	Kravyets	Tailor.
Lotnictwo	Lotneetstvo	Aviation.
Lotniczy	Lotneetchi	Aviation (adj.).
Lotnik	Lotneek	Aviator.
Lotnisko	Lotneesko	Aerodrome.
Lufa	Loofa	Barrel (of a gun or rifle).
Łączność	Wontchnoshtch	Liaison, contact.
Ładować	Wadovatch	Load.
Ładunek	Wadoonek	Bursting charge (of shell) also cartridge.
Łódź, podwodna	Woodj, podvodna	Boat, submarine.
Łopata	Wopata	Spade.
Magazynierz	Magazinyezh	Storeman.
Mapa	Mapa	Map.
Marsz	Marsh	Quick march.
Marszałek	Marshawek	Field-Marshal.
Marynarka	Marinarka	(1) Navy. (2) Field service jacket.
Maska przeciwgazowa	Maska pshetcheevgazova	Anti-gas mask.
Meldować	Meldovatch	To report.
Meldunek	Meldoonek	Report (in the field).
Miecz	Myetch	Sword.
Miotacz min	Myotatch meen	Minenwerfer.
Mobilizacja	Mobilizatsya	Mobilization.
Most	Most	Bridge.
Moździeż	Mozhdzhyezh	Mortar.
Munsztuk	Moonshtook	Bit (of a bridle).
Muzyka	Moozika	Band.
Naboj	Naboy	Round (of ammunition).
Naczelnik	Natchelnik	Commander, head, chief.
Napad	Napad	Attack (subs.).
Napad gazowy	Napad gazovi	Gas attack.
Nalewo	Nalevo	To the left.
Naprawo	Naprahvo	To the right.
Narzędzie	Narzhendzhye	Tools.
Natarcie	Natartshye	Attack (subs.).
Niepodległość	Nyepodlegwoshtch	Independence.
Nieprzyjaciel	Nyepshiyatchyel	Enemy.
Niewola	Nyevola	Captivity.
Niszczyć	Neeshtchitch	Destroy.
Niższy	Neezhshi	Inferior.

THE POLISH ARMY

Oblegać	Oblegatch	Besiege.
Oblężenie	Oblenzhenye	Siege.
Obrona	Obrona	Defence.
Obsadzić	Obsadzhitch	Occupy.
Obszar	Obshar	Area.
Obsługa	Obswooga	Crew, gun detachment.
Obuwie	Oboovye	Boots.
Ochotnik	Okhotnik	Volunteer.
Odbić	Odbeetch	Beat off, repulse.
Odciąć	Odtchyontch	Cut off.
Odćinek	Odtcheenek	Sector.
Oddział	Oddziaw	Detachment, section.
Odległość	Odlegwoshtch	Distance, range.
Odrzut	Odzhoot	Recoil.
Odwód	Odvood	Reserve.
Odznaka	Odznaka	Badge.
Oficer	Ofeetser	Officer.
Oficer sztabowy	Ofeetser shtabovi	Field (not staff) officer.
Oficer sztabu (generalnego)	Ofeetser shtaboo (generalnego)	Staff officer.
Ogień	Ogyeny	Fire.
Ogniomistrz	Ognyomistsh	Serjeant-major (artillery).
Ogólny	Ogulni	General.
Okop	Okop	Entrenchment.
Opor	Opor	Resistance.
Oporo-powrotnik	Oporo-povrotnik	Recoil buffer and springs.
Ordynans	Ordinans	Batman.
Oś	Osh	Axle.
Osłona	Oswona	Protection, covering.
Otworzyć	Otvozhitch	Open: a door, fire.
Palić	Paleetch	Burn.
Pancerny	Pantserni	Armoured.
Pas	Pass	Belt.
Patrol	Patrol	Patrol.
Pieszy	Pyeshi	On foot, dismounted.
Pika	Peeka	Lance.
Pionier	Pyonyer	Pioneer.
Pionowy	Pyonovi	Vertical.
Piorunujący	Pyoroonooyontsi	Fulminating, detonating.
Placówka	Platsoovka	Picquet.
Pluton	Plooton	Platoon, troop.
Plutonowy	Plootonovi	Serjeant.
Płaszcz	Pwashtch	Greatcoat.
Płatnik	Pwatnik	Paymaster.
Płatowiec	Pwatovyets	Aeroplane.
Pociąg	Potshyong	Train (railway).
Pocisk	Potchisk	Shell.
Poddać się	Poddatch she'n	To surrender (one's self).
Podkuć	Podkootch	To shoe (a horse).
Podkuwacz	Podkoovatch	Shoeing smith.
Podlegać	Podlegatch	Be under the orders of.
Podległy	Podlegwi	Subordinate to.
Podoficer	Podofeetser	Non-commissioned officer.
Podporucznik	Podporootchnik	Second Lieutenant.
Podpułkownik	Podpoowkovnik	Lieutenant-Colonel.
Podsłuchowy	Podswookhovi	Listening, sound-ranging (adj.).
Pokój	Pokooy	Peace.
Położenie	Powozhenye	Situation, position.

Porucznik	Porootchnik	Lieutenant.
Porządek	Pozhondek	Order, arrangement.
Pościg	Poshtchig	Pursuit.
Powódz	Povudj	Inundation.
Powstanie	Povstanye	Insurrection.
Poziomy	Pozyomi	Horizontal.
Pozycja	Pozeetsya	Position.
Prawy	Pravi	Right.
Proch	Prokh	Powder.
Przodek	Pshodek	Limber.
Przeciwlotniczy	Pshetcheevlotneetchi	Anti-aircraft (adj.).
Przeciwnik	Pshetcheevnik	Enemy.
Przedmoście	Pshedmoshtchye	Bridgehead.
Przepis	Pshepees	Order, instruction.
Przerwa	Psherva	Pause, interruption
Przestrzeń	Pshestsheny	Space, extent.
Przeszkoda	Psheshkoda	Obstacle, jump.
Przeznaczać	Psheznatchatch	Appoint, destine.
Przydzielony—lić	Pshidzhyeloni—litch	Attached—attach.
Pułk	Poowk	Regiment.
Pułkownik	Poowkovnik	Colonel.
Punkt obzerwacyjny	Poonkt observatseeni	Observation point.
Puszkarz	Pooshkazh	Armament officer (gun).
Radjo-Telegraficzny	Radyo-telegrafeetchni	Wireless (adj.).
Raport	Raport	Report.
Reflektor	Reflektor	Searchlight.
Rotmistrz	Rotmistsh	Captain (cavalry and horse artillery).
Rower	Rover	Bicycle.
Rozkaz	Rozkaz	Order.
Rozpoznanie	Rozpoznanye	Reconnaissance.
Rozsypać się	Rozsipatch she'n	To extend, deploy.
Rozwinięty	Rozveenyenti	In line (deployed).
Ruszać	Rooshatch	(1) Touch. (2) Move.
Rusznikarz	Rooshneekazh	Armourer (small arms).
Rymarz	Rimazh	Saddler.
Samochód	Samokhud	Motor vehicle.
Samochód ciężarowy	Samokhud tchyenzharovi	Lorry.
Samochód osobisty	Samokhud osobeesti	Motor car.
Samochód pancerny	Samokhud pantserni	Armoured car.
Samodzielny	Samodzyelni	Independent.
Samolot	Samolot	Aeroplane.
Siarka	Shyarka	Sulphur.
Siekiera, siekierka	Shyekyera—ka	Hand axe.
Sierżant	Shyerzhant	Serjeant-major (infantry, etc.).
Sila	Sheela	Strength.
Skład	Skwad	(1) Composition. (2) Store.
Skrzydło	Skshidwo	Wing, flank.
Slepy	Shlepi	Blind, blank (cartridge).
Służba	Swoozhba	Service, duty.
Sluzba sanitarna	Swoozhba sanitarna	Medical service.
Spieszony	Shpyeshoni	Dismounted.
Sprzymierźoni	Spzhimyezhoni	Allied.
Srodek	Shrodek	(1) Means. (2) Middle.
Stan	Stan	Strength.

THE POLISH ARMY

Sterowiec	Sterovyets	Dirigible.
Stopień	Stopyeny	Rank (status).
Stosować się	Stosovatch she'n	Comply with, obey.
Strata	Strata	Loss, casualty.
Straż	Strazh	Guard.
Straż boczna	Strazh botchna	Flank guard.
Straż przednia	Strazh pshednya	Advanced guard.
Straż tylna	Strazh tilna	Rear guard.
Strażnica	Strazhneetsa	Guard house.
Strzał	Stzhaw	Shot, round (that is fired).
Strzelec	Stzhelets	Rifleman.
Sygnalizacja optyczna	Signalizatsya opteetchna	Visual signalling.
Szabla	Shabla	Sword.
Szereg	Shereg	Rank (front or rear).
Szeregowi (plural)	Sheregovi	Rank and file.
Szeregowiec	Sheregovyets	Private soldier.
Szewc	Shevts	Shoemaker.
Szczególny	Shtchegulni	Special, detailed.
Szosa	Shosa	Metalled road, chaussée.
Szpieg	Shpyeg	Spy.
Szrapnel	Shrapnel	Shrapnel.
Szwadron	Shvadron	Squadron (cavalry).
Szybkość początkowy	Sheebkoshtch potchontkovi	Initial velocity.
Tabor	Tabor	Transport.
Tabor bojowy	Tabor boyovi	Regimental transport, 1st and 2nd lines.
Tabor żywnościowy	Tabor zhivnostchovi	Supply transport.
Tajemnica (subs.)	Tayemnitsa	Secret.
Tajnie (adj.)	Tainye	Secret.
Tamburmajor	Tamboormayor	Drum-major.
Tarcza ochronna	Tartcha okhronna	Gun shield.
Telefon	Telefon	Telephone.
Telegraf	Telegraf	Telegraph.
Tlen	Tlen	Oxygen.
Torpedowiec	Torpedovyets	Torpedo boat.
Trębacz	Trembatch	Trumpeter.
Trzon	Tzhon	Breech block.
Ubezpieczyć	Oobezpyetchitch	Make secure.
Ubranie	Oobranye	Clothing.
Uciekać	Ootchyekatch	Flee.
Uderzeniowy	Oodezhenyovi	Percussion (of a fuze).
Uderzyć	Ooderzheetch	Strike.
Udział	Oodzhyaw	Part, share.
Ujemny	Ooyemni	Unfavourable.
Ułan	Oowan	Uhlan, lancer.
Umierać	Oomyeratch	Die.
Urlop	Oorlop	Leave, furlough.
Uzbroić	Oozbroeetch	To equip, fit out.
Uzbrojenie	Oozbroyenye	Armament, equipment.
Uzupełnienie	Oozoopewnyenye	Reinforcement.
Wachmistrz	Vakhmistsh	Serjeant-major (cavalry).
Walka	Valka	Fight, combat.
Wiadomość	Vyadomoshtch	Information.
Wjnao	Voyna	War.
Wjskoo (pl. wojska)	Voysko, voyska	Army, troops.

Polish	Pronunciation	English
Wóz	Vooz	Wagon.
Wózek	Voozek	Cart.
Wróg	Vrug	Enemy.
Współdziałać	Vspoowdzhyawatch	Co-operate.
Współdziałanie	Vspoowdzhyawanye	Co-operation.
Współdzielnia	Vspoowdzhyelnya	Co-operative, canteen.
Wycofać	Vitsofatch	Withdraw.
Wydać	Vidatch	Surrender (arms).
Wyładować	Viwadovatch	Unload.
Wyrzutnik	Vizhootnik	Extractor.
Wywiadowcza (służba)	Vivyadovtcha	Intelligence (service).
Zaczepny	Zatchepni	Offensive.
Zadanie	Zadanye	Task.
Zająć	Zayontch	To occupy, conquer.
Załoga	Zawoga	Garrison.
Zamek	Zamek	Breech (of a gun) castle.
Zamiar	Zamyar	Intention.
Zaopatrzenie	Zaopatzhenye	Supply.
Zapalnik	Zapalnik	Fuze (of a shell).
Zapalnik uderzeniowy	Zapalnik oodezhenyovi	Percussion fuze.
Zapas	Zapas	Reserve.
Zarządzenie	Zazhondzenye	Disposition, arrangement.
Zastępca	Zastemptsa	Deputy.
Zawiadomienie	Zavyadomyenye	Intelligence report.
Zbieg	Zbyeg	Deserter.
Zbiórka	Zbyoorka	Assembly.
Zdobycz	Zdobitch	Booty.
Zmiana	Zmyana	Relief.
Zwyzięstwo	Zvitchyenstvo	Victory.
Zwyciężyć	Zvitchyenzhitch	To conquer, defeat.
Zwyczaj	Zvitchai	Custom.
Żywność	Zheevnoshtch	Food supplies.

APPENDIX III.

ABBREVIATIONS USED IN THE POLISH ARMY.

Abbreviation.	Polish Full Name.	Meaning.
A.S.	Adjutant Sztabowy	Staff Adjutant.
Baon.	Bataljon	Battalion.
C.S.Czołg.	Centralna Szkola Czolgow	Central Tank School.
C.S.Kaw.	Centralna Szkola Kawalerji	Central Cavalry School.
C.S.S.	Centralna Szkola Strzelnicza	Central Musketry School.
c.k.m.	ciężki karabin maszynowy	Heavy machine gun.
C.Skł.Amm.	Centralny Skład Ammunicji	Central Ammunition Depot.
C.Skł.Br.	Centralny Skład Broni	Central Arms Depot.
C.Skł.U. (Uzbr.)	Centralny Skład Uzbrojenia	Central Armament Depot.
C.Z.Gaz.	Centralny Zakład Gazowy	Central Gas Establishment.
C.Z.Lot.	Centranlne Zakłady Lotnicze	Central Aviation Establishments.

THE POLISH ARMY

D.A.K.	Dywizjon Artylerji Konnej	Horse Artillery Group.
D-ca.	Dowodca	Commander (G.O.C.).
D.K.	Dywizja Kawalerji	Cavalry Division.
D.O.K.	Dowodstwo Okręgu Korpusowego	Military District Headquarters.
D.P.	Dywizja Piechoty	Infantry Division.
Dstwo., D-wo.	Dowodstwo	Headquarters (of a Division, etc.).
K.O.P.P.	Korpus Obrony Pogranicznej Panstwowej.	Frontier Guard Corps.
K.P.A.	Kompanja Pomiarow Artylerjskich	Artillery Ranging Company.
K.S.	Korpus Sądowy	Corps of Justice (applied to officers).
K.U.K.	Komenda Uzupełnien Koni	Remount Depot.
l.k.m.	lekki karabin maszynowy	Light machine gun.
L.O.P.P.	Liga Obrony Powietrznej Panstwowej.	Aerial Defence League.
M.S.W. (Wojsk)	Ministerstwo Spraw Wojskowych	Ministry of War.
Nacz.D-wo	Naczelnie Dowodstwo	General Headquarters.
Ob.S.Art.	Oboz Szkolny Artylerji	Artillery Instructional Camp.
O.E.	(1) Okręg Etapowy	Line of Communication District.
	(2) Oficer Ewidencyjny	Registration Officer (in P.K.Us.).
Ob.S.W.Łącz.	Oboz Szkolny Wojsk Łącznosci	Signal Training Camp.
O.K.	Okrąg Korpusowy	Military District.
O.S.Art.	Oficerska Szkoła Artylerji	Officers' School of Artillery.
O.S.dla P.	Oficerska Szkoła dla Podoficerow	Officers' School for N.C.Os.
O.S.Inz	Oficerska Szkoła Inżynierji	Officers' School of Engineering.
O.Z.G.	Okręgowy Zakład Gospodarczy	District Supply Store.
O.Z.M.	Okręgowy Zakład Mundurowy	District Clothing Store.
O.Z.U.	Okręgowy Zakład Uzbrojenia	District Armament Store.
P.A.C.	Pułk Artylerji Ciężkiej	Heavy Artillery Regiment.
P.A.G.	Pułk Artylerji Górskiej	Mountain Artillery Regiment.
P.A.N.	Pułk Artylerji Najcięższkiej	Heaviest Artillery Regiment.
P.A.P.	Pułk Artylerji Polowej	Field Artillery Regiment.
P.A.Pl.	Pułk Artylerji Przeciwlotniczej	Anti-Aircraft Artillery Regiment.
P.K.U.	Powiatowa Komenda Uzupełnien	District Recruiting Office.
płdn.	południe	South.
płn.	północ	North.
P.Łącz.	Pułk Łącznosci	Signal Regiment.
P.Lot.	Pułk Lotniczy	Aviation Regiment.
P.P.	Pułk Piechoty	Infantry Regiment.
P.P. (Leg.)	Pułk Piechoty Legjonowej	Infantry Regiment, Legion.
P.P.A.	Pluton Pomiarow Akustycznych	Sound Ranging Platoon.
P.P.O.	Pluton Pomiarow Optycznych	Visual Ranging Platoon.
P.S.D.	Park Saperski Dywizji	Divisional Engineer Park.
P.S.K.	Pułk Strzelcow Konnych	Mounted Rifle Regiment (Cavalry).
P.S.P.	Pułk Strzelcow Podhalanskich	Mountain Rifle (Infantry) Regiment.
P.Sap.	Pułk Saperow (Saperski)	Engineer Regiment.
P.Szwol.	Pułk Swoleżerow	Chevauzleger Regiment.
P.U.	Pułk Ułanow	Lancer Regiment.
P.U.A.	Park Uzbrojenia Armji	Army Armament Park.
P.U.D.	Park Uzbrojenia Dywizji	Divisional Armament Park.
r.k.m.	ręczny karabin maszynowy	Hand machine gun.

S.G.	Sztabu Generalnego		Of the General Staff (applied to officers).
Szk.Pchor.	Szkoła Podchorążych		Cadet School.
Szk.Pil.	Szkoła Pilotów		Pilots' School.
T.B.1	Tabor Bojowy, 1		Fighting Transport, 1st Echelon.
T.B.2	Tabor Bojowy, 2		Fighting Transport, 2nd Echelon.
T.Z.	Tabor Żywnościowy		Supply Train.
U.	—		—
W.P.(Wojsk.Pol.)	Wojska Polskie		Polish Army.
W.S.I.	Wyższa Szkoła Intendantury		Supreme Intendance School.
W.S.Woj.	Wyższa Szkoła Wojenna		Supreme War School.
wsch.	wschód		East.
Z-ca.	Zastępca		Deputy.
zach.	zachód		West.

APPENDIX IV.—WAR ESTABLISHMENTS.

ARMY HEADQUARTERS.

War Establishment.

	Officers.	Other Ranks.	Horses.	Vehicles.	Motor Cars.
Commander	1	7	8	2	—
Army Staff	38	105	79	12	—
Army Artillery Staff	4	17	17	2	—
Artillery Services	9	25	14	2	—
Engineer Staff	4	19	9	3	—
Signal Staff	4	13	5	1	—
Intendance Services	8	44	18	9	—
Medical Services	6	19	6	3	—
Veterinary Services	2	9	4	1	—
Remount Services	1	4	3	—	—
Motor Transport Service	2	10	—	—	—
Horse Transport Service	2	9	7	1	—
Chaplains' Service	2	6	2	1	—
Court Martial	5	25	8	4	—
Gendarmerie	3	66	30	1	—
Post Office	2	11	4	2	—
Treasury	1	10	4	2	—
Supply and Transport duties for A.H.Q.	1	28	11	4	—
A.H.Q. Supply Column	—	30	60	30	—
Camp Commandant	1	13	2	—	—
Headquarters Company	1	141	8	4	—
Field Topographical Station (Section)	24	97	49	14	—
Grand Total Army Headquarters	122	776	381	99	—

CORPS HEADQUARTERS.

War Establishment.

	Officers.	Other Ranks.	Horses.	Vehicles.	Motor Cars.
Commander	1	6	6	1	1
Corps Staff	14	51	35	4	2
Artillery Staff	4	17	17	2	1
Corps Medical Officer	1	4	—	—	—
Corps Intendant	1	1	—	—	—
Supply and Transport duties at Corps Headquarters	1	15	7	2	—
Corps Headquarters Supply Column	—	10	20	10	—
Treasury	1	8	4	2	—
Camp Commandant	1	5	1	—	—
Headquarters Company	1	138	8	4	—
Total Corps Headquarters	25	255	98	25	4

DIVISIONAL HEADQUARTERS.

War Establishment.

	Officers.	Other Ranks.	Horses.	Vehicles.	Motor Cars.
Commander	1	6	6	1	1
Divisional Staff	7	29	22	3	1
Divisional Infantry Headquarters	3	12	12	1	—
Divisional Artillery Headquarters	4	17	15	2	—
Signal Officer	1	2	2	—	—
Intendance Service	3	12	6	3	—
Medical Service	2	7	5	1	—
Veterinary Service	2	7	4	1	—
Horse Transport Service	1	4	5	1	—
Chaplain	1	4	2	1	—
Court Martial	2	13	4	1	—
Platoon Gendarmerie	1	60	12	1	—
Post Office	2	11	4	2	—
Treasury	1	8	4	2	—
Divisional Headquarters Supply Officer and Supply Column.	1	35	39	18	—
Headquarters company	2	147	9	4	—
Total Divisional Headquarters	34	374	151	42	2

War Establishment of a Division.

Unit.	Officers.	Other Ranks.	Total.	Horses.	Vehicles.	Guns.	Light M.G. or Auto. Rifles.	Heavy M.Gs.	Mortars.	Infantry Guns.	Road Space in yards. With Fighting Transport only. T.B.1 & T.B.2.	Road Space in yards. With Fighting Transport and Supply Train.
Divisional Headquarters	32	374	406	150	44	—	—	2	—	—	500	770
3 Infantry Regiments—												
(a) With auto. rifles	222	8,100	8,322	1,375	516	—	324	108	9	9	9,300	11,550
(b) With light M.Gs.	222	8,250	8,472	1,440	678	—	324	108	9	9	—	—
Divisional Cavalry	13	380	393	410	33	—	8	2	—	—	500	770
1 Artillery Regiment	67	1,730	1,797	1,570	337	36	—	18	—	—	5,300	6,600
Armament Park	5	138	143	15	11	—	—	—	—	—	165	220
Divisional Engineers	17	650	667	250	120	—	—	4	—	—	1,875	2,200
Signal Units	6	220	226	62	23	—	—	—	—	—	440	500
Medical Units	14	320	334	180	81	—	—	—	—	—	1,500	1,650
Intendance Park	2	94	96	28	13	—	—	—	—	—	385	440
Transport Columns	9	922	931	1,267	577	—	—	—	—	—	6,600	7,200
Total (a)	387	12,900	13,287	5,307	1,755	36	332	134	9	9	29,000	35,000
Total (b)	387	13,100	13,487	5,372	1,917						16¾ miles	20 miles

THE POLISH ARMY

CAVALRY DIVISIONAL HEADQUARTERS.

War Establishment.

	Officers.	Other Ranks.	Horses.	Vehicles.	Motor Cars.
Commander	1	7	8	2	1
Divisional Staff	7	28	32	3	1
Divisional Artillery Staff	3	13	15	1	—
Signal Officer	1	5	5	1	—
Intendance Service	3	14	8	3	—
Medical Service	1	6	4	1	—
Veterinary	1	7	6	1	—
Horse Transport Service	1	5	5	1	—
Chaplain	1	2	2	1	—
Court Martial	2	13	4	1	—
Gendarmerie	1	60	62	1	—
Post Office	2	11	4	2	—
Treasury	1	8	4	2	—
Cavalry Division Headquarters Supply Officer and Supply Column.	1	30	36	14	—
Headquarters Squadron	2	67	81	6	—
Total Cavalry Divisional Headquarters	28	276	276	40	2

War Establishment of a Cavalry Division.

	Personnel.			Horses.	Vehicles.	Guns.	Auto. Rifles or Light M.Gs.	Heavy M.Gs.
	Officers.	Other Ranks.	Total.					
Cavalry Division Headquarters	28	276	304	276	42	—	—	—
3 Cavalry Brigades	230	5,450	5,680	6,050	534	—	96	72
2 groups Horse Artillery	44	1,280	1,324	1,440	140	24	—	12
Armament Park	5	138	143	15	11	—	—	—
Pioneer Squadron	5	150	155	150	18	—	—	—
Signal Units	6	150	156	145	20	—	—	—
Medical Units	14	300	314	200	80	—	—	—
Intendance Park	2	94	96	28	13	—	—	—
Transport Column	9	922	931	1,267	577	—	—	—
Total	345	8,800	9,145	9,600	1,435	24	96	84

INDEPENDENT CAVALRY BRIGADE HEADQUARTERS.
War Establishment.

	Officers.	Other Ranks.	Horses.	Vehicles.	Motor Cars.
Commander	1	6	6	1	1
Staff	5	20	25	2	1
Intendance Service	2	10	7	2	—
Medical Service	1	7	4	1	—
Veterinary Service	1	4	3	—	—
Court Martial	2	13	4	2	—
Gendarmerie	1	60	62	1	—
Post Office	1	13	4	2	—
Treasury	1	8	4	2	—
Brigade Headquarters Supply Officer and Supply Column.	1	37	46	20	—
Headquarters Squadron	2	73	83	3	—
Total Independent Cavalry Brigade Headquarters	18	254	252	36	2

ARTILLERY.
War Establishments.

	Officers.	Other Ranks.	Horses.	Guns.	Ammn. Wagons.	Wagons.	Motors.	Heavy M.Guns.
Headquarters Field Artillery Regiment	10	135	164	—	—	67	—	—
Headquarters Group 75's	6	45	30	—	—	5	—	—
Battery 75's	4	140	110	4	4	10	—	2
Amm. Col. Group 75's	1	75	110	—	—	50	—	—
Group 75's	19	530	460	12	12	85	—	6
Headquarters Group 105 mm. Howitzers	6	45	30	—	—	5	—	—
Battery 105's	4	140	110	4	4	10	—	2
Amm. Col. Group 105's	1	90	140	—	—	65	—	—
Group 105's	19	540	490	12	12	100	—	6
Field Artillery Regiment	67	1,730	1,570	36	36	337	—	18

DISTRIBUTION OF TRANSPORT.
Field Artillery Regiment.

Fighting Transport—1st Echelon.

Per battery	4 guns 4 ammunition wagons 2 wagons with telephone equipment 1 wagon with engineer stores 2 wagons with machine guns	*Vehicles.* 117
Per Amm. Col., 75's	45 ammunition wagons	90
Per Amm. Col., 105's	60 ammunition wagons	60
Per Group 75's or 105's	2 wagons with telephone equipment 1 wagon with med. and vet. equipment	9
Per Regimental Hdqrs.	1 wagon with telephone equipment 1 wagon with med. and vet. equipment	2
	Total	278

THE POLISH ARMY

	Fighting Transport—2nd Echelon.	*Vehicles.*
Per Battery and Amm. Col.	1 field kitchen 1 cooks' wagon 1 baggage wagon 1 forage wagon	48
Per Group	1 baggage wagon	3
Per Regimental Hdqrs.	1 field kitchen 1 cooks' wagon 3 wagons, baggage and office 1 forage wagon 1 C.Os.' wagon 1 treasury wagon	8
	Total	58

ARTILLERY.

Heavy Artillery Regiment.

	Officers.	Other Ranks.	Horses.	Guns.	M. Guns.	Amm. Wagons.	Other Wagons.
Regimental Headquarters	10	144	184	—	—	—	77
Group Headquarters	6	43	30	—	—	—	5
Battery 105 mm. guns	3	120	88	2	2	10	10
Battery 155 mm. howitzers	4	172	148	4	4	28	10
Group Ammunition Column	1	91	138	—	—	60	5
Total Group (1 battery 105's, 2 batteries 155's and Ammunition Column)	18	600	560	10	6	126	40
Heavy Artillery Regiment	64	1,950	1,850	30	18	378	197

ALLOTMENT OF TRANSPORT.

	Fighting Transport—1st Echelon.		*Total in Regiment.*
Per 105 mm. battery	10 ammunition wagons 2 for telephone equipment 1 for engineer stores 2 for machine guns	15	45
Per 155 mm. battery	28 ammunition wagons 2 for telephone equipment 1 for engineer stores 2 for machine guns	33	198
Per Group Ammunition Column	60 ammunition wagons	60	180
Per Regimental Headquarters	1 telephone wagon 1 for med. and vet. equipment	2	2
			434

THE POLISH ARMY

Fighting Transport—2nd Echelon.

			Total in Regiment.
Per Battery or Ammunition Column	1 field kitchen 1 cooks' wagon 1 baggage wagon 1 forge wagon	4	48
Per Group Headquarters ..	1 baggage wagon ..	1	3
Per Regimental Headquarters ..	1 field kitchen 1 cooks' wagon 3 baggage wagons 1 forge wagon 1 treasury wagon 1 personal carriage	8	8
			59

Supply Column and Forage Wagons.

Per Battery	.. 1 forage wagon		9
Per Ammunition Column..	.. 1 forage wagon		3
Per Group Headquarters..	.. 1 forage wagon		3
Per Regimental Headquarters ..	1 forage wagon 66 supply and meat wagons	67	67
			82

Summary.

Fighting Transport, 1st Echelon	..	..	..	..	434 wagons.
Fighting Transport, 2nd Echelon	..	..	..	..	59 ,,
Supply Column ..	..	..	..	..	82 ,,
	Total ..	..	..	..	575 ,,

APPENDIX V.

LIST OF POLISH PLACE NAMES, WITH THEIR CORRESPONDING NAMES UNDER THE PARTITIONING POWERS.

Polish Name.	Former Name.
A.—Russian Poland.	
Brzesc-nad-Bugiem (Brzesc on the Bug) ..	Brest-Litovsk.
Modlin	Nowo Georgievsk.
Dęblin	Ivangorod.
B.—Austrian Poland.	
Nowy Sącz	Neu Sandez.
Lwow	Lemberg.
Nowy Targ	Neumarkt.
Oswięcim	Auschwitz.
Cieszyn	Teschen.
Sląsk	Schlesien (Silesia).
C.—German Poland.	
Brodnica	Strasburg (Westpreusen).
Bydgosc (Bydgoszcz)	Bromberg.
Chełmno	Culm.
Chełmza	Culmsee.
Chodziez	Colmar.

Polish Name.						Former Name.
Chojnice	..	..	..	..	..	Konitz.
Działdowo	..	..	..	..	..	Soldau.
Gdansk	..	..	..	..	..	Danzig.
Gniew	..	..	..	..	..	Mewe.
Gniezno	..	..	..	..	..	Gnesen.
Gory Tarnowskie	..	..	..	..	..	Tarnowitz.
Grudziądz	..	..	..	..	..	Graudenz.
Inowraclaw	..	..	..	..	..	Hohensalza.
Kcynia	..	..	..	..	..	Exin.
Kępno	..	..	..	..	..	Kempen.
Koscierzyna	..	..	..	..	..	Berent.
Leszno	..	..	..	..	..	Lissa.
Lidzbark	..	..	..	..	..	Lautenburg.
Łubawa	..	..	..	..	..	Lobau.
Notec (river)	..	..	..	..	..	Netze.
Nowe	..	..	..	..	..	Neuenburg.
Nowe Miasto	..	..	..	..	..	Neumark.
Pomorze	..	..	..	..	..	Pommern (Pomerania).
Poznan	..	..	..	..	..	Posen.
Pszczyna	..	..	..	..	..	Pless.
Puck	..	..	..	..	..	Putzig.
Radzyn	..	..	..	..	..	Rehden.
Rogozno	..	..	..	..	..	Rogasen.
Ryczywoł	..	..	..	..	..	Richtenwalde.
Rynarzewko	..	..	..	..	..	Netzwald.
Skarszewy	..	..	..	..	..	Schoeneck.
Srem	..	..	..	..	..	Schrimm.
Sroda	..	..	..	..	..	Schroda.
Swiecie	..	..	..	..	..	Schwetz.
Szamotuly	..	..	..	..	..	Samter.
Tczew	..	..	..	..	..	Dirschau.
Ujscie	..	..	..	..	..	Usch.
Wąbrzezno	..	..	..	..	..	Briesen.
Wejherowo	..	..	..	..	..	Neustadt.
Więcborek	..	..	..	..	..	Vandsberg.
Wrzesnia	..	..	..	..	..	Wreschen.
Zbąszyn	..	..	..	..	..	Bentschen.

And many other villages.

APPENDIX VI.

ORDER OF BATTLE AND PEACE STATIONS OF THE POLISH ARMY.

Military District (D.O.K.) I : Warsaw.

Unit.	Location.	Remarks.
8th Division	Warsaw.	
13th Infantry Regiment	Pultusk.	
21st Infantry Regiment	Warsaw.	
32nd Infantry Regiment	Modlin.	
32nd Infantry Regiment, 3rd Battalion	Dzialdowo.	
8th Field Artillery Regiment	Plock.	

Military District (D.O.K.) I : Warsaw—continued.

Unit.	Location.	Remarks.
18th Division	Lomza.	
33rd Infantry Regiment	Lomza.	
42nd Infantry Regiment	Bialystok.	
42nd Infantry Regiment, 3rd Battalion	Ossowiec.	
71st Infantry Regiment	Zambrow.	In D.O.K. III.
18th Field Artillery Regiment	Ostrow Lomzynsk.	
18th Field Artillery Regiment, 1st Group	Zambrow.	
28th Division	Warsaw.	
15th Infantry Regiment	Deblin.	
36th Infantry Regiment	Warsaw.	
72nd Infantry Regiment	Radom.	
28th Field Artillery Regiment	Deblin.	
28th Field Artillery Regiment, 2nd Group	Rembertow.	
2nd Cavalry Division	Warsaw.	
1st Cavalry Brigade	Warsaw.	
1st Chevauxlegers	Warsaw.	
1st Mounted Rifles	Garwolin.	
12th Cavalry Brigade	Ostrolęka.	
5th Ulans	Ostrolęka.	
7th Ulans	Minsk Mazowiecki.	
13th Cavalry Brigade	Plock.	
11th Ulans	Ciechanow.	
4th Mounted Rifles	Plock.	
1st Horse Artillery Group	Warsaw.	
12th Horse Artillery Group	Ostrolęka.	
2nd Divisional Pioneer Squadron	Warsaw.	
2nd Armoured Car Squadron	Warsaw.	
Non-divisional Units.		
Manœuvre Battalion	Rembertow.	
1st Heavy Field Artillery Regiment	Modlin.	
1st Heaviest Artillery Regiment	Warsaw.	
1st Anti-aircraft Regiment	Warsaw.	
1st Aviation Regiment	Warsaw.	
1st Sapper Regiment	Modlin.	
Pontoon Battalion	Modlin.	
Electro-technical Battalion	Modlin.	
2nd Railway Regiment	Jablonna.	
1st Signal Regiment	Zegrze.	
Wireless Telegraph Regiment	Warsaw.	
Wireless Telegraph Regiment, 1st Battalion	Benjaminow.	
1st Medical Battalion	Warsaw.	
1st Group Gendarmerie	Warsaw.	
1st Train Squadron	Warsaw.	
1st Motor Transport Group	Warsaw.	
Units in the District belonging to other Formations.		
30th Infantry Regiment	Warsaw.	To 10th Division.
2nd Sapper Regiment	Pulawy.	To D.O.K. II.

Military District (D.O.K.) II : Lublin.

Unit.	Location.	Remarks.
3rd (Legion) Division	Zamosc.	
7th (Leg.) Infantry Regiment	Chelm.	
8th (Leg.) Infantry Regiment	Lublin.	
9th (Leg.) Infantry Regiment	Zamosc.	
9th (Leg.) Infantry Regiment, 3rd Battalion	Tomaszow Lubelski.	
3rd (Legion) Field Artillery Regiment	Zamosc.	

THE POLISH ARMY

Unit.	Location.	Remarks.
13th Division	Rowne.	
43rd Infantry Regiment	Dubno.	
43rd Infantry Regiment, Mob. Stores	Brody.	In D.O.K. VI.
44th Infantry Regiment	Rowne.	
44th Infantry Regiment, Mob. Stores	Wlodzimierz Wolynski.	
45th Infantry Regiment	Rowne.	
45th Infantry Regiment, Mob. Stores	Wlodzimierz Wolynski.	
13th Field Artillery Regiment	Rowne.	
13th Field Artillery Regiment, Mob. Stores	Luck.	
13th Field Artillery Regiment, 1st Group	Luck.	
27th Division	Kowel.	
23rd Infantry Regiment	Wlodzimierz Wolynski.	
24th Infantry Regiment	Luck.	
50th Infantry Regiment	Kowel.	
50th Infantry Regiment, 3rd Battalion	Sarny.	
27th Field Artillery Regiment	Wlodzimierz Wolynski.	
2nd Independent Cavalry Brigade	Rowne.	
12th Ulans	Krzemieniec.	
12th Ulans, Reserve Squadron	Zamosc.	
19th Ulans	Ostrog.	
19th Ulans, Reserve Squadron	Wlodzimierz Wolynski.	
21st Ulans	Rowne.	
21st Ulans, Reserve Squadron	Luck.	
2nd Horse Artillery Group	Dubno.	
2nd Brigade Pioneer Squadron	Rowne.	

Non-divisional Units.

Unit.	Location.	Remarks.
2nd Heavy Field Artillery Regiment	Chelm.	
2nd Sapper Regiment	Pulawy.	In D.O.K. I.
2nd Medical Battalion	Lublin.	
2nd Group Gendarmerie	Lublin.	
2nd Train Squadron	Lublin.	
2nd Motor Transport Squadron	Lublin.	

Units in the District belonging to other Formations.

Unit.	Location.	Remarks.
17th Cavalry Brigade	Hrubieszow.	
24th Ulans	Krasnik.	
2nd Mounted Rifles	Hrubieszow.	

Military District (D.O.K.) III : Grodno.

Unit.	Location.	Remarks.
1st (Legion) Division	Wilno.	
1st (Leg.) Infantry Regiment	Wilno.	
1st (Leg.) Infantry Regiment, Mob. Stores	Bialystok.	
5th (Leg.) Infantry Regiment	Wilno.	
6th (Leg.) Infantry Regiment, Mob. Stores	Sokolka.	
1st (Leg.) Field Artillery Regiment	Wilno.	
1st (Leg.) Field Artillery Regiment, Mob. Stores	Bialystok.	
19th Division	Nowowilejka.	
77th Infantry Regiment	Lida.	
85th Infantry Regiment	Nowowilejka.	
86th Infantry Regiment	Molodeczno.	
86th Infantry Regiment, Mob. Stores	Nowowilejka.	
19th Field Artillery Regiment	Nowowilejka.	
19th Field Artillery Regiment, 2nd Group	Molodeczno.	
19th Field Artillery Regiment, 3rd Group	Lida.	

THE POLISH ARMY

Military District (D.O.K.) III : Grodno—*continued*.

Unit.	Location.	Remarks.
29th Division	Grodno.	
41st Infantry Regiment	Suwalki.	
41st Infantry Regiment, Mob. Stores	Sokolka.	
76th Infantry Regiment	Grodno.	
81st Infantry Regiment	Grodno.	
81st Infantry Regiment, 2nd Battalion	Sokolka.	
29th Field Artillery Regiment	Grodno.	
29th Field Artillery Regiment, 1st Group	Suwalki.	
1st Cavalry Division	Bialystok.	
4th Cavalry Brigade	Suwalki.	
2nd Ulans	Suwalki.	
2nd Ulans, Reserve Squadron	Bialystok.	
3rd Chevauxlegers	Suwalki.	
3rd Chevauxlegers, Reserve Squadron	Grodno..	
11th Cavalry Brigade	Augustow.	
1st Ulans	Augustow.	
1st Ulans, Reserve Squadron	Bialystok.	
9th Mounted Rifles	Grajewo.	
9th Mounted Rifles, Reserve Squadron	Bialystok.	
18th Cavalry Brigade	Bialystok.	
10th Ulans	Bialystok.	
3rd Mounted Rifles	Wolkowysk.	
4th Horse Artillery Group	Suwalki.	
8th Horse Artillery Group	Bialystok.	
1st Divisional Pioneer Squadron	Bialystok.	
1st Armoured Car Squadron	Bialystok.	
3rd Independent Cavalry Brigade	Wilno.	
4th Ulans	Podbrodzie.	
4th Ulans, Reserve Squadron	Wolkowysk.	
13th Ulans	Nowowilejka.	
13th Ulans, Reserve Squadron	Wolkowysk.	
23rd Ulans	Wilno.	
3rd Horse Artillery Group	Wilno.	
3rd Brigade Pioneer Squadron	Wilno.	
Non-divisional Units.		
3rd Heavy Field Artillery Regiment	Wilno.	
3rd Anti-aircraft Artillery Group	Wilno.	
11th Aviation Regiment	Lida.	
3rd Sapper Regiment	Wilno.	
3rd Medical Battalion..	Grodno.	
3rd Group Gendarmerie	Grodno.	
3rd Train Squadron	Sokolka.	
3rd Motor Transport Group	Grodno.	
Units in the District belonging to other Formations.		
42nd Infantry Regiment	Bialystok. }	To 18th Division.
42nd Infantry Regiment, 3rd Battalion	Ossowiec. }	

Military District (D.O.K.) IV : Lodz.

Unit.	Location.	Remarks.
7th Division	Częstochowa.	
25th Infantry Regiment	Piotrkow.	
25th Infantry Regiment, 2nd Battalion	Tomaszow Mazowiecki.	
27th Infantry Regiment	Częstochowa.	
74th Infantry Regiment	Lubliniec.	
74th Infantry Regiment, Mob. Stores	Piotrkow.	
7th Field Artillery Regiment	Częstochowa.	

THE POLISH ARMY

Unit.	Location.	Remarks.
10th Division	Lodz.	
28th Infantry Regiment	Lodz.	
30th Infantry Regiment	Warsaw.	In D.O.K. I.
31st Infantry Regiment	Lodz.	
10th Field Artillery Regiment	Lodz.	
10th Field Artillery Regiment, 3rd Group	Rozany.	In D.O.K. IX.
26th Division	Skierniewice.	
10th Infantry Regiment	Lowicz.	
10th Infantry Regiment, 3rd Battalion	Skierniewice.	
18th Infantry Regiment	Skierniewice.	
37th Infantry Regiment	Kutno.	
37th Infantry Regiment, 3rd Battalion	Lęczyca.	
26th Field Artillery Regiment	Skierniewice.	
26th Field Artillery Regiment, 2nd Group	Wloclawek.	In D.O.K. VII.

Non-divisional Units.

Unit.	Location.	Remarks.
4th Heavy Field Artillery Regiment	Lodz.	
4th Heavy Field Artillery Regiment, 2nd Group	Częstochowa.	
4th Sapper Regiment	Sandomierz.	In D.O.K. X.
4th Medical Battalion	Lodz.	
4th Group Gendarmerie	Lodz.	
4th Train Squadron	Lodz.	
4th Motor Transport Group	Lodz.	

Military District (D.O.K.) V : Krakow.

Unit.	Location.
6th Division	Krakow.
12th Infantry Regiment	Wadowice.
12th Infantry Regiment, 3rd Battalion	Krakow.
16th Infantry Regiment	Tarnow.
16th Infantry Regiment, 3rd Battalion	Krakow.
20th Infantry Regiment	Krakow.
6th Field Artillery Regiment	Krakow.
21st (Mountain) Division	Bielsko Biala.
1st Mountain Rifle Regiment	Nowy Sącz.
1st Mountain Rifle Regiment, 3rd Battalion	Nowy Targ.
3rd Mountain Rifle Regiment	Bielsko Biala.
3rd Mountain Rifle Regiment, 3rd Battalion	Krakow.
4th Mountain Rifle Regiment	Cieszyn.
21st Field Artillery Regiment	Bielsko Biala.
21st Field Artillery Regiment, 3rd Group	Oswięcim.
23rd Division	Katowice.
11th Infantry Regiment	Gory Tanrowskie.
11th Infantry Regiment, 2nd Battalion	Będzin.
11th Infantry Regiment, Mob. Stores	Będzin.
73rd Infantry Regiment	Katowice.
73rd Infantry Regiment, 2nd Battalion	Oswięcim.
73rd Infantry Regiment, Mob. Stores	Oswięcim.
75th Infantry Regiment	Krolewska Huta.
75th Infantry Regiment, 2nd Battalion	Rybnik.
75th Infantry Regiment, 3rd Battalion	Wielkie Hajduki.
75th Infantry Regiment, Mob. Stores	Oswięcim.
23rd Field Artillery Regiment	Będzin.
23rd Field Artillery Regiment, 2nd Group	Zory.
5th Independent Cavalry Brigade	Krakow.
3rd Ulans	Gory Tarnowskie.
3rd Ulans, Reserve Squadron	Bochnia.
8th Ulans	Krakow.
5th Horse Artillery Group	Krakow.
5th Brigade Pioneer Squadron	Krakow.
5th Armoured Car Squadron	Krakow.

Military District (D.O.K.) IV : Lodz—continued.

Unit.	Location.	Remarks.
Non-divisional Units.		
5th Heavy Field Artillery Regiment	Krakow.	
5th Anti-aircraft Group	Krakow.	
2nd Aviation Regiment	Krakow.	
5th Sapper Regiment	Krakow.	
1st Railway Regiment	Krakow.	
5th Independent Signal Battalion	Krakow.	
5th Medical Battalion	Krakow.	
5th Gendarmerie Group	Krakow.	
5th Train Squadron	Krakow.	
5th Motor Transport Group	Krakow.	
Units in the District belonging to other Formations.		
5th Mounted Rifles	Tarnow.	To 8th Ind. Brigade.
5th Mounted Rifles, 3rd and 4th Squadrons	Bochnia.	

Military District (D.O.K.) VI : Lwow.

Unit	Location	Remarks
5th Division	Lwow.	
19th Infantry Regiment (Defenders of Lwow)	Lwow.	
19th Infantry Regiment, 3rd Battalion	Rawa Rusha.	
26th Infantry Regiment	Lwow.	
26th Infantry Regiment, 2nd Battalion	Kamionka Strumilowa.	
40th Infantry Regiment	Lwow.	
5th Field Artillery Regiment	Lwow.	
11th Division	Stanislawow.	
48th Infantry Regiment	Stanislawow.	
49th Infantry Regiment	Kolomyja.	
53rd Infantry Regiment	Stryj.	In D.O.K. X.
11th Field Artillery Regiment	Stanislawow.	
11th Field Artillery Regiment, 1st Group	Kolomyja.	
12th Division	Tarnopol.	
51st Infantry Regiment	Brzezany.	
52nd Infantry Regiment	Zloczow.	
54th Infantry Regiment	Tarnopol.	
54th Infantry Regiment, Mob. Stores	Brzezany.	
12th Field Artillery Regiment	Zloczow.	
12th Field Artillery Regiment, 1st Group	Tarnopol.	
4th Cavalry Division	Lwow.	
10th Cavalry Brigade	Przemysl	
20th Ulans	Rzeszow.	
20th Ulans, 2nd, 3rd, 4th Squadrons	Dębica.	In D.O.K. X.
10th Mounted Rifles	Lancut.	
10th Mounted Rifles, 3rd, 4th Squadrons,	Hruszow.	
16th Cavalry Brigade	Lwow.	
14th Ulans	Lwow.	
6th Mounted Rifles	Zolkiew.	
17th Cavalry Brigade	Hrubieszow.	
24th Ulans	Krasnik.	In D.O.K. II.
2nd Mounted Rifles	Hrubieszow.	
10th Horse Artillery Group	Jaroslaw.	In D.O.K. X.
13th Horse Artillery Group	Lwow.	
4th Divisional Pioneer Squadron	Lwow.	
4th Armoured Car Squadron	Lwow.	

THE POLISH ARMY

Unit.	Location.	Remarks.
6th Independent Cavalry Brigade	Stanislawow.	
6th Ulans	Stanislawow.	
9th Ulans	Czortkow.	
9th Ulans, 1st, 3rd, 4th Squadrons	Trembowla.	
9th Ulans, Reserve Squadron	Stanislawow.	
22nd Ulans	Brody.	
22nd Ulans, Reserve Squadron	Zloczow.	
6th Horse Artillery Group	Stanislawow.	
6th Brigade Pioneer Squadron	Stanislawow.	

Non-divisional Units.

Unit.	Location.	Remarks.
6th Heavy Field Artillery Regiment	Lwow.	
6th Anti-aircraft Artillery Group	Lwow.	
6th Aviation Regiment	Lwow.	
6th Sapper Regiment	Przemysl.	In D.O.K. X.
6th Medical Battalion	Lwow.	
6th Gendarmerie Group	Lwow.	
6th Train Squadron	Lwow.	
6th Motor Transport Group	Lwow.	

Military District (D.O.K.) VII : Poznan.

Unit.	Location.	Remarks.
14th Division	Poznan.	
55th Infantry Regiment	Leszno.	
55th Infantry Regiment, 2nd, 3rd Battalions	Rawicz.	
55th Infantry Regiment, Mob. Stores	Poznan.	
57th Infantry Regiment	Poznan.	
58th Infantry Regiment	Poznan.	
14th Field Artillery Regiment	Poznan.	
17th Division	Gniezno.	
68th Infantry Regiment	Wrzesnia.	
68th Infantry Regiment, 3rd Battalion	Konin.	
69th Infantry Regiment	Gniezno.	
70th Infantry Regiment	Plesew.	
70th Infantry Regiment, 1st Battalion	Jarocin.	
17th Field Artillery Regiment	Gniezno.	
25th Division	Kalisz.	
29th Infantry Regiment	Kalisz.	
29th Infantry Regiment, 2nd, 3rd Battalions	Szczypiorno.	
56th Infantry Regiment	Krotoszyn.	
56th Infantry Regiment, Mob. Stores	Jarocin.	
60th Infantry Regiment	Ostrow Poznanski.	
25th Field Artillery Regiment	Kalisz.	
25th Field Artillery Regiment, 1st Group	Ostrow Poznanski.	
3rd Cavalry Division	Poznan.	
7th Cavalry Brigade	Poznan.	
15th Ulans	Poznan.	
17th Ulans	Leszno.	
17th Ulans, Reserve Squadron	Poznan.	
14th Cavalry Brigade	Bydgosc.	In D.O.K. VIII.
16th Ulans	Bydgosc.	
7th Mounted Rifles	Poznan.	
7th Mounted Rifles, 1 Squadron	Zbąszyn.	
15th Cavalry Brigade	Grudziądz.	In D.O.K. VIII.
18th Ulans	Grudziądz.	
18th Ulans, Reserve Squadron	Torun.	
8th Mounted Rifles	Chelmno.	
8th Mounted Rifles, Reserve Squadron	Wloclawek.	

THE POLISH ARMY

Military District (D.O.K.) VII : Poznan—*continued*.

Unit.	Location.	Remarks.
7th Horse Artillery Group	Poznan.	
11th Horse Artillery Group	Bydgosc.	In D.O.K. VIII.
3rd Divisional Pioneer Squadron	Poznan.	
3rd Armoured Car Squadron..	Poznan.	

Non-divisional Units.

Unit.	Location.
Machine Gun Battalion	Biedrusko.
7th Heavy Field Artillery Regiment	Poznan.
7th Anti-aircraft Artillery Group	Poznan.
3rd Aviation Regiment	Poznan.
7th Sapper Regiment	Poznan.
7th Independent Signal Battalion	Poznan.
7th Medical Battalion..	Poznan.
7th Gendarmerie Group	Poznan.
7th Train Squadron	Poznan.
7th Motor Transport Group	Poznan.

Military District (D.O.K.) VIII : Torun.

Unit.	Location.	Remarks.
4th Division	Torun.	
14th Infantry Regiment	Wloclawek.	
63rd Infantry Regiment	Torun.	
67th Infantry Regiment	Brodnica.	
67th Infantry Regiment, Mob. Stores	Torun.	
4th Field Artillery Regiment	Inowraclaw.	
15th Division	Bydgosc.	
59th Infantry Regiment	Inowraclaw.	
61st Infantry Regiment	Bydgosc.	
62nd Infantry Regiment	Bydgosc.	
15th Field Artillery Regiment	Bydgosc.	
16th Division	Grudziądz.	
64th Infantry Regiment	Grudziądz.	
64th Infantry Regiment, Mob. Stores	Wloclawek.	
65th Infantry Regiment	Starogard.	
65th Infantry Regiment, 2nd Battalion	Gniew.	
65th Infantry Regiment, Mob. Stores	Inowraclaw.	
66th Infantry Regiment	Chelmno.	
66th Infantry Regiment, 3rd Battalion	Grudziądz.	
16th Field Artillery Regiment	Grudziądz.	
8th Independent Cavalry Brigade	Starogard.	
2nd Chevauxlegers	Starogard.	
2nd Chevauxlegers, Reserve Squadron	Torun.	
5th Mounted Rifles	Tarnow.	In D.O.K. V.
5th Mounted Rifles, 3rd, 4th Squadrons	Bochnia.	In D.O.K. V.
1st Rifle Battalion	Chojnice.	
2nd Rifle Battalion	Starogard.	

Non-divisional Units.

Unit.	Location.
8th Heavy Field Artillery Regiment	Torun.
8th Anti-aircraft Artillery Group	Torun.
4th Aviation Regiment	Torun.
Balloon Battalion	Torun.
8th Sapper Regiment	Torun.
8th Medical Battalion..	Torun.
8th Gendarmerie Group	Torun.
8th Train Squadron	Torun.
8th Motor Transport Group	Bydgosc.

THE POLISH ARMY

Unit.	Location.	Remarks.
Units in the District belonging to other Formations.		
14th Cavalry Brigade	Bydgosc.	
16th Ulans	Bydgosc.	
15th Cavalry Brigade	Grudziądz.	
18th Ulans	Grudziądz.	To 3rd Cavalry Division.
18th Ulans, Reserve Squadron	Torun.	
8th Mounted Rifles	Chelmno.	
8th Mounted Rifles, Reserve Squadron	Wloclawek	
11th Horse Artillery Group	Bydgosc.	

Military District (D.O.K.) IX : Brzesc-Nad-Bugiem.

9th Division	Siedlce.
22nd Infantry Regiment	Siedlce.
34th Infantry Regiment	Biala Podlaska.
35th Infantry Regiment	Brzesc-Nad-Bugiem.
35th Infantry Regiment, 1st Battalion	Lukow.
9th Field Artillery Regiment	Biala Podlaska.
9th Field Artillery Regiment, 3rd Group	Bereza Kartuzka.
20th Division	Slonim.
78th Infantry Regiment	Baranowicze.
78th Infantry Regiment, Mob. Stores	Bereza Kartuzka.
79th Infantry Regiment	Slonim.
80th Infantry Regiment	Slonim.
20th Field Artillery Regiment	Pruzany.
30th Division (Siberian)	Kobryn.
82nd Infantry Regiment	Brzesc-Nad-Bugiem.
83rd Infantry Regiment	Kobryn.
84th Infantry Regiment	Pinsk.
84th Infantry Regiment, 3rd Battalion	Luniniec.
30th Field Artillery Regiment	Wloclawek.
9th Independent Cavalry Brigade	Baranowicze.
25th Ulans	Pruzany.
25th Ulans, Reserve Squadron	Lukow.
26th Ulans	Baranowicze.
27th Ulans	Nieswiez.
27th Ulans, Reserve Squadron	Baranowicze.
9th Horse Artillery Group	Baranowicze.
9th Brigade Pioneer Squadron	Baronowicze.
Non-divisional Units.	
9th Heavy Field Artillery Regiment	Siedlce.
9th Heavy Field Artillery Regiment, 1st Group	Brzesc-Nad-Bugiem.
9th Sapper Regiment	Brzesc-Nad-Bugiem.
9th Independent Signal Battalion	Brzesc-Nad-Bugiem.
9th Medical Battalion	Siedlce.
9th Gendarmerie Group	Brzesc-Nad-Buglem.
9th Train Squadron	Brzesc-Nad-Bugiem.
9th Motor Transport Group	Brzesc-Nad-Bugiem.

Military District (D.O.K.) X : Przemysl.

2nd (Legion) Division	Kielce.
2nd (Leg.) Infantry Regiment	Pinczow.
2nd (Leg.) Infantry Regiment, 1st, 3rd Battalions	Staszow.
3rd (Leg.) Infantry Regiment	Jaroslaw.
3rd (Leg.) Infantry Regiment, 2nd Battalion	Nisko.
4th (Leg.) Infantry Regiment	Kielce.
2nd (Leg.) Field Artillery Regiment	Kielce.

214   THE POLISH ARMY

Military District (D.O.K.) X : Przemysl—continued.

Unit.	Location.	Remarks.
22nd (2nd Mountain) Division	Przemysl.	
2nd Mountain Rifle Regiment	Sanok.	
2nd Mountain Rifle Regiment, 3rd Battalion	Dębica.	
5th Moutain Rifle Regiment	Przemysl.	
5th Mountain Rifle Regiment, 2nd Battalion	Sambor.	
6th Mountain Rifle Regiment	Stryj.	
6th Mountain Riffe Regiment, 3rd Battalion	Drohobycz.	
22nd Field Artillery Regiment	Rzeszow.	
22nd Field Artillery Regiment, 3rd Group	Grodek Jagiellonski.	
24th Division	Jaroslaw.	
17th Infantry Regiment	Rzeszow.	
38th Infantry Regiment	Przemysl.	
39th Infantry Regiment	Jaroslaw.	
39th Infantry Regiment, 1st, 2nd Battalions	Lubaczow.	
24th Field Artillery Regiment	Jaroslaw.	

Non-divisional Units.

1st Tank Regiment	Przemysl.	
10th Heavy Field Artillery Regiment	Przemysl.	
10th Sapper Regiment	Przemysl.	
10th Medical Battalion	Przemysl.	
10th Gendarmerie Group	Przemysl.	
10th Train Squadron	Przemysl.	
10th Motor Transport Group	Przemysl.	

Units in the District belonging to other Formations.

53rd Infantry Regiment	Stryj.	To 11th Division.
10th Cavalry Brigade	Przemysl.	
20th Ulans	Rzeszow.	
20th Ulans, 2nd, 3rd, 4th Squadrons	Dębica.	To 4th Cavalry Division.
10th Mounted Rifles	Lancut.	
10th Mounted Rifles, 3rd, 4th Squadrons	Hruszow.	
10th Horse Artillery Group	Jaroslaw.	
4th Sapper Regiment	Samdomierz.	To D.O.K. IV.
6th Sapper Regiment	Przemysl.	To D.O.K. VI.

Schools.

Supreme War School (Staff College)	Warsaw.
Supreme Intendance School	Warsaw.
Cadet School	Warsaw.
Infantry Officers' School	Warsaw.
Experimental Training Centre	Rembertow.
Cadet Corps No. 1	Lwow.
Cadet Corps No. 2	Ostrow.
Cadet Corps No. 3	Rawicz.
Non-commissioned Officers', Officers' School	Bydgosc.
Non-commissioned Officers' School	Chelmno.
Central Musketry School	Torun.
Central School of Gynmastics and Sport	Poznan.
Central Tank School	Przemysl.
Central Cavalry School	Grudziądz.
Artillery Officers' School	Torun.
Artillery Ranging School	Torun.

THE POLISH ARMY

Unit.	Location.	Remarks.
Artillery Training Camp	Torun.	
Engineer Officers' School	Warsaw.	
Engineer Training Camp (Kosciuszko's)	—	
Aviation Officers' School	Grudziądz for Dęblin.	
Aviation School	Bydgosc for Dęblin.	
Aviation Mechanics' School	Bydgosc.	
Signal Training Camp	Zegrze.	
Railway Troops Training Camp	Jablonna.	
Motor Transport Training Camp	Warsaw.	
Gendarmerie School	Grudziądz.	
Military Medical School	Warsaw.	
Medical Non-commissioned Officers' School	Przemysl.	
Gas Warfare School	Warsaw.	
Armourers' School	Warsaw.	
Topographical School	Warsaw.	
Central Shoeing School	Warsaw.	
School of Administration	Krakow.	

PLATE I.

DISTINGUISHING SHIELDS OF HEADQUARTERS.

HEADQUARTERS.	SHIELDS.	REMARKS.
ARMY CORPS.	Star, 3 metres	The width of the black stripes = 4·5 c.m.
DIVISIONS.	1st Div., 2nd Div., 3rd Div., 4th Div. OF A CORPS. (3 metres)	
1st BRIGADE.	1st Div., 2nd Div., 3rd Div., 4th Div. (3 metres)	The width of the black stripes and squares = 40 c.m.
2nd BRIGADE.	1st Div., 2nd Div., 3rd Div., 4th Div. OF A CORPS. (3 metres)	Cavalry (not on the move) use the same shields, with the addition of the general cavalry shield; 2 metres square with a red circle in the centre with a diameter of 1 metre.
REGIMENTS.	1st Regt, 2nd Regt, 3rd Regt, 4th Regt. OF A DIVISION. (3 metres)	
BATTALIONS.	1st Batt., 2nd Batt., 3rd Batt., 4th Batt. OF A REGIMENT.	

THE POLISH ARMY

Plate IIa.

[*To accompany paragraph No. 56.*

ORDINARY SIGNALS FROM AEROPLANES.

Number.	Meaning.	Nature.
1	"I am your aeroplane"	Identification marks on the aeroplane and identification signal made by aviator: shown in plan of communication.
2	"Show your position"	6 stars—signal lights.
3	"Understood—furl cloths"	3 stars—signal lights.
4	"Enemy is preparing an attack (counter-attack) from the direction in which I (the aeroplane) am in."	Yellow smoke.
5	"Position in which I (the aeroplane) am in is lightly held—you may attack (take advance to this position)."	Black smoke.
6	"Attack, in order"	Signals 6, 7, 8, 9 alternated, combinations of them, together with the signal "caterpillar."
7	"Attack postponed"	Shown in plan of communication.
8	"Can you hear my wireless well?"	—
9	"Caterpillar" signal	Signal light in the form of long threads with which are mingled several 8–12 star lights.

Plate II_B

SIGNALS OF INFANTRY H.QRS. (from battalions upwards) MADE WITH DISTINGUISHING SHIELDS OF H.QRS. AND TWO SIGNALLING CLOTHS AND ANSWERS TO THEM IN MORSE CODE FOR WIRELESS TELEGRAPHY.

MEANING OF SIGNALS.	BATTALION.	REGIMENT.	BRIGADE (DIVISION)	WIRELESS SIGNALS.	REMARKS.
	Shewn from ground to aviators.			*The aviator transmits by wireless, giving the number of the battalion (regiment, brigade, etc.).*	*These 11 signals can also be given by commanders of infantry (cavalry) in the first line of battle by means of artificial lights.*
GENERAL. 1. "I am ready to attack."				· · · · ·	
2. "I will not be ready to attack at the appointed hour."				— — · · — ·	*The code of these light signals will be given in the plan of communication, and will be CHANGEABLE, as the enemy will also be able to see them and will very quickly understand their meanings.*
3. "The objective ordered has been obtained."				· · · —	
4. "I want ammunition."				— · — —	
5. "I want grenades."				— — · —	
TO ARTILLERY. 6. "I want fire in preparation for an attack"					*The wireless signals given here can in some cases, be given optically (to be seen) and acoustically (to be heard); but in every case they must be repeated several times in order to prevent mistakes.*
7. "I am attacking, increase range."				· · · · — — — —	
8. "I want harassing fire."				— — — —	
9. "I am being fired on by our field artillery."				— · · · ·	
10. "I am being fired on by our heavy artillery."				· · · · — · · · —	
11. "Message received" or "Understood."				· · · — — · — · · · · — ·	

Malby & Sons

Plate IIc

SIGNALS MADE WITH 3 SIGNALLING CLOTHS AND ANSWERS TO THEM IN MORSE CODE.

NUMBERS.	CLOTH SIGNS. *Shewn from the ground to aviators.*	WIRELESS SIGNS. *Given by aviators.*	REMARKS.
1 – ONE	▭ ▭ ▭	· ─ ─ ─ ─	1.) Numbers form conditional and modifiable signals, whose meaning is given in the plan of communication or in orders for special instances.
2 – TWO	⌐	· · ─ ─ ─	
3 – THREE	III	· · · ─ ─	Numbers and similar signs are also used by artillery for the information of observers in aeroplanes who are fixing ranges. (See Regulations for Communication between Artillery and Aviators).
4 – FOUR	IV	· · · · ─	
5 – FIVE	V	· · · · ·	2.) The width of cloths and the distances between them must not be less than :- 0.50 m. for infantry cloths. 2 m. for field artillery. 3 m. for long range heavy artillery.
6 – SIX	▽I	─ · · · ·	
7 – SEVEN	⌐	─ ─ · · ·	
8 – EIGHT	LI	─ ─ ─ · ·	
9 – NINE	IX	─ ─ ─ ─ ·	3.) The "T" Signal ⊤ (Direction of Wind) is only used to shew aviators suitable places for landing.
10 – TEN	X	─ ─ ─ ─ ─	
0 – ZERO	─ <	─ ─ ─ ─ ─ ─	

Plate III.

INFANTRY PRIVATE—Marching Order.

221

CAVALRYMAN—Marching Order.

222

Plate VI.

MACHINE GUN DETACHMENT—Infantry

Plate V.

MACHINE GUN DETACHMENT—Cavalry.

www.ingramcontent.com/pod-product-compliance
Ingram Content Group UK Ltd.
Pitfield, Milton Keynes, MK11 3LW, UK
UKHW022122230426
12048UKWH00011BA/667